WEST EUROPEAN COMMUNISM
AND
AMERICAN FOREIGN POLICY

WEST EUROPEAN COMMUNISM AND AMERICAN FOREIGN POLICY

MICHAEL A. LEDEEN

Transaction Books
New Brunswick (U.S.A.) and Oxford (U.K.)

Copyright © 1987 by Transaction, Inc.
New Brunswick, New Jersey 08903

All rights reserved under International and Pan-American Copyright Conventions. No part of this book may be reproduced or transmitted in any form or by any means, electronic or mechanical, including photocopy, recording, or any information storage and retrieval system, without prior permission in writing from the publisher. All inquiries should be addressed to Transaction Books, Rutgers—The State University, New Brunswick, New Jersey 08903.

Library of Congress Catalog Number: 87-5977
ISBN: 0-88738-140-5
Printed in the United States of America

Library of Congress Cataloging in Publication Data

Ledeen, Michael Arthur, 1941-
  West European communism and American foreign policy.

  Bibliography: p.
  Includes index.
  1. Partito comunista italiano.   2. Communist parties—Europe.   3. United States—Foreign relations—Italy.   4. Italy—Foreign relations—United States.
5. United States—Foreign relations—Europe.
6. Europe—Foreign relations—United States.   I. Title.
JN5657.C63L375   1987   324.245′075   87-5977
ISBN 0-88738-140-5

Contents

Introduction	vii
1. The Communists and the Italian Resistance	1
2. The Cold War in Italy	29
3. The American Response	49
4. The Opening to the Left	71
5. The Italian Communist Party	103
6. The Myth of Eurocommunism	133
7. The Question of American Policy	161
Index	191

Introduction

This is a book about European Communism—primarily the Italian Communist party—and the United States of America. That a book could be written about such a subject indicates the importance of the Communist party of Italy (PCI), for there is no other political party in Europe that has required the United States to devise—for more than forty years—a political strategy in order to prevent or at least forestall its arrival in the corridors of national executive power. Yet this has been a major problem for American policy makers ever since the United States entered the Italian theater in the Second World War, when the Communists' preeminent role in the Italian Resistance compelled the leaders of the Office of Strategic Services (OSS) to analyze the nature of the PCI in the midst of the fighting.

From the war to the present, American diplomats, military men, and intelligence officials have been afraid that if the PCI entered the Italian Cabinet, there would be a sea-change in the relationship between the United States and Italy. This change would, in the virtually unanimous view of all American officials who have been involved in this problem, stem from two inevitable consequences of the PCI's arrival in Italian ministries: increasing Soviet influence over Italian policy (and access to Western secrets), and a systematic threat to Italian democracy. American policy has therefore aimed at preventing the kind of electoral gain by the PCI that would enable it to claim a share of executive power.

In chronicling and analyzing this fascinating duel, it is necessary to focus on several elements: What was the nature of the Italian Communist party? What were its objectives, and to what extent were the desires and intentions of the Italian Communists subject to external (primarily Soviet) influence and control? What did the Americans think was going on? What did they do about it? Finally, there is the Italian context itself: What were the real alternatives available to American and Italian policy makers?

I do not for a moment believe that this is the last word on the subject, although I hope that I have contributed some new information and perhaps some useful insights of my own. Much remains unknown on both sides of the matter, ranging from the nature of Italian communism to the content of American views and actions. Yet with the passage of time, a useful body of information has become available, and it seems a good moment to attempt an overall view.

I have been able to find considerable documentary material that has not previously seen the light of day. Much of this information was obtained thanks to the Freedom of Information Act, which enabled me to find previously classified CIA biographies and analyses, State Department intelligence studies, cables from the 1940s and 1950s, memoranda of conversations from the 1960s, and so forth.

Other material came from numerous interviews, generally with persons who have requested anonymity. I have abided by their requests, and rather than resort to the usual euphemisms ("a former high-ranking State Department official" and other such unhelpful constructs), I have simply taken responsibility myself for the information in question. I have done my best to check it, and whatever errors remain should be attributed either to the inaccuracies of the memories of my sources or my own inability to confirm the considerable quantity of new material I obtained.

I wish to thank the John M. Olin Foundation for a research grant in support of this project. Thanks are also due to many people in Italy and the United States who helped me understand this subject. They are too numerous to list here, but particular gratitude is due to Francesco Cossiga, president of the Italian Republic; Bettino Craxi, president of the Council of Ministers; Spartaco Vanoni, Eugenio Reale, Enzo Bettiza, Alberto Ronchey, Claire Sterling, Renato Mieli, Henry Kissinger, Graham Martin, William Colby, James Angleton, Raymond Rocca, William Friend, James Schlesinger, William Hyland, Helmut Sonnenfeldt, Richard Gardner, Giorgio Amendola, Ugo Stille, Renzo de Felice, and Rosario Romeo.

Above all, I want to thank Irving Louis Horowitz for his support and encouragement, without which this book would never have been completed. Friendship also consists of this, and I am profoundly grateful.

This is the first in a series of books dealing with the struggle for democracy in Latin Europe in the postwar period. I soon hope to finish a second volume—on the transition from dictatorship to democracy in Spain.

Chevy Chase, Md.
March 1987

1

The Communists and the Italian Resistance

> *The American Government discovered to its surprise that few of its citizens possessed any expert knowledge of contemporary Italy.*
> —H. Stuart Hughes, OSS

Moving slowly from South to North in 1943, the Americans were hardly in a position to evaluate the culture, the politics, and the passions that characterized the Italian peninsula under Nazi and Fascist control. While few Americans had any real understanding of the country, the British had very strong opinions about Italian character and politics, and Churchill insisted upon a quick stabilization of the country, preferably under the king and politicians known and trusted in London—above all, Marshall Badoglio.[1]

At first, Roosevelt preferred to defer to Churchill in the Mediterranean theater, but with the passage of time many Americans challenged the British evaluation and urged a more progressive policy. Indeed, the conflicts between the Americans and the British were among the most intense political battles of the period.[2] Their differences surfaced first over the question of the Resistance. All observers recognized that the driving force of the Italian Resistance was the underground Italian Communist party, and thus to strengthen the military role of the partisans would inevitably increase the political weight of the PCI, both during the fighting and afterwards. The military advantages of obtaining full cooperation from the partisans seemed considerable (most analysts had an inflated opinion of partisan strength[3]), but it was unattractive to fight an extended campaign in Italy, only to find the country politically hostile at the end of the war.

Thus, from the onset of the Italian campaign, the question of the Resistance was ineluctably linked to the political future of the country.

In one of the earliest available documents on the partisan question,[4] the OSS Research and Analysis Branch (R&A) observed that the participation of the Resistance forces was closely linked to the political stand of the

Allies. It was hardly possible to enlist the enthusiastic participation of the partisans if Allied political strategy rested on the restoration of the pre-Fascist ruling class under the leadership of (in American eyes, at least) a widely discredited king and Marshall Badoglio.[5] According to the OSS document, if the Allies wanted full cooperation from the Resistance, it would be necessary to tolerate radical political change after the war:

> The use of an underground movement is, on the whole, incompatible with insistence on the political and social status quo. An underground operation in a Fascist state is in its very essence a revolutionary operation. Its aim is the subversion of the existing machinery of force.

Support of the partisans thus implied toleration of radical change in postwar Italy—precisely what Churchill wanted to avoid, both because of his conservative outlook and because of his fear that this would give the Soviet Union considerable leverage over Italy. Many in OSS, however, disagreed. The military campaign did not go as well as initially hoped, and the addition of a fifth column behind Nazi lines was attractive. But the partisans could not be expected to support Badoglio, particularly "the most active political groups who would have to bear the brunt of subversive activity, sabotage and open resistance in support of allied military operations."[6] Would it not be better to call for a people's war of national liberation, and encourage the more radical forces in the North to fight passionately for the Allied victory?

Moreover, the OSS analyst suggested that a conservative political line might actually produce one of the results it was ostensibly designed to prevent:

> The popular resistance movements, if persuaded that the Anglo-American armies intend only to restore a slightly refurbished model of the old regime, will inevitably turn to quarters where they can expect help in their mission of social reconstruction—that is, to Soviet Russia . . . the stake is not simply Italy. It is likely to be the political allegiances of resistance movements everywhere in Europe.

Much of subsequent American strategy in Italy was based on this model, for many Americans believed it was best to work with the popular Resistance movements. The Churchill strategy was rejected on two grounds by such people: it would weaken the war effort, and it would drive partisans toward the Russians for support. Many Americans urged their government to enlist the Resistance.

To be sure, any characterization of American "policy" during the Italian campaign must be tentative, since the military government of the peninsula was so chaotic. In some areas individual officers, whether of the regular Army or the OSS, simply made their own policies, and the range of actions was wide indeed. But there was certainly no blanket anticommunism on the part of the Americans (indeed, OSS chief William Donovan at one point had to warn his men about recruiting Italians whose loyalty to the king was in doubt[7]). By late 1943, both OSS and at least some of the British Special Operations Executive (SOE) in Italy had decided to organize an anti-Fascist fighting force under the leadership of General Pavone, a man recommended by none other than the distinguished liberal philosopher Benedetto Croce.[8] This initiative was blocked in the winter, but still had its supporters as late as the following March. Ironically, it was finally dropped when Communist party leader Palmiro Togliatti returned from the Soviet Union and announced his full support for the king and Badoglio.

The United States was thus quite willing to contemplate radical change in postwar Italy. Indeed, OSS actively enlisted known Communists in its ranks. Several members of the Lincoln Brigade held important posts in OSS,[9] and even in 1944-45, when American hostility to the Italian Communists had substantially increased, OSS would continue to work closely with Communist partisan groups. Thus, it is hardly surprising to hear from one of the participants that in the fall of 1943, the most heated debates among Americans in Italy were those over the British view of the situation.[10]

The American plan to create an anti-Fascist military force failed for a variety of reasons: British opposition, bickering among Italians, and the stalled Allied advance. With the long delay in achieving victory, some sections of the populace began to turn against the Americans. In late 1943, OSS reported "a loss of hope in the Anglo-American forces and a growth of emotional antagonism,"[11] particularly in the North. And for the first time, there was a suggestion that the major beneficiary of this hostility was not the German enemy, but the Soviet ally. "Opinion on Russian capabilities and aims . . . seems friendly. Several arguments are brought forward to support the contention that Russia will be predominant in postwar Europe."[12]

Surprisingly, this shift in public opinion was *not* attributed to the Communists, who were expected to cooperate with the Allies at least until the country had been fully liberated. And the OSS analyst went on to suggest that the Russians had no intention of getting deeply involved in postwar Italian affairs, since Rome was so far away from Moscow.[13]

Was this simple confusion or something more sinister? The OSS report coincided with the sort of thing that Stalin was telling other Allied leaders,[14] but there was ample evidence that the Russians intended to be quite busy in Italy after the conflict. Andrei Vishinsky was the Soviet representative on the Allied Advisory Council (the body that was nominally in charge of decisions in that area), and he was later replaced by Bogomolov, another major Soviet figure. When it came time to negotiate the unconditional surrender of Italy, the Russians demanded their full share: substantial reparations, and a whopping one-third of the Italian Navy. This latter provision caused such a stir in Italy that Churchill had to deny its existence, but in fact the ships were turned over to the Soviets when the peace treaty was initialled in 1947.

The first clear sign of Soviet intentions came in March 1944, when Russia unexpectedly announced that it was normalizing relations with Italy. Shortly thereafter the Soviets requested permission to establish an air base on the peninsula. Both of these moves were taken without any consultation with the British or the Americans,[15] and the Allied representatives in Italy took a dim view of them. British General Noel MacFarlane, the head of the Allied Control Commission, sent a top secret cable on March 23,[16] warning that Soviet recognition of the Badoglio government was having a considerable effect on the Italian political situation. The clearest sign of this effect was to be seen in the behavior of the PCI, which hitherto had called for the abdication of the king, and the creation of a "democratic government." MacFarlane's cable neatly summarized the remarkable about-face in Communist tactics:

> Prior to the sixteenth March the Communist Party had not only publicly announced that the Russian decision had made no difference to their policy but had continued to be the prime movers in demanding that the three party petition should go forward on a junta basis. They had even offered privately to pay a third of the expenses, or, if necessary, the entire amount. At the meeting of the junta on the sixteenth March, however, they completely changed their attitude and the Secretary now tells us that in his opinion the proposal for a petition is being shelved. Moveover, in a speech at Bari on the nineteenth March, Tedeschi (code name for Spano, M.L.) completely altered the line of argument contained in his previous speeches. ... At Bari he refrained from attacking the King and Badoglio and argued that the only necessity was that Italy should have a strong government.

MacFarlane was not entirely certain that a fundamental change had, in fact, occurred. Certainly such a shift in Communist behavior would have the gravest consequences in the short term, since it would strengthen the hand of the monarchy against those moderate anti-Fascist forces who were pressing for the creation of a more representative government. As Carlo Sforza angrily told another member of the Control Commission a few days later, in the long run the Communist strategy threatened to prolong the "neofascist rule of the King" and have the dangerous side effect of increasing Soviet influence. Sforza acidly observed that the Allies were now paying the price for their failure to back the advocates of "a more democratic settlement of the local Italian question,"[17] that is, himself.

For his part, Badoglio told the Allies that while he was not particularly happy to have normalized relations first with the Soviet Union, he could hardly deny normal ties with one of the three Allies. At the same time, he felt that the Americans were showing insufficient concern over the future of Italy (a sentiment that would be expressed by every Italian leader from that moment forward), and accused them of leaving the field open to the Russians and the British by withdrawing "your good Eisenhower and sympathetic General Smith."[18]

The Russian initiatives in Italy in the spring of 1944 involved one further ingredient, which the Americans watched with mixed concern and fascination—the return of Togliatti from exile. The arrival of the leading member of the Italian Communist party was a major event, and MacFarlane felt that, if nothing else, Togliatti's actions would finally give the Allies a clear indication of Soviet strategy in Italy. For the Americans were remarkably well-informed about the general secretary of the PCI.[19] They knew that he was the complete Stalinist, his loyalty and ruthlessness having been demonstrated in countless difficult moments as second secretary of the Comintern. He unquestioningly carried out instructions from the Kremlin, even when this entailed the sacrifice of loyal comrades in Spain and elsewhere. It was Togliatti who had transmitted the suicidal orders from Moscow to the clandestine PCI in 1929—the so-called *svolta*—that announced the existence of a "revolutionary situation" in Italy and called upon the Communists to lead an insurrection.[20]

The Americans could hardly have been expected to know about this particular episode (which produced the destruction of much of the clandestine Communist organization and the imprisonment of many of its leaders), but they knew in a general way of Togliatti's participation in the purges that characterized Stalin's rule, even on the verge of the war. The Americans also knew that Togliatti had played a major role in the internal purge of PCI leaders in 1937, an operation that stretched from Moscow to New York. As the purges began in Moscow, orders were given for the elimination of possible Fascist infiltrators and potentially disloyal elements from the PCI's enfeebled ranks. The party headquarters in Paris was the scene of discussions concerning the possible transfer of PCI leaders to New York, where several major figures of the anti-Fascist "concentration" had already gone, a clear symptom of the pessimism with which prospects for action in Italy were viewed at the time. The action of the Comintern thus came at a particularly delicate moment, when the Communists in Paris were already under considerable internal pressure.

The orders for the purge were passed to Togliatti from M.A. Trilisser, the chief NKVD officer for Western Europe, who served as a Soviet representative on the Comintern Secretariat under the pseudonym of Moskvin.[21] Through his extensive network of European agents, Trilisser had gathered detailed information on PCI leaders (in part, apparently, from Soviet double agents within Italian intelligence services; however, it is also possible that some of the targets for the purge were provided by Fascist "disinformation," inducing the Russians to crack down on persons who were actually loyal to the Comintern), and Togliatti was the channel for the orders to purify party ranks. The three primary targets were Ruggiero Grieco (chief of the clandestine party headquarters in Paris), Giuseppe Dozza (head of "Organization," then, as now, one of the most delicate positions in any Communist party), and Emilio Sereni (one of the leading intellectuals in the party, and brother of the famous Zionist Enzo Sereni, who was killed by the Nazis in the last days of the war while carrying out an operation behind German lines).

The purge of the Paris group was entrusted to Giuseppe Berti, one of the most highly trusted apparatchiks. Berti had been the head of the Italian Communist Youth organization in 1921, was arrested by the Fascists two years later, sent to "confinement" for several years, and then emigrated, first to France and then to Moscow. His return to the West represented an extension of the purges to Paris, and he carried out his role with professional discipline. Dozza and Grieco were removed from the Party Secretariat, and the Central Committee was dissolved. Sereni was lured to Moscow by a subterfuge, and escaped death only thanks to a remarkable letter to Stalin in which Sereni hailed the purges, even if they produced the elimination of "involuntary traitors" like himself.[22] Released from a Moscow jail, Sereni was sent back to Paris where he was tried again and found innocent.

The leadership of the PCI was thus fully Stalinized by the outbreak of the war; there were no major figures at liberty who were not fully loyal to the Soviet dictator. Togliatti's role was to place the Italian party at the service of the Soviets, and more specifically—as his close working relationship with Trilisser demonstrated—at the service of the secret intelligence services of the U.S.S.R.:

> Togliatti . . . permitted the secret services of the Soviet state to replace the Communist International and the leadership of the PCI who belonged to it, exercising a ruthless and uncontrolled power under cover of the Comintern, and, so far as the Italian Communists were concerned, the apex of the PCI. In the last analysis, this was the price for survival.[23]

The imposition of strict Soviet control over the PCI was not an easy matter, for relations between the Kremlin and the Italian Communists had passed through at least one very strained period. This came in the late 1920s and early 1930s, over the *svolta*. Instructed by the Kremlin to treat social democrats as if they were fascists, and advised that the long-awaited moment of the great crisis in world capitalism had finally arrived, the Communist parties of Western Europe abandoned collaboration with moderate socialists in favor of an all-out assault on enemies ranging from Hitler to moderates within their own ranks. In Italy, the *svolta* was contested by two of the founding fathers of the party: Umberto Terracini and Antonio Gramsci, both of whom were in prison at the time. In addition, among those Communists outside prison, opposition was so intense that three others were expelled from the party.[24]

At the very same time, there was another conflict between the Kremlin and some Italian Communists. The Italians had long been aware that many of their own members were recruited for espionage work by the NKVD, and this was considered a serious problem. In an ongoing discussion with their Russian comrades, the Italian Communists asked to be shielded from such penetration and their members freed to conduct revolutionary activity in their own country rather than being used as agents for Soviet spying. But recruitments continued, and Soviet intelligence played a continuing role in the relations between Russia and the PCI.[25] Soviet intelligence organizations maintained surveillance over the ranks of the PCI, both through its own agents within the party, and through a widely articulated network of spies and double agents throughout Europe. Thus the tension between Russia and the Italian Communist party was not merely at the ideological level, nor restricted to the menacing problems arising from Stalin's control of the Soviet Union and the International.[26]

The PCI which emerged from fascism was consequently under great Soviet control. Further, despite the internal shakeups, the leadership was in large part physically intact, thanks to Togliatti's efforts to limit the human damage of Stalin's wilder moods. As Giorgio Amendola has observed,[27] while the party was wracked by the purges, with few exceptions leading Italian Communists were spared the murders that plagued so many other European parties. The PCI was therefore blessed with experienced and disciplined leadership, as exemplified by Ercoli himself. Once he returned to Italy, the party changed its tactics from demanding the abdication of the king to a more malleable approach which is strikingly similar—in both style and content—to the Eurocommunism of the 1970s.

Togliatti and the Communists: the Spring of 1944

On April 20, 1944, MacFarlane cabled his account of what appears to be the first encounter between the chief commissioner and the "world's number one Italian Communist."[28] The cable was a masterpiece of understatement:

> Togliatti alias Ercoli called on me this afternoon. . . . We were in complete agreement that the formation of a government to include all the political parties was a most urgent necessity. Togliatti stated definitely that his party were very ready to serve under Badoglio as Prime Minister. In his opinion Badoglio had a perfectly clean record.[29]

These laconic words described an encounter that warranted far more colorful language, for Ercoli's return to Italy had produced a sensational effect, as MacFarlane was well aware. Just four days earlier an analyst at the commission had observed that the events of the preceding month had documented "the strength of the Communist party in influencing politics in Allied-occupied Italy and the influence of the Soviet Union in determining the policy of the party."[30] The sequence of events to which the anonymous analyst referred was indeed impressive. A month prior to the encounter between MacFarlane and Togliatti, the PCI was one of the most belligerent parties in Italy, demanding the creation of a republic. Led by Eugenio Reale, Communists in Naples had called for an anti-Badoglio strike in early March, and had been "prime movers behind the proposal that the six parties should organize a petition in support of the Bari resolutions for the abdication of the king and the formation of a broad based government."

In mid-March, the Russians announced normalization of relations with Italy, and the PCI attitude changed. After a couple of days during which party leaders stoutly maintained that the Russian action would have no effect on PCI policy, Communist leaders suddenly backed away from their demands for abdication. Togliatti arrived on March 26, and called a meeting of Communist leaders for the first of April. After that meeting, "it was made clear that the Italian Communist party did not wish to insist on either (abdication or withdrawal of the king) as a necessary precondition."[31]

The effect of these maneuvers was electric. The other parties could not sustain their own calls for abdication, and the monarchy survived. The most intense immediate reaction came from the Action party, a liberal group largely composed of pro-Western intellectuals and upper-middle-class representatives under the leadership of Count Carlo Sforza. Sforza had been foreign minister prior to Mussolini's March on Rome, and had spent the Fascist period in comfortable exile in London and New York, where he maintained contacts with the leading representatives of moderate antifascism, such as Salvemini, Tarchiani, and Ascoli. As soon as the Communist decision was known, Sforza told the Americans that:

It was clear that the party decision had been taken under orders from Moscow and that in the long run it would destroy the basis of democratic government in Italy by prolonging the neofascist rule of the king and that it would merely serve to increase the influence of Soviet Russia not only as regards Italy but in other liberated areas of Central and Western Europe as well. He deeply regretted that the Allied governments had lost the opportunity of bringing about a more democratic settlement of the local Italian question.[32]

Sforza's analysis was excellent both regarding the failure of the Allies to encourage a quick democratic solution to the Italian political crisis and concerning the effectiveness of Communist tactics. Nobody really believed that the PCI was indifferent about the monarchy (nor could anybody take seriously Togliatti's astonishing claim that Badoglio had a clean record), but the status quo favored Communist chances, as the analyst at MacFarlane's headquarters pointed out. The PCI, he observed, was the wealthiest and best organized political party in southern Italy, having considerable financial resources ("some are derived from legitimate subscription. . . . In addition there have almost certainly been subsidies from Soviet sources") and having collected additional funds in the form of "insurance" from citizens eager to acquire anti-Fascist credentials. But Togliatti's strength was not limited to the South, for it was clear that "the only strong and well-disciplined party in northern Italy is the Communist party and that it plays a dominating role insofar as resistance is concerned."[33]

MacFarlane's analyst went so far as to speculate that the Fascist seizure of power might now be repeated by the Communists:

More than twenty years ago a similar situation provoked the March on Rome, and gave birth to Fascism. We are now about to stage another March on Rome. We must make up our minds and that quickly whether or not we wish to see this second March developing into another "ism."

The Russians had made a daring and successful gesture; the absence of Soviet troops in Italy spared them the friction and hostility from the populace that accompanies military occupation; and the march of Russian troops through the Balkans could project Soviet power into the Italian peninsula. Thus was the vision of MacFarlane's analyst within weeks of Togliatti's return to Italy. Henceforth, whatever Ercoli might say about his intentions, the Allies would remain convinced that any increase in Communist strength in Italy represented an extension of Soviet power into the peninsula. It therefore appeared to most Americans that Togliatti's proposal of support for the monarchy was a deception, masking the real strategy of organizing the party for a Leninist insurrection at some later date. Even though the Communists continued to give lip service to the notion of democratic behavior, the Americans for the most part belived that Communist strategy hinged on preparations for the ultimate assault.[34]

We do not know the truth of the matter. Lacking access to Soviet archives (or, at a minimum, to those of the Western Communist parties in this period), the question cannot be resolved. But nothing we know about Soviet strategy in this phase militates against the idea that the Russians might have been planning militant action once the field was clear. Indeed, the Soviet Union pursued just such a course in all countries where there was a reasonable chance for success. The initial period of cooperation with other parties served to strengthen the Communist organizations and lay down a detailed plan for the seizure of power; it also permitted the Communists effectively to infiltrate the government and other political parties, so that when the "X hour" arrived, Communists would be placed throughout the power structure.

Interestingly—especially given the Allies' fear of a mass movement growing out of the Resistance—the one strategy systematically rejected by Stalin in the immediate postwar period was that of using anti-Fascist partisans as the core of an insurrectionary force. The Kremlin vigorously rejected the notion of a partisan revolution.[35] In part, this was undoubtedly because Stalin feared the development of armed conflict in which the Allies would be tempted to intervene (fully justified, as events in Greece confirmed). But it was also due to broader strategic considerations.

For a full decade, the Soviet Union had argued that the Communist revolution would come about in two stages: a first stage of broad "democratic" coalition, and a second stage during which the seizure and consolidation of power by the Communist party would occur. The most elegant description of Soviet strategy comes from the maverick Spanish Communist, Fernando Claudin:

> Stalin's policy during the Second World War was based on two main strategic rules.... The first, which was formulated towards the end of the 1920s ... and derives from the theory of "socialism in one country," can be stated as the subordination of revolutionary action in any part of the world to the interests of the Soviet state. The second, which came into being in the thirties after the defeat of the German proletariat by Nazism, was the result of the loss of confidence in the revolutionary capacity of the Western proletariat, and called for giving priority to the exploitation of contradictions between the imperialist powers, and the subordination of any revolutionary action to this priority. The second rule is no more than the practical application of the first, in view of the inability of the Western proletariat to create a revolution.[36]

The "two stage theory" was therefore both a check against a sort of insurrectionary "adventurism," which might produce a threat to Soviet national interests, and a control of the real evolution of the situation in European countries. Quite clearly, the Russians would be delighted by a successful Communist revolution in the West. But they were skeptical about the capacities of the Western Communists, and wished to avoid false starts.

Along with these general considerations, one must add a specifically Italian element of particular importance in the development of "Eurocommunism": the Gramscian-Togliattian theory of the long march through the institutions. It will be described in greater detail later, but its salient points can be simply stated. Whereas traditional Leninist theory held that the Communist revolution would be organized and led by a "vanguard" (the party), and communism would then be imposed upon the society from the top, Togliatti (relying heavily upon the writings of Antonio Gramsci) suggested that the process in Western Europe would be different. In this view, the role of the party was to create a Communist "hegemony" over the society as a whole, thus converting the great bulk of the populace to Communist values. Piece by piece, institution by institution, the society would be communized from within. At the end of this process, the party would simply assume its historic role and formalize what had already in fact taken place. Entry into government, in this view, would be the last act in the historic drama, rather than the first step in the revolution.

This brilliant theory fit well with Stalin's international requirements, for it meant that any attempt at insurrection would necessarily be delayed until some later date. Moreover, the strategy of a long march through the institutions was quite attractive to Soviet national interests, for it meant that the Italian Communist party would attempt to gradually expand their participation in all the institutions of the country, thereby offering excellent opportunities for espionage and subversion. Finally, the gradualist approach did not compromise insurrectionary opportunities. If a genuinely attractive situation developed, there would be time enough to exploit it, provided that the PCI (and, to the extent that the theory could be generalized, other Western Communist parties) maintained a structure capable of executing an effective insurrection.

Thus, Togliatti (like his counterpart, Maurice Thorez in France) embarked upon a dual strategy. On the one hand, he called for the creation of *il partito nuovo*, the New party,[37] based on a far broader base than that dictated by tradition. This party would not only attempt to recruit the proletarian masses, but would seek allies in all classes. In like manner, it would pursue National Front governments wherever possible, both to prevent the outbreak of civil war and to legitimize the party itself among all strata of the population.

On the other hand, the party had to maintain an insurrectionary force, armed and trained for the Leninist uprising. Given the political requirements of the Gramscian model, this insurrectionary force would have to be clandestine, for knowledge of its existence would frighten too many potential allies; these had to be wooed, not cowed into participation.

In concrete terms, this meant that the party would undertake to behave in a moderate fashion, assuaging fears of insurrection. At the same time, however, the clandestine fighting force had to be organized, other parties had to be infiltrated, and all sectors of institutional activity had to be subject to Communist influence and eventual control. In this manner a maximum flexibility would be obtained without risking a potentially fatal, open conflict with superior forces, whether foreign or domestic.

As for the partisan movement, the task was clear: maximize Communist control (avoiding adventures by the true believers), and prepare for the future. This meant diverting some strength from the war against the Nazis, and this is precisely what took place. To take one of the most detailed reports in the hands of OSS intelligence officers in late 1944, information from the Interrogation Center in November 1944 produced the following testimony:

> Sources became aware of another curious phenomenon, viz. that weapons were disappearing. They themselves asked to be given weapons, their duties as doctors involving long journeys alone in unfrequented districts. They were promised weapons, but never received them. It was thus that they learned that many weapons were being sent from the mountains down to the plains, to be concealed in readiness for the time when the ideas which were being preached every day would be imposed by force. To quote the actual words of a commissar: "The allies of today may become the enemies of tomorrow and we must be ready to fight them." Sources cannot give exact locations of these secret stores of weapons, but know that large numbers of weapons destined for the Partisans were NOT used by them, but were sent to secret stores in the vicinity of MODENA.[38]

By the time this report was filed, enough was known about Communist strategy throughout the war zone to permit a reader to scribble in the margin, "universal partisan preaching."

The war also permitted other forms of Communist infiltration and control, some of it originating outside the peninsula. OSS discovered early on, for example, that Italian prisoners of war were being given courses in Communist indoctrination in Soviet POW camps.[39] These classes reportedly involved several thousand "students," who were then sent into Italy to carry on various tasks for the Soviets. Once discovered, of course, the products of this training could often be "turned" by Allied counterintelligence, and become active sources for the West. This happened in many cases.[40]

In addition, Allied counterintelligence organizations uncovered an elaborate network of Communist couriers, travelling by sea and ground, which permitted the Comintern (and the Russians after the dissolution of the Comintern in 1943) to maintain an efficient communications network.[41] American analysts noted that the Russians seemed to have much better information about Italy than the Allies did,[42] even though half the country was under Anglo-American occupation, and the Russians were far removed from the scene. One explanation was that the clandestine Communist organizations in Italy were passing information through Yugoslavia to Moscow,[43] but one was forced to recognize that the system was extremely widespread, for Italian Communists in New York were able to stay on top of the latest shifts in party tactics and always knew precisely what was expected of them.[44] OSS was convinced that most of the couriers operated under cover of shipping activities, and estimated that there were many hundreds of couriers masked as merchant seamen operating through the port of Genoa as of the end of the war.[45]

The Communists and the United States

The determining factor in the evolution of American policy toward the Italian Communist party was the recognition that the Communists were anti-American. While communism itself never achieved great popularity in the United States, the kind of visceral anticommunism that one associates with the worst moments of the Cold War or the various Red Scares is difficult to find in the documents of the 1943-45 period. Indeed, within OSS there were many who favored very "progressive" solutions. In general terms, the Research and Analysis Division of OSS was basically pro-socialist, while the covert and operational groups (SI, SO, and S-2) tended to be more conservative.[46] This meant that several analysts and political counsellors urged the United States to endorse a more liberal solution to the Italian political problem, and on several occasions they were successful. For example, the first Bonomi government following the Allied capture of Rome was installed, thanks to American insistence upon a non-Badoglio government with anti-Fascist credentials. This was achieved despite Churchill's protests (and the Americans finally yielded to Churchill's demand that Sforza not be foreign minister).

Unlike the British, the Americans favored an anti-Fascist campaign. But in the first few months of the campaign in the South, the Allies failed to capitalize on a clear opportunity to rid the *Mezzogiorno* of both reactionary and mafia hegemony,[47] and many in the South felt they were simply turned over from one set of antidemocratic masters to another, albeit of a rather more traditional sort. In many cases, as Senator Adlai Stevenson remarked after his fact-finding tour of Sicily at the head of an American economic commission in late 1943, "public opinion complained to the commission that the allied military government had failed to remove the worst Fascists from their positions."[48] The Americans remained sensitive to the problem, but any hopes of installing a more progressive government were ruined by Togliatti's *svolta di Salerno*. Not only did Togliatti's line prevent installation of a more liberal government, but his drive for a mass party entailed signing up many former Fascists. This weakened the later "purification" campaign, despite intense Communist anti-Fascist rhetoric.[49] Finally, by the time that the Resistance took on real substance (in the 1944-45 period, when it was certain that the Allies would win), the Communists were violently anti-American. In an OSS report dated 9 November 1944, the matter was described in some detail:

> 1. On 5 November, Dr. Rodano, head of the Catholic Communists . . . stated confidentially that the Communist party has received instructions from Togliatti that the work and influence of the Americans in Italy must be hindered as much as possible. Moreover, that any commercial or political penetration of the Italian peninsula by the United States must be impeded. Togliatti is quoted as saying: "Today there is only one enemy, the Americans."
>
> 2. It would seem that similar instructions have been sent by the Communist party to all other European states. This violent attitude seems to be a consequence of the Moscow conferences. This is contrary to what has been previously reported, i.e. that the Communists were to maintain an attitude of friendly collaboration with the Anglo-Americans in Italy.[50]

Communist historians—along with several distinguished scholars—have claimed that the partisans turned against the United States because of a conviction that the Americans actually sought to weaken the Resistance. More specifically, it has been argued[51] that OSS and SOE deprived the partisans of supplies and support, because the Allies feared the creation of an armed partisan movement similar to Tito's army in Yugoslavia. The Allies *did* urge the Resistance to keep its groups small, and the partisans would have done well to follow this advice. The Germans could not be defeated by a frontal assault by the partisans, yet the Resistance amassed mini-armies and even created partisan republics near Switzerland in the autumn of 1944. The result was precisely what the Allies had predicted: the partisans were slaughtered by Kesselring's superior forces. At this point, General Alexander made his celebrated call to the partisans to lay low for the winter, an appeal widely regarded as a betrayal. But in the words of a recent study, "in truth there was no other strategy the partisans could have adopted once they had been defeated; it was only common sense to prevent further unnecessary losses."[52] Indeed, the warning against forming large units was echoed by no less a figure than "Gallo"—Luigi Longo, later president of the PCI, and one of the two leading figures in the northern Resistance.

From the American standpoint, then, the partisans were politically dangerous and militarily foolhardy. The Americans had attempted to work with them, and would continue to do so, even when this entailed great danger. The Americans ran supply operations to the partisans, and attempted to coordinate the actions of the politically divided Resistance, and some American officers continued to help the partisans even after having their lives threatened when Allied supplies failed to live up to expectations.[53]

From the purely military standpoint the partisans were a mixed blessing. They performed heroically on occasion (especially in acts of sabotage, and transmitting military intelligence), but they were only really useful in the conduct of the war when they acted in parallel with major Allied advances. As B.H. Liddell Hart has written, "at other times they were less effective than widespread passive resistance."[54] Furthermore, their incessant activism often provoked the worst excesses of the Nazi occupation. "Terror produced counter-terror," as Walter Laqueur has observed,[55] "and given the heavy demands on their manpower, the Germans lacked the soldiery to destroy the partisans if these operated in favorable conditions." Thus, rather than attempting to track down the partisans, the Germans wreaked vengeance on the civilian population. The infamous massacre at the Ardeatine Caves in Rome in the spring of 1943, which cost the lives of 335 Italians, was the most dramatic case.[56] It was in response to a partisan terrorist attack against a platoon of German soldiers in the center of Rome.

But such observations are those of historians writing years after the fact; for the participants, especially the Americans, the partisans were brave allies, and if they were Communists, so be it. In a lengthy discussion of the Resistance,[57] the R&A branch of OSS estimated the effective strength of the partisans at half a million. And although it granted that the Communists were the most effective political force within the Resistance, "it is reported that not more than 30 percent of the membership of bands so organized is actually enrolled in the Communist party, or even committed to the Communist ideology." Thus, Communist control over the partisans was downplayed, anti-Americanism hardly mentioned (and when it was mentioned, it was often ascribed to American neglect), and the motives of the partisans themselves often glorified:

> It seems clear . . . that relations between the Italian government and the partisans are based on the one hand upon the determination of the latter to protect their political position, and on the other, upon Allied determination

to preclude patriot-inspired postliberation disorders. The dual problem is apparently to be dealt with by propaganda designed to ingratiate the government in the eyes of the patriots and render Allied opposition to consolidation of the partisans publicly unpopular.

Here, the partisans have become the "patriots" and their goals are those of the OSS analyst, even when they conflict with Allied policy. To be sure, very few Americans felt comfortable with Italian communism, and for the most part American liberal sympathies went either to the Action party or to the Socialists. This identification with the Socialists—above all with the most charismatic figure in the party, Pietro Nenni—became a leitmotif of American policy for some thirty years, as many American officials earnestly sought for a legitimate, democratic Socialist party in Italy. The monarchy was discredited, the new Christian Democratic party—even with the extraordinary leadership of De Gasperi—was not attractive to American liberals, and the Communists were unacceptable, both because of their links to Moscow and because of their anti-Americanism and their internal organization and collectivist programs. The Action party was by far the most attractive, but was so weak that it could not prevail.

This left the Socialists, and the problem with them was that they appeared to be firmly in the pocket of the PCI.[58] Not only did Nenni himself line up with Togliatti in an "Action Pact," but he simply refused to take meaningful steps toward social democracy. On many issues, Nenni was well to the left of the PCI, even though most observers believed that the Socialists were "really" more moderate than the Communists.

Thus for decades the Americans would continue to hope that the Socialists were other than what they appeared to be. The Americans' dilemma was well described in a report of a conversation between Nenni and an American OSS officer in October 1944:

> Asked whether the Socialist party in alliance with the Communist party could become anything but a satellite of the latter, Nenni refrained from answering directly. . . . According to Nenni, either the Socialists are good friends with the Communists, or inevitably they become bitter enemies. Should they break with the Communists, the latter would concentrate their whole strength in attacking the Socialists.
>
> Asked if the Socialist party would not have better chances of assuming a leading role if it undertook a close alliance with the other democratic parties, instead of the present alliance . . . Nenni asked in return with what could the Socialist party ally itself. He stated that the Action party has no future, but he admitted that the Christian Democratic party would like very much to reach a closer understanding with the Socialist party. . . . Nenni agreed without comment with Ruini's suggestion that the chances for a democratic front or bloc in Italy depend entirely upon the attitude of the Socialist party.[59]

Nenni's remarks were important not so much for what was stated, but for what lay behind the words. Nenni's first reply was a euphemism for his real concerns, and related to the recent history of the Communist International. From Nenni's perspective, the worst case was to repeat the fate of Bukharin. He did not know in 1944 what we now know—that the United States was prepared to exert tremendous pressure to prevent a Communist triumph in Italy. Nenni made a political calculation that Togliatti's chances for success were excellent. As he later remarked to at least two separate Christian Democratic friends, "You, as the traditional enemies (of the Communists) at worst would have ended in jail; I, as the traitor of the working class, would have gotten a bullet in the back of the neck."[60]

Nenni's other option was to throw in with the Americans, but would they protect him if his decision turned out to be disastrous? And would the Americans offer him more than moral encouragement and physical protection if he were threatened? This last is not merely rhetorical, for numerous sources have stated that Nenni had become financially dependent on the Soviet Union, through the good offices of the PCI.[61] If he intended to switch camps, Nenni needed some financial assistance from the United States.

The matter of American dollars to the PSI would become an ongoing problem. First raised in conversations between Nenni and American intelligence officers in Switzerland in 1943, it lasted until the early 1970s, if not later. Throughout the period, Socialist leaders—above all, Nenni himself—received clear indications that the Americans would help if Nenni would move the party to a more independent position. But even though such assurances were given, Nenni was not inclined to break his Action Pact with the Communists in the closing months of the war, or in the immediate postwar period.

Nenni seriously miscalculated the political future of Italy. He expected that the PCI would be the dominant postwar poliltical force, and he wanted to be on the winning side.[62] In recent years, he admitted to such errors, but claimed [63] that the *svolta di Salerno* actually represented an evolution in the PCI away from the ideological domination of the Soviet Union (!). If Nenni held such a view in the late 1970s, the Action Pact in the 1940s was a firm bond indeed.

The Soviet Union in Italy, 1943-45

The conventional wisdom has it that the Russians had arranged to divide Europe into two spheres of influence, with Italy in the Western, non-Soviet zone. It follows from this that the Allies would have a free hand in Italy, come what may, and that the Russians would not meddle. Yet there was abundant evidence that the Russians' intentions were not so benign. One of the most significant bits of information was provided by a tour of southern Italy by a Soviet labor delegation in October 1944. Invited by the Communist trade union leader Giuseppe di Vittorio, the Russians spent the better part of the month travelling under the auspices of the *Confederazione Generale Italiana del Lavoro* (CGIL), dominated then, as now, by the PCI. Since a similar tour had been arranged earlier for an Anglo-American labor group, the Control Commission cooperated with the Russians in setting up their trip. The Soviet delegates were accompanied by an extremely observant and well-informed ACC labor relations officer named Scicluna, who filed a detailed report on the tour the following month.[64]

Scicluna's report left little doubt that the Russians had been sent for several reasons. First, they were intent on bolstering the Soviet image in Italy, particularly with the working class. Second, they wanted to support the CGIL throughout the South. Third, they wanted to make it unmistakably clear that the PCI was the Soviet spokesman in Italy. Fourth, they wished to support the Popular Front strategy, especially as regarded the trade union movement. Fifth, they wanted to sabotage efforts by other trade unions to build strength. Last, they used the tour to "further the spread of Soviet ideals and creating a spirit of confidence and respect for Soviet Russia, rather than as an opportunity for the Soviet delegates to see the conditions of the working classes and to study the trade union organization in liberated Italy."

The Soviets maneuvered to avoid any Allied surveillance. The itinerary for each day was announced only in the morning, and the schedule prepared by the ACC was frequently ignored. Whenever the Socialist delegate was absent, both the Russians and di Vittorio took more violent rhetorical positions than when the Socialist was present. The Christian Democrat who accompanied the group was twice abandoned (once he was forced to hitchhike to catch up with the tour, while the second time Scicluna went back to fetch him). Once in a new city, the Russians would closet themselves with local Communist and CGIL leaders, excluding the non-Communists from the meetings, and Scicluna was constantly impressed with the financial resources available to the Communists:

> The delegation was everywhere lavishly entertained at banquets attended by many Communists and a small minority of the "white" trade union. Expenses in connection with these entertainments as well as for hotel accommodations were ostensibly being defrayed by the local "Camera del Laboro" though circumstantial evidence suggests other sources.

Scicluna was also able to observe the quite substantial traffic in firearms that was going on under the cover of the partisan movement, even though the Allied military government had passed legislation requiring that all partisans turn over their weapons as soon as their area had been liberated.

> Between the arms legitimately obtained . . . and those seized from the disintegrating Italian Army, the Rome Socialist-Communist partisan groups, one is reliably informed, had in their possession hand grenades, some motorcycles and armoured cars, as well as approximately 30,000 firearms . . . of which some 10,000 were distributed to the sectional leaders while the remainder was held in reserve.

This military strength enabled the partisans—in concert with the trade union organizations and the political wing of the Resistance (the *Comitati di liberazione*)—to exert tremendous pressure on employers. (Communists in liberated areas got some of their commissars appointed to high positions in private industry, and they encouraged the formation of powerful union groups within the factories. This was part of a carefully designed strategy that was laid down in detail by di Vittorio at each stop along the tour.)

Scicluna concluded that the United States would be forced to challenge the Russians for the future of Italy, and that the Americans should "force the revolutionary issue before the withdrawal from Italy of the Anglo-American troops." In this connection Scicluna made two main recommendations:

> 1. The Americans should attempt to exploit the internal divisions within the Socialist party by discrediting Nenni. "One has reason to believe that there is a great deal that could be said of Nenni, who has been in the pay of Russia while in Paris, and is cunningly directing the Socialist movement towards political absorption by the Communist party."
>
> 2. In the trade union field, the United States should encourage the anarcho-syndicalists and more moderate Socialists, in order to block the hegemony of the Communists. The United States should also attempt to undermine the strategy of a unified trade union organization, which would in all likelihood come under Communist control.

Finally, Scicluna insisted that steps be taken to counter Soviet claims that Russia had become the paradise of the working classes, and urged the Americans to enlist the Vatican in this effort.

Scicluna was well ahead of his time; much of his strategy would be applied by the United States during the frantic election campaign of 1948. In 1944, however, Italy was simply not a major question for the United States (nor for Great Britain either, aside from its use as a conduit for Allied troops), and such an elaborate operation could not be mounted. Furthermore, when the war ended, American fears were calmed when the great majority of the partisans simply turned in their arms, and the Communists brought the Resistance under control. With rare exceptions, there was no sign of a radical insurrection.[65]

To be sure, few Americans believed that the Communists had ceased to extend Soviet influence in Italy, but they were impressed at the rapid demilitarization of the partisans. The Americans knew that this was not particularly popular (especially since some of it occurred at a time when there was still risk of attack from Nazi forces), but they also knew that Togliatti had given strict instructions that Allied orders be obeyed.

It is worth noting that the Americans were not alone in the view that the Communists were dissembling a peaceful strategy; many comrades held the same view. For many years, tens of thousands of Communists held themselves in readiness for the inevitable insurrection, their view of revolution being based on accounts of the storming of the Winter Palace and the creation of the Soviets.[66] But this was not to be, whether by design or by force of circumstance. Above all, Stalin did not want it, at least in the latter days of the war, and the PCI was not about to challenge his desires.

Soviet control of the "revolutionary" emotions of some Italian Communists[67] does not, however, mean—as the likes of Gabriel Kolko have suggested[68]—that the Communists saved capitalism. Kolko says that "where the Russians could control indigenous, powerful Communist parties, they served an essentially moderating and conservative function, compelling the world Communist parties to choose between obedience and success." The purported reason for this Soviet conservatism was a desire to consolidate their hold on Eastern Europe ("their essential security interests"), and because the Russians "were aware by mid-1944 of numerous Anglo-American acts of resistance to the Left."[69]

These claims do not stand up. First of all, the Soviet tactics in Western Europe were simply a continuation of the Comintern line, which had been constant since the mid-thirties. The Soviets had no reason to alter this strategy, since the real choice in countries like Italy and France was not between "obedience and success," but rather between a rational strategy for achieving power, and folly.

Moreover, the insurrectionary option was not abandoned, but rather deferred; this is the significance of the clandestine hoarding of weapons during the Resistance. For while Togliatti publicly advocated a parliamentary strategy ("the long march"), the PCI simultaneously created a clandestine army, the so-called *Partito Armato*. The story of this secret army belongs to a later chapter, but the fact of its existence, and the Americans' knowledge of the fact, were significant at war's end.[70]

The Americans believed that the Communists were planning for an armed assault someday, but they also believed that the basic cause of communism lay in the social and economic spheres. They were thus inclined to look for economic solutions to the Communist threat; there was little interest in turning Italy into an American garrison.

L'envoi

At the end of his tour as chief commissioner, Rear Admiral Ellery Stone sent a long analysis of the Italian situation to the Supreme Allied Commander. Dated 23 June 1945,[71] it well summarizes the model on which subsequent American policy would be based.

> Italy is at the parting of the ways . . . she has had five governments since September 1943; a million of her men have been in exile either as slave labor or as prisoners of war; more than half a million of her people have suffered dislocation of home; her financial position is precarious; her economy has been totally disrupted . . . without coal and raw materials she faces unemployment amounting to several millions; the country is full of arms illegally held. Like other European countries devastated by the war, the ground in Italy is fertile for the rapid growth of the seeds of an anarchical movement fostered by Moscow to bring Italy within the sphere of Russian influence. Already there are signs that, if present conditions long continue, communism will triumph—possibly by force.

Yet Stone was convinced that communism could not be defeated by "restrictive or repressive measures. Since the conditions which engender it are both material and moral, the only hope of restraining it in Italy is to ameliorate these conditions. . . ." Stone therefore recommended a policy that would improve economic conditions (aid), raise Italian morale (by lifting some of the harsh terms of the armistice), and encourage the spread of democratic values. As Stone warned, "Unless they receive help and guidance from the democracies . . . they will inevitably turn to the U.S.S.R. and join the group of 'police' states."

Stone made detailed recommendations about the treatment of Italian armed forces. Finally, he felt it important for the Allies to carry out training programs for the armed forces and the police, this last in order to remove Fascist elements: "It is essential . . . that immediate steps be taken to overhaul and possibly reconstitute the whole of the public security agencies in Italy, based on democratic principles."

For all of the fear of insurrection, then, the primary weapons against the Communist threat in Italy were to be economic assistance and democratic education. At times of great tension (such as the electoral campaign of 1948, or the Communist offensive against the Marshall Plan the previous year), the Americans would take more direct action, even fomenting divisions with the labor movement and supporting moderate Socialists to break with Nenni. But such actions were rare, and almost always taken in response to Italian initiatives. Finally, and perhaps most important, was the general American ignorance about and lack of interest in Italian problems.[72]

Thus, for all of the intelligence work carried out by OSS, for all the fine analysis of Communist intentions and Socialist acceptance of PCI domination, for all the suggestions of promising lines of action for the United States in Italy, by and large the Americans dealt with Italy as a small corner of Europe. There would be no real American initiative specifically designed for Italy until 1947, when the crisis came to a head. It was not until then that the United States finally discarded an attitude that is termed *abulia*,[73] a pathological form of lack of will.

Notes

A general note on sources: Some of the information used in this book comes from confidential interviews. Rather than use some awkward and unsatisfying reference like "confidential interview," I have simply omitted the reference.

1. The best sources on the war years in Italy remain the memoirs of the major participants. Thus, for the nature of British policy see Churchill's memoirs, as well as Pietro Badoglio, *Italy in the Second World War* (London, 1948), Mark Clark, *Calculated Risk* (New York, 1950), and the highly polemical but still indicative writings of Luigi Longo and Pietro Secchia about the relations between the Allies and the Resistance.
2. See, for example, the OSS Report on British policy written in the summer of 1944: OSS, Research and Analysis Branch (henceforth OSS/R&A) #2318, "British policy in Italy." The thrust of this document is that "British views and aims in regard to Italy do not always coincide with those of the other Allied powers."

    In fact, OSS was highly critical of the British, as a later statement in the same document shows: "It is clear that the apparent British aim of reducing Italy to a position of political and military subserviency runs counter to the hopes and aspirations of the great majority of Italians, whose repudiation of Fascism does not imply surrender of their claim to national independence."

    Many in OSS believed that the British were heavily responsible for the growth in Communist strength: "The spectacular growth of the Italian Communist party during the past year seems to be attributable, in large measure, precisely to the British policy of supporting the monarchy and its reactionary adherents." The author of these words seems not to have considered the irony that the PCI held precisely the same position as the "reactionary" British—an error that would be repeated many times in the future by American analysts.
3. See, for example, OSS/R&A #2993, "Contributions of the Italian partisans to the Allied War Effort," 31 March 1945.
4. OSS/R&A #1448, "Political Dilemma in Italy," 15 October 1943. The quotation that follows in the text is from p. 17.
5. For a discussion of Churchill's position, as viewed from the Italian side, see

Antonio Gambino, *Storia del Dopoguerra; dalla liberazione al potere DC* (Rome and Bari, 1975), especially 26-29, and Lamberto Mercuri, *1943-1945, Gli Alleati e l'Italia* (Naples, 1975). These two books complement each other: Gambino is excellent on the political maneuvers of the period, but does not pay sufficient attention to the purely military and administrative problems facing the Allies, while Mercuri—who has performed a real service in looking at the questions of military government—is weaker on the Italian political scene.

6. "Political Dilemma in Italy," *op. cit.*, 10. The subsequent quotation is from pp. 19-20.
7. On the other hand, Donovan recognized that this was impossible. According to a recent study, Donovan could never quite make up his mind about the political requirements of OSS activity in Italy and France, where the Communists were the dominant underground force. Anthony Cave Brown, *The Secret War Report of the OSS* (New York, 1976), 5-6. On loyalty to the king, cf. p. 195.
8. Norman Kogan, *Italy and the Allies* (Cambridge, 1956), 99 ff.
9. R. Harris Smith, *OSS: The Secret History of America's First Intelligence Agency* (Berkeley, Los Angeles, London, 1972). "Donovan found that political leftists were often the most valiant field officers in his espionage and sabotage branches. When the FBI triumphantly presented the general with dossiers of three OSS employees with Communist party affiliations and demanded their ouster from the organization, Donovan responded, 'I know they're Communists; that's why I hired them.' The men in question had fought with the Abraham Lincoln Brigade for the Republican Loyalists in the Spanish Civil War of 1936-1939" (p. 11). Two of the officers in question were undoubtedly Vincent Lassowski and Irving Goff, later accused of having been chairman of the Louisiana Communist party and of the Veterans Committee of the New York Communist party. Brown, *op. cit.*, 193.

The current availability of documentation does not permit any serious evaluation of the role played by Communists in OSS (or, for that matter, in the British SOE in the same period). It may eventually be demonstrated that some of these acted as Soviet agents of influence within OSS. It appears that this may have happened in Yugoslava, where SOE officers slanted information in such a way to induce Churchill to switch his support from Mihailovich to Tito. See David Martin, *Patriot or Traitor; The case of General Mihailovich* (Stanford, 1978), 117 ff.
10. Conversations with Max Salvadori and H. Stuart Hughes.
11. OSS/R&A #1681, "The Radical Trend in German-occupied Italy," n.d. (but clearly December 1943), 2.
12. *Ibid.*, 3.
13. *Ibid.*, 4.
14. The documentation on the "spheres of influence" theory is enormous. The best recent study of Soviet diplomacy in the period—and a healthy corrective to some of the "revisionist" views of Stalin—is Vojtech Mastny, *Russia's Road to the Cold War* (New York, 1979). As Mastny notes, "In the last analysis (Stalin's) hands were tied by the Soviet system which had bred him and which he felt compelled to perpetuate by his execrable methods; that system was the true cause of the Cold War" (p. 306). According to Mastny, the "spheres" never really existed in any firm form (and surely not in the form claimed by Churchill in his memoirs); Stalin had ambitions but no grand design, and any agreement at any time was open to unilateral revision as the "objective situation" changed.

Furthermore, it turns out that the "spheres of influence" were very different indeed from the account given by Churchill, and accepted by the conventional wisdom as an element of fundamental importance in Communist behavior in the West. For if Stalin had granted the British and the Americans the primary responsibility for Western Europe, there could by definition be no Soviet-guided insurrection. This hypothesis falls when it is realized that the Americans were not privy to the "deal" in the first place, and did not approve it when they learned about it. "Indeed, the United States was not even completely informed of the terms. And the Department of State was left to shift for itself in running down the details. Roosevelt and Hull showed a puzzling lack of curiosity in not directly asking the British or the Soviets for details. . . ." Albert Resis, "The Churchill-Stalin Secret 'Percentages' Agreement on the Balkans, Moscow, October 1944," in *The American Historical Review*, Vol. 83, #2, April 1978, 384-385.

Finally, and perhaps most importantly, there was no American understanding about spheres of influence outside the highest levels of the government. Stuart Hughes, at the time the head of the Division of Research for Europe in the State Department, had no knowledge of the deal (if such it was), and claims to have learned of its existence only five years afterwards when Churchill wrote about it for the first time. Nonetheless, they shared its basic assumptions. "We reached the notion of spheres of influence on our own." H. Stuart Hughes, "The Second Year of the Cold War," in *Commentary*, August 1969, 28.

15. Gambino, *op. cit.*, 38.
16. The cable, #5607, has only recently been declassified.
17. Cable from MacFarlane to AFHQ 3 April 1944. See also Murphy's cable from Algiers to the secretary of state, 27 April, referring to a conversation he had with Sforza on 7 April in Naples.
18. Murphy to the secretary of state, 22 April 1944. The cable begins, "Last evening Badoglio beaming with satisfaction told me of his labors during the past week in working what he described as 'the alchemy of politics'. . . ."
19. There are several excellent OSS profiles on "Ercoli" that show great understanding of Togliatti's role in the Communist International. Indeed, some of the Americans had a better understanding of the matter than many of Togliatti's Italian comrades. One of the best OSS studies, dated 25 February 1944 (that is, even before Togliatti's formal reentry) and entitled "Communists in Italy," is an outstanding example of political prediction. While many leading Communists believed that an insurrectionary strategy suited the Italian situation, the OSS knew differently: "In some ways the ideological evolution of the Comintern and the P.C.I. is reflected in the evolution of Ercoli's personal qualities. In the twenties he appeared to be quite sectarian and bitter. Since the middle thirties, he has apparently become softer, more 'reasonable' and more cooperative in his manner as well as in his views and he has shown considerable agility in observing and in trying to manipulate non-Communist persons and movements." The same document presumed that Ercoli would return to Italy in the near future, and accurately forecast the effects within the PCI leadership of this event.
20. On the *svolta* see, above all, Umberto Terracini, *Intervista sul comunismo difficile* (Rome and Bari, 1978), 81 ff.
21. Renato Mieli, "Stalinismo all'Italiana," in *il Giornale nuovo*, 4 July 1978. Mieli's various historical articles in *il Giornale* are among the most important contributions to an accurate history of the PCI. A former editor of *l'Unità*, Mieli broke with the party in the 1950s.

22. *Ibid.*
23. *Ibid.* See also Renato Mieli, "Un testimone del terrore," in *il Giornale nuovo*, 20 March 1979.
24. Terracini, *op. cit.*, 14.
25. At the end of the war, American intelligence officers in Italy captured a vast quantity of documentation dealing with the relations between the clandestine PCI apparatus in Italy during the Facist period and Soviet "control" abroad. This documentation, which remains classified, included the evidence of serious conflicts between PCI members—naively convinced that they would be allowed to pursue a genuinely independent course of action—and Soviet intelligence. After the war, the discussions continued. Indeed, it was commonplace in some foreign intelligence services that the Soviets recruited agents among the ranks of Western European Communist parties only in extremeis; as a general principle, this was not done. However, according to several Western intelligence sources, the Soviets not only did not end the practice, but made formal promises to the Europeans to terminate such recruitment on at least two occasions: once shortly after the death of Stalin, and again in the mid-1960s.
26. It is unfortunately typical of much of what passes for political analysis these days, that there is virtually no mention of the problem of Soviet intelligence control over foreign Communist parties in any of the current literature on "Eurocommunism." As will be shown, this myopia is not restricted to the academic or journalistic communities; it reflects a shift in reporting by American embassies and American intelligence agencies as well. But anyone interested in the question of "independence from Moscow" by the Western European Communist parties must come to grips with this problem.

    To anticipate slightly what follows, there has certainly been a change in the relationship between Russia and the European Communists. This change is reflected in the use of European Communists for intelligence purposes. But the Soviet attempt to maintain control has certainly not ended, and the relationship thus remains, at best, an uneasy one, for those European Communists who do not wish to function as the *lunga manus* of the Kremlin.
27. Giorgio Amendola, *Intervista sull'antifascismo* (Rome and Bari, 1976), 118-120.
28. The phrase comes from a letter written by G.D. Horner in Allied Force HQ to Samuel Reber in Washington, 7 April 1944: "(Togliatti) is known as the world's number 1 Italian Communist and one of the world's top leading international Communists."
29. MacFarlane, "Top Secret," 20 April 1944.
30. "Memorandum" from OSS/R&A, 16 April 1944, on the Communists and the U.S.S.R. in Italy.
31. *Ibid.*
32. MacFarlane, 3 April 1944 (Fatima M134).
33. "Memorandum," *op. cit.* This document is cited by Kolko, but only the last paragraph is quoted (the part referring to the March on Rome). Kolko typically ignores all the discussion of active Soviet penetration of Italy, and consequently makes the author of the document look like a visceral anti-Communist. In fact, the author demonstrated a reasoned anticommunism.
34. The Americans, as has been shown, were not alone; most Italian Communists were similarly convinced that Togliatti's appeals to moderation and to the politics of national unity were a trick. As Gambino has put it—with a fine sense

of paradoxes involved—this led to a situation in which the PCI actually had two doctrines:

"In the PCI a relationship is established between the esoteric doctrine, that is secret, and the exoteric doctrine, that is vulgar. This relationship is more subtle and contorted than that of the most refined Oriental sects. The affirmations of Togliatti—that the Communists have no ulterior motives, are not awaiting the X hours, and want to work for a national policy, etc.—for all that they reuttered publicly and repeated every week, are really (because not truly believed by the majority of the members) the secret doctrine. Meanwhile, the exoteric and public doctrine is that which the PCI militants communicate, apparently secretly, by hints." Gambino, *op. cit.* 160 n.

35. Mastny has caught the irony of Stalin's attitudes in late 1943 and early 1944: "There was a certain amount of snobbery in the preference that Stalin, the revolutionary upstart, showed for dealing with established leaders. But this preference had practical advantages, too, provided his loyal Communist lieutenants could be used to make those leaders more pliable. Ideally, he wanted Communists to become powerful enough to be influential, but not so powerful that they would develop ambitions of their own. Rather than holding the power in their countries, they were to hold the key to its balance, which could then be manipulated conveniently from Moscow." Mastny, *op. cit.*, 143-144.
36. Fernando Claudin, *The Communist Movement* (London, 1975), 387.
37. The best description of the doctrine of the *Partito nuovo*—and one written with enthusiasm that would have warmed Togliatti's heart—is in a doctoral dissertation by Lawrence Gray for the School of Advanced International Studies, Johns Hopkins University. See note 49.
38. The document was produced for the Allied Control Commission. The National Archives of the United States (henceforth NAUS), Record Group #331 10,000/143, Box 10.
39. OSS "Control" document, 30 November 1944, "Several Thousand Prisoners of War in Russia Enrolled in Communist Propaganda Schools," NAUS, ID Documents, Record Group #319.
40. Interviews with former OSS officers.
41. OSS/R&A #1632.15, "Communists in Italy," 27 May 1944.
42. *Ibid.*
43. See, for example, OSS/R&A #1632.8 and 1632.10.
44. OSS Foreign Nationalities Branch, 21 August 1943, "The Communists and the Italian Crisis," NAUS, Record Group #84, Box 604.
45. OSS/R&A #1632.15, *op. cit.*, and interviews.
46. Interviews, with, among others, H. Stuart Hughes. There is an interesting follow-up to this division within American intelligence: Immediately after the war, much of the OSS/R&A was dismantled, and its practitioners went back to the universities within a few years (Hughes, Langer, Marcuse, Manuel, and others would come to constitute a sort of Who's Who of American intellectual life). The people involved in operations made up the core of the new CIA. Thus, by the time the Italian crisis of the spring of 1948 rolled around, the intelligence community was rather more hard-headed than the R&A people had been a few years before. Later in the 1950s, of course, CIA became a haven for liberals, since Allen Dulles shielded the agency from McCarthyism in a way the State Department did not. By the mid-1950s, the analyses in CIA were more liberal—by a long shot—than those in State. This will be seen in the chapter on the Opening to the Left.

47. Mercuri, *op. cit.*, 56-96. These are among the finest pages dedicated to the subject of the Allies in Italy.
48. The Stevenson Report is found in "Adlai Stevenson's Report on the Allied Military Government," in *The Bridgeport Sunday Herald Magazine,* 9 September 1956. See also Elena Aga-Rossi, "La politica degli Alleati verso l'Italia nel 1943," in *Storia Contemporanea,* III, #4 (1972).
49. Lawrence Gray, unpublished dissertation for the Johns Hopkins University, "The Pluralist Tradition of Italian Communism" (Baltimore, 1976), 207.
50. OSS "Control" Document #L49196, 9 November 1944, NAUS Record Group #226.
51. Among others, Gambino, Mercuri, and Kogan believe that the Allies could—and should—have done a lot more to support the Resistance.
52. Walter Laqueur, *Guerilla* (Boston and New York, 1978), 212.
53. Smith's account *(op. cit.)* is typical of dozens of similar cases:
"The partisans expected more of the OSS men and their disappointment was simply that much greater when plane-loads of American materiel failed to arrive. A few OSS officers, like the Lincoln Brigaders . . . remained on good terms with leftist guerrillas. Other Americans were less fortunate. A 26-year-old OSS major of German descent who dropped into northwestern Italy reported that the Garibaldini leaders were '10 percent for liberation and 90 percent for Russia. We soon found that they were burying the German arms they had captured, to save them for use after the war was over and the Americans had pulled out of Italy. What the Italians did after the war was over was their own business,' he added, 'but we were dropping weapons to the partisans for the purpose of saving American lives. I wanted our weapons used for this.' In return for his protests, the major discovered that the local Communist political commissar was plotting to have him murdered. He barely escaped. But in spite of all his mishaps, the major, like most OSS officers, retained an unswerving admiration for the rank-and-file of the resistance" (112).
54. B.H. Liddell Hart, *Strategy* (New York, 1967), 368-369.
55. Laqueur, *op. cit.,* 215.
56. On the Ardeatine Cave Massacre, see Attilio Ascarelli, *Le Fosse Ardeatine* (Rome, 1974).
57. 31 March 1945.
58. Nenni's apology for this behavior is to be found in Pietro Nenni, *Intervista sul socialismo italiano* (Rome and Bari, 1977).
59. OSS Document #A-42544, 27 October 1944, "Conversation with Pietro Nenni."
60. Quoted in Gambino, *op. cit.,* 124 n.
61. Among the available sources, see the lengthy document cited in note 64.
62. Gambino, *op. cit.,* 123-125.
63. Nenni, *op. cit.,* 65.
64. "Memorandum on the Soviet Labour Delegation to Italy," 18 November 1944, NAUS, Allied Control Commission Italy, Record Group #331 10,000/109/198, Box 6.
65. Nonetheless, in Italy (as in France) the myth of a "revolution betrayed" remains a very live issue. The only question for many Italians is whether "the revolution" was betrayed by the Allies or by Togliatti and Stalin.
66. This is one of the supreme ironies of the period, since it was undoubtedly the Russians—via Togliatti—who stifled any possibility of an attempt at insurrection.

67. The three most notorious figures in the PCI who were identified—rightly or wrongly—with this view were Pietro Secchia, Luigi Longo, and Cino Moscatelli.
68. Gabriel Kolko, *The Politics of War* (New York, 1969).
69. *Ibid.*, 36. I have chosen Kolko as an exemplar of a whole school of rhetoric, because the thesis is stated in its baldest form.
70. See OSS, Internal Dissemination Document #A-57485, 21 June 1945, "General Outline of the Communist Party Military Organization in the Milan Area," NAUS, Record Group #226, L57208.
71. NAUS, Allied Control Commission Italy, Record Group #331 10,000/109/313, Box 9.
72. Interviews with, among others, H. Stuart Hughes, James Dunn, and Henry Tasca.
73. Gambino, *op. cit.*, 335.

2

The Cold War in Italy

> *(The expulsion of the Communists from the governments of Italy and France in May 1947), rather than a consequence of American intervention, must be attributed to an objective similarity between the two situations, and to the polarization in both countries between the parties of the Center-Right and the Center-Left on the one hand, and the Communists on the other.*
> —Antonio Gambino[1]

From 1945 to 1949, the United States government slowly and reluctantly came to realize that American intervention in Europe was necessary if European democracy were to be effectively defended. The American actions began with largely indirect pressure on the Europeans in 1946, and culminated in the Marshall Plan, the Truman Doctrine, and the considerable American involvement in the Italian election campaign of 1948. Contrary to much of the conventional wisdom, these activities did not stem from a desire to support conservative governments in Western Europe. Rather, American policy was a reaction to what the Americans took to be a clear pattern of Soviet initiatives; the information reaching Washington showed in detail a Soviet-guided movement in Western Europe, aimed at the installation of radical governments that would be particularly vulnerable to Communist influence and eventual Communist domination.

Despite the abundant evidence, the United States acted quite slowly. The public was tired of war, and had no desire to leave many American soldiers behind in the old world to fight against the surrogates of our former Soviet ally. The low level of support in 1946-47 for vigorous American action abroad would not be reached again until the post-Vietnam period, and it is consequently easy to sympathize with the slow pace of the Truman administration. It is also easy to understand why, when Truman decided to support the West Europeans (and Iranians) against the Soviets and their proxies, he cast the policy in terms of the most dire necessity. The public, or so it must have seemed to the White House, simply would not support foreign action unless it were presented as a matter of life and death.

This is not to say that the grim warnings were necessarily false, for American officials throughout Europe received convincing information suggesting that the Communist parties, in coordination with the Soviet Union, were planning a series of steps leading to a Communist seizure of power. This coordinated action was said to have been scheduled for late 1947 and early 1948. Was the American government misinformed, or did Stalin really plan such a vast operation? The answer may lie in the Soviet archives, but such scattered information as we have indicates that the possibility was a very real one. This was a period of heightened labor agitation, particularly in France and Italy. It was also a moment of aggressive Soviet action in Czechoslovakia, Greece, and Finland (where a coup d'etat ordered by Stalin in early 1948 was foiled, thanks to the defection of the Communist minister of the interior). Stalin may very well have given instructions to prepare for a big push in Western Europe before the Marshall Plan's results could be seen.[2]

It may of course eventually be demonstrated that the Americans were wrong and that no such Soviet intentions existed. Much of the information reaching American intelligence officials in the West came from European governments that had every reason to overstate the threat. It was evident to the likes of De Gasperi, Sforza, Blum, and Ramadier that the Americans were more likely to give economic assistance if they believed that massive spending was required to save Europe from communism. It is important to note, for example, that these Europeans generally spoke in much more alarmist tones about communism to Americans than they did to their own citizens—at least until the overheated atmosphere of 1948, by which time the representatives of the Communist parties of France and Italy had been expelled from their respective governments for a year, and the Cold War was on.

Whatever the precise details, the threat to democracy in France and Italy—and therefore to American interests in Western Europe—was clear enough, and an American reaction was desperately needed. Interestingly, for those inclined to believe that the United States was basically shoring up conservative governments, the tone of most of the documents is quite different, stressing the need for greater liberalization and even structural reform in order to combat the extension of Soviet power and totalitarianism. As will be seen, the concern of the American officials was not based on ideology, but on a vast body of evidence regarding Soviet espionage, military and paramilitary activities under Communist and Soviet control, and Communist infiltration of other political parties and of the trade union movement.

American activities in Italy in the immediate postwar period were accordingly concentrated in areas where Soviet moves were most menacing: intelligence and counterintelligence, support for those elements of the Left that were prepared to break with the Communists, and support for non-Communist trade union organizations. For the most part, this support was kept secret, for a series of good reasons. First, it enhanced the efficiency and reliability of information-gathering. Second, it protected American friends from embarrassment and possible violent reprisals. And third, since a good part of the program was aimed against Communist clandestine actions, it made sense to have the response equally secret.

The Italian Communist Military Underground

Throughout the period following the *svolta di Salerno*, while Togliatti preached the merits of cooperation and moderation, the Communist party was building an armed force to support a seizure of power. The two PCI officials in charge of this task were Luigi Longo and Pietro Secchia.[3] Longo had had extensive military experience as one of the two leading Communist military commanders in the Spanish Civil War, and had been the head of the Garibaldi Brigades during the Resistance. Secchia, whose name came to be identified with the whole enterprise, demonstrated outstanding organizational abilities, and his deep commitment to Leninist revolutionary goals made him the ideal chief of the organization, which the Americans referred to as the *Apparato militare* (the Italians generally called it the *Partito Armato*).

Togliatti organized the *Partito Nuovo* while Secchia created the *Partito Armato*. Secchia thus played Trotsky to Togliatti's Lenin, by training the clandestine cadres who would have to fight in the event of open conflict. Secchia organized a network of couriers who transported the documents of the party to Prague, where the PCI archives remained until well after the death of Stalin (thus providing the Kremlin with an additional element of control over the party, for all the secrets of the members were in the custody of Soviet agents in Czechoslovakia). And Secchia managed the secret funds of the party, smuggled into Italy in the diplomatic pouches of Soviet and East European diplomats for decades following the war. Divided into smaller parcels, the millions of dollars (generally in American banknotes) were deposited in safes in the homes of party faithful, to be withdrawn and used as needed.[4]

All these activities were supervised by Secchia from his post as the head of PCI Organization from 1945 to 1954. And while he was under Togliatti's control, Secchia acquired an imposing personal power base. From the end of the war until the autumn of 1947 (when the party was instructed by the

Comintern to adopt a more aggressively anti-American line), while Togliatti played Lenin the moderate Secchia preached the sermon of violent resistance, supervised the arming and training of the partisan formations that were brought under party control, and rehearsed the armed struggle. For many within the PCI, Secchia represented the true revolution. Togliatti was complex, devious, and intellectual; Secchia was unambiguous and spoke a familiar, aggressive language most party members fully approved. These comrades looked to him for instructions, awaiting his command to storm the barricades.

The history of the *Partito Armato* remains to be written. In part, this is due to a paucity of reliable information, in part because of the understandable preference of historians and apologists to deal with the more attractive and intellectually more stimulating political and cultural aspects of Togliatti's party. But in so doing they have failed to analyze an ingredient of prime importance within the PCI. As Giorgio Bocca, one of the most honest students of Italian communism, has written:

> Togliatti has his politics, and we know what they are. But he cannot reject *a priori*, or ignore, the X hour, which is not the mythical revolution, but may be atomic war, or a conventional conflict in Europe, or an anti-Communist coup.[5]

In an interview with Bocca in the 1970s, Secchia insisted that his organization was not a "party within the party," but an attempt to create a tightly organized group of totally loyal followers. Former partisans were placed in key sectors of the trade union movement, for example, where they could be used as labor organizers. In addition, in Secchia's words:

> In all the federations, we carried out a sort of partisan census in order to know, place by place, which elements could be trusted. The hiding of arms was a secondary element. When a mass organization exists, the weapons can always be found.[6]

Yet the *Partito Armato* was more than a small group of former Resistance fighters, and from time to time its real face was seen. The most spectacular case was that of the infamous *Volante Rossa*, which flourished from 1945 to 1949. This was a mixed bag of "legal" and clandestine party members who became particularly active following the aggressive turn in PCI strategy in the autumn and winter of 1947-48. The *Volante Rossa* was a sort of Pretorian Guard for the PCI, providing security at the Six Party Congress in 1948 and serving as bodyguards for foreign dignitaries, ranging from the Soviet representatives to French Communist leader Maurice Thorez. The members of this quasi-autonomous band were renowned for their unrestrained violence, and many of them were forced to go into exile (as a general rule to Czechoslovakia, where some of the them went to work at Radio Prague) after being condemned for murder and armed assault. The leader of the *Volante Rossa*, Giulio Paggio, himself went into Czech exile to avoid imprisonment.[7]

The *Volante Rossa* was closely tied to the PCI, although Togliatti was careful not to give the organization a formal stamp of party legitimacy. The story is told that at the 1948 Congress some of the group asked Togliatti for his autograph on their bright red identity cards. He reportedly replied, "not on these cards, but on party membership cards, yes."[8] The two PCI officials who maintained close working relations with the *Volante* were Secchia and Giuseppe Alberganti, who was the official in charge of the Milan Communist Federation in the late 1940s.

While the existence of the *Volante Rossa* was hardly a secret (even though it had a clandestine wing), the bulk of the *Partito Armato* was not nearly so visible. Evidence for its existence comes from personal testimony of the participants, from documents of the American government and its intelligence agencies (some of which came from Italian and other foreign sources), and from the one spontaneous appearance of the clandestine paramilitary organization in the streets of Italy following the attempted assassination of Togliatti in July 1948.

The Americans received considerable information about the Armed party, but although they were certain it existed, they were less confident about its precise strength and the identity of its leaders. A cable from Dunn to Washington in June 1947, is typical:

> There have recently been reports, often from reliable sources, of large potential military and paramilitary formations under Communist control in Italy, especially the North. There is no doubt that Communist Party has military organization based on former Communist controlled partisan formations... the number of these armed Communist elements has been placed as high as 150,000 men. The Embassy believes that this figure is too high insofar as actually armed elements are concerned. It is of opinion that there are in neighborhood of 50,000 trained men equipped with light weapons and side arms at disposition of CPI. This does not include however unarmed or semi-armed men who might rally to Communist banner in case of insurrection.[9]

The sources of American information are not always known.[10] One was the Italian military intelligence organization, SIM; another was SIFAR, the reconstituted political police (following the dissolution of the Fascist OVRA); yet another was the *Carabinieri*, the elite paramilitary force who often served an intelligence function. There were also many "walk-ins," people who had done work for OSS or British Intelligence during the war, or opportunists simply looking for a way to make some money and acquire some useful friends at a time when jobs were scarce. It took some time for the Americans to sort out the reliable sources, and also to identify the so-called disinformation agents put out by the Communists and the Soviets to deceive the American officials.

In addition to these external information sources, the Americans had organizations of their own, ranging from the relatively visible operation coming out of the military attache's office to a deep cover group that had no contact with the embassy at all. This latter organization was run by James J. Angleton, a former top official of X-2, the OSS counterintelligence group, and by all accounts was one of the best-designed and best-informed organizations in Europe at the time.

The information arriving from reliable sources in Italy identified an Armed party that was based largely in the North, was well armed and fairly well trained, and was in constant touch with Soviet advisers and control agents. It is worthwhile to consider a fairly typical dispatch at some length, in order to get the flavor of the phenomenon. It came from the Florence Consulate in mid-October 1947:

> Reliable sources report that Communists in Florence are in possession of approximately 300 submachine guns, 10 heavy machine guns, 1500 carbines and a great many hand-grenades. Although it could easily be supposed that former partisans would constitute the nucleus of Communist action groups, it has been ascertained that Communist leaders are not inclined to be completely confident concerning their control of the partisans and, therefore, these are kept as a reserve force. The minimum estimate concerning Communist forces that can enter into action immediately is slightly more than 1,000 men. Several Russian officers have been in Florence for varying periods of time, sometimes several months, for the purpose of military instruction of these semimilitary units. These Communist organizations have disguised themselves under various forms such as the "Red Carnation" which pretends to be a welfare organization. Other secret Communist agents visit the city periodically for the purpose of purchasing supplies on the local market which are then shipped to Yugoslavia. It has been ascertained that stolen American military material has sometimes formed part of these shipments.
>
> The efforts of the police to conduct investigations with reference to the activities of foreign agents have not proved to be particularly successful inasmuch as the latter are furnished with forged documents, many times with the connivance of public officials in other parts of Italy, notably Bologna. However, it has been reported that shortly before the demonstration scheduled for 20 September 1947, five Yugoslav agents from Trieste were in Florence for a short visit.[11]

There was clearly a substantial Communist military organization, closely linked to the Soviet Union. The Soviet connections were not limited to the occasional military adviser or clandestine agent from Yugoslavia; there were also Soviet agents within the PCI. There were several top Communist officials with intimate relations with the Kremlin: Togliatti, with his long years in Moscow; Longo, with his experience in the International Brigade in Spain; Secchia, who had supported Stalin's commands for the suicidal *svolta* and was widely regarded as the Russians' man in Rome; Moscatelli, one of the leaders of the Garibaldi Brigades during the Resistance, nicknamed the "murderous colonel" during the late years of the war; and Antonio Roasio, the head of the Central Cadre Office in Rome until late 1948, when he took over the Emlia-Romagna organization. In late 1948, the Americans uncovered some information about Roasio that threw additional light on the Armed party, and on the PCI as well:

> During the purges which took place in the Soviet Union in 1937, Hon. Antonio Roasio gave rise to some suspicion regarding his loyalty to the Bolshevist cause. He, as well as other Italian emigrants, was arrested by the NKVD (now called MVD). He was kept in prison until irrefutable evidence of his Communist orthodoxy had been obtained. Afterwards, however, he became an active collaborator of the Soviet police. He carried out his assignments with such ability and shrewdness that he obtained wide praise and recognition and was even granted an officer rank in the NKVD hierarchy.[12]

In the American evaluation of this information, said to originate from "PCI circles," was "B-3." This meant that the source was quite reliable, and the information "probable." It was therefore not certain that Roasio was a Soviet intelligence agent, but the hypothesis was credible. Given Roasio's position, and the other evidence of Soviet penetration of Italy, the possibility had to be taken seriously. The Central Cadre Office in Rome was one of the most important elements in the party structure, and vied with "Organization" as the key to the formation of the PCI hierarchy. The official PCI school in the Alban Hills outside Rome was under Roasio's control and, as the American document indicated, the Cadre Office was "in charge of espionage and CE activities."

Whatever his role in the Soviet intelligence service, Roasio was certainly well liked by the Russians, and long after he became a relatively minor figure in the party structure he continued to participate in activities meaningful to the Soviet Union. He was part of the official PCI delegation to Mocow for Stalin's funeral, as well as for the celebration of the fiftieth anniversary of the October Revolution in 1977. And Togliatti himself, when asked why Roasio continued to hold positions of honor in later years, bluntly replied, "because the Russians like him."[13]

In addition to firsthand observation of the Soviet hand within the Armed party, the Americans received a series of highly detailed reports on the international structure within which the PCI's military wing functioned. According to these reports (some of which originated outside Italy, others from the Christian Democratic party, and still others from the *Carabinieri*), the Armed party was one element in an international organization reporting to the Soviet Politburo. These documents[14] (which, however, were never given maximum credibility by the embassy) claimed that the PCI was controlled through Lubiana, Yugoslavia, "which is linked laterally with the subcentrals of Geneva (for France) and of Lisbon (for the Iberian Peninsula). The union of the three subcentrals constitutes the 'Latin Horizontal.'"[15] The reports went on to give names of Soviet control agents, intermediaries, reliable elements within the PCI, military commanders in Italy, and so forth.

This vision of a centrally controlled continental military conspiracy may have seemed exaggerated to some of the American analysts, but there was some intriguing supporting information. As early as January 1944, the Americans were receiving alleged intercepts of communications to Italian Communist groups in northern Italy coming from Yugoslavia.[16] Some of the messages were said to arrive by courier (even, on occasion, by submarine), while others came by radio. The content of the messages was interesting: instructions for political and paramilitary action, infiltration of specified targets, intelligence operations directed against British, American, and Zionist groups,[17] and indications of the impending arrival of Soviet inspection teams. It is not known if these intercepts were genuine, or if the Americans and Italians acted on them, but the very existence of the information enhanced the overall picture of a vast, underground network.

To be sure, there was also considerable evidence of independence by some PCI leaders, and public occasions on which party members openly criticized the Soviet Union. So that even if there was an international Communist network under Soviet control, and even if many Italian Communists were Russian agents, one still had to account for the "deviations" from the Kremlin line. One possible explanation was that the apparent independence of some Italians was a deception, designed to lull their opponents or to test the true loyalty of other party members. Such strategic deception was a well-known Soviet method,[18] and could not be ruled out in the case of the PCI.

Another explanation was that there were really two Communist parties: the visible, "legal" one led by Togliatti, and the clandestine structure that would emerge only after the seizure of power. In this view, such apparently moderate figures as Togliatti and Terracini would be permitted to conduct political disinformation and to construct a mass party, but behind these figures stood others, with the full force of the Kremlin and the Soviet secret police behind them. In a report that originated at high levels of the *Carabinieri* in mid-1947, one finds the claim that the real chief of the PCI was Pietro Secchia.

> Togliatti is automatically the head of the party. But . . . in reality the power to deliberate is in the hands of Secchia who enjoys the confidence of the "politburo" whose instruction he interprets . . . Longo and Moscatelli are advisers on matters of a military nature.[19]

A similar picture of the PCI, albeit with a different candidate for the "real" party leader, was sketched out in the State Department Division of Biographic Information the following year, in its biography of Luigi Longo:

> According to some observers, Longo is the real power in the Communist party, while Togliatti is merely the nominal head. It has been said that Longo is the Italian Communist who enjoys the greatest influence with Stalin and other Soviet leaders. He is regarded as the only link between the political and military branches of the party and the only one who knows the secrets of both. . . .
>
> In addition to commanding the . . . Communist paramilitary organization, Longo is reportedly inspector of schools for theoretical and practical instruction in clandestine warfare, is nominal head of recruiting and arming of volunteers for the "International Brigade," and is national director of an autonomous corps of eliminators and saboteurs formed in August 1947.[20]

The view that there was a secret leader of the PCI was shared by many at the time. In their view, Togliatti seemed ill-suited to lead a Leninist insurrection or to govern a Communist state. He seemed too flexible, too intellectual, and lacking in toughness to install a Stalinist regime. Moreover, he hardly seemed the sort to organize and command the military apparatus that had been created in Italy.

The theory was intellectually attractive, but false. The error stemmed from the lack of evidence regarding Togliatti himself, particularly about his work on Stalin's behalf during the war years. The Americans had not yet pieced together Togliatti's actions in Spain during the Civil War, where he played a major role as the Kremlin's prime representative in the field prior to the final debacle. And, above all, the Americans were unaware of Togliatti's heavy responsibilities for the Great Purge in Russia. It was not until the PCI in 1979 published a volume of Togliatti's works from the thirties and early forties that it was finally established that "Ercoli" not only knew what was going on around him, but actively participated in the horrors:

> Togliatti . . . follows the development of the trials very closely, attends numerous sessions, probably discusses them with Stalin himself to give his own

opinion or to receive orders. In the Comintern offices ... near Red Square, Togliatti writes incendiary articles ... for the communists of the entire world ... Togliatti also coordinates and controls the public relations production ... destined for European readers and prepared by some of his own collaborators: he receives the articles of Humbert-Droz, stimulates Fischer.[21]

We now know that there was no question about Togliatti's capabilities, whether in the field of propaganda, in military strategy, or Stalinist repression. But Togliatti's problems were quite different from Stalin's. He was the leader of a party, not a nation; he did not have the option of resorting to systematic terror within the PCI (although there were some purges); and he was eager to create a mass party, not narrow his base to a handful of loyalists. In apparent accord with Stalin, Togliatti therefore embarked upon the creation of the *Partito Nuovo* in order to swell the ranks of the party, but at the same time the *Partito Armato* was being readied for other purposes. This dual structure of the party was well described by Secchia some thirty years afterwards:

> A Communist Party, a revolutionary party, must have two organizations, one large, mass, articulated organization, visible to all, and one small and secret. This is necessary even in times of the most ample democracy and legality, because one should never have confidence in the plans of the enemy. We want to proceed along a peaceful path advancing towards socialism. But does the enemy agree? Will he stand by and watch? It is necessary to prepare for every eventuality, and this can be done by having both a propagandistic apparatus (to orient public opinion) and an organizational one (for relations with both our soldiers and officials and those of the adversary), along with a structure adequate to face any development.[22]

The full extent of Togliatti's involvement in all aspects of Communist activities, including the nastiest of Stalin's actions, was kept secret from the world until well after his death, and even to most of his close friends and associates Togliatti had the image of a Stalinist *malgré lui*, a man who reluctantly carried out orders, but who had never been one of the leading participants in terror. The image of an innocent Togliatti was important for both internal and external reasons. Within the PCI it was necessary to present Togliatti as one who was trusted by Stalin and who transmitted Stalin's orders to the party, but also a man who represented a milder, Latin version of communism. To be sure, for most of his life it was advantageous for Togliatti to pass as a loyal Stalinist, but even so most party members were ignorant of the full extent of Togliatti's activities. The case of Giuseppe Berti[23] is typical in this regard.

Long considered the second most important figure in the PCI's clandestine international apparatus during the Fascist period, Berti purged the Central Committee at the PCI's foreign center in Paris in the late thirties, and took charge of the operation there. Berti and Togliatti had agreed that if the Germans marched on Paris, the PCI foreign headquarters should be shifted to New York. The move was duly carried out in June 1940.

Unluckily for Berti, Stalin was infuriated by the move, and Togliatti quite predictably told the Soviet dictator that the decision to move the center to America and been Berti's alone, and that the party would take appropriate disciplinary measures once normality was reestablished. Thus, after the war, Berti was denounced for "abandoning his post of combat in the face of the enemy," and was driven from the inner circles of the PCI. Berti in vain requested an open hearing, hoping that Togliatti would eventually explain the action in 1940. The hearing never came.

The treatment of Berti served several purposes. First and foremost, it protected Togliatti, both within the party and vis-à-vis the Kremlin. Second, it reinforced internal discipline, stressing the need for members to unquestioningly obey orders and live with their consequences. Third, it strengthened the image of the PCI as a great "anti-Fascist" party, an image of great importance for the party's cultural strategy. Berti was never rehabilitated, even after the most obvious cause of his mistreatment—the fear of Stalin himself—had disappeared. In fact, following Stalin's death Berti was vilified even more as the "worst of the Stalinists," and he died unmourned by the party in the late 1970s.

The action against Berti must also be viewed within the context of the PCI in the immediate postwar years. Togliatti's purge of Berti both strengthened his control and enhanced his "moderate" image, permitting him to appear both Stalinist and moderate, severe disciplinarian and tolerant leader, pro-Soviet and "polycentrist." Togliatti was playing to many audiences, and he used members of the party to stage dramatic scenes according to his needs. Another such scene came in October 1947, and Togliatti's co-star was Umberto Terracini, a man notorious for his independence and willingness to challenge the party line. Terracini had rebelled against the *svolta* in the thirties, and later protested the Hitler-Stalin pact. For his failure to submit to party discipline, Terracini was expelled from the PCI, but once he was released from Fascist prison after the overthrow of Mussolini, Terracini joined the Resistance and was readmitted to the party. Although he promised to be more disciplined, Terracini's pugnacity soon reappeared.

In October Terracini, who was then president of the National Assembly, gave an interview to Kingsbury Smith of the International News Service, in which he said that the United States should stop interfering in the internal affairs of European countries, and then added that "this rule also applies to Russia as well. European nations should be allowed to work out their own internal affairs without interference by the Great Powers."[24]

Togliatti's reaction was swift. Terracini was called before the Central Committee and was roundly denounced. Terracini made a formal apology to the party, while in public he was permitted to make a vague statement that somewhat saved face. All of this greatly impressed the Americans. Ambassador James Dunn was certain that the interview had accurately presented Terracini's views. "Had he desired unequivocally to disassociate himself from INS interview as reported," Dunn cabled Washington on October 26, "he could have simply said that interpreter did not properly interpret his remarks." Terracini's recall to party discipline thus made a strong impression:

> Nevertheless, abject submission of Terracini . . . to the Party directorate on a point involving not (repeat not) Communist doctrine but the prestige of U.S.S.R. a foreign state is another glaring example of the complete mechanization of thought and expression demanded by the Communist Party of its members.[25]

Two weeks later Dunn reported information obtained by American sources within the PCI:

> Prassenti, Chief of Communist cell in Banco di Roma, told reliable informant that many Communists seriously concerned re future of Party in Italy and have been deeply impressed by the threats of physical violence with which Terracini . . . was compelled to retract his statement. . . . Fear was expressed that physical violence would be exercised against member of Communist Party who did not measure up to mark.[26]

This account corresponds to the recollections of another participant in the Central Committee meeting at which Terracini was brought to discipline (although, interestingly enough, Terracini later passed off the entire episode as a minor inconvenience when he reflected on it in the late 1970s). Renato Mieli, later the editor of *l'Unità*, was so deeply moved by Terracini's humiliation that he could not understand why Terracini stayed in the party.[27]

For many of the best observers in Italy then, the Terracini affair demonstrated that the full force of the PCI would be brought to bear on any party member who challenged the prestige of the U.S.S.R. The image of the Soviet Union was thus untouchable for the party, and Terracini's independence was unacceptable.

Or was it? Pietro Secchia, who certainly knew what was going on, was never convinced that the episode was what it appeared to be. "It was not possible," he wrote, "that a comrade from the Directorate like Terracini could, in that moment, take such a position without the assent of the

Secretary General of the party." And Secchia made a further point, "this was certainly the interpretation that the Soviets gave to the episode."[28]

In all probability, the Terracini affair had been staged by Togliatti. Despite all the rhetoric, Terracini's "punishment" was surprisingly mild, especially since from the party's point of view Terracini was a three-time loser: first the *svolta*, then the Hitler-Stalin Pact, and now the suggestion that the Soviet Union should stay out of Italian affairs. Terracini had been expelled once before, and one might reasonably have expected the PCI to rid itself of this troublesome Jewish hothead once and for all. Instead, Terracini got off with a mere reprimand, remained among the party elite, and stayed on as assembly president.

The incident was probably staged for three different audiences: the Russians, the party, and the public at large (including the Americans). As will be seen, the fall of 1947 marked a shift in the Soviet line, and the Western Communist parties were ordered to become more aggressive toward the United States. The Terracini affair could well have been an object lesson to the party, serving notice that henceforth the PCI would attack all American actions in Italy, while encouraging Soviet initiatives. Moreover, Togliatti's melodramatic condemnation of Terracini enhanced his own image with the Soviets as a leader capable of conducting a tough campaign against the United States. Finally, the discipline meted out to Terracini strengthened the secretary general's hand within a PCI that contained powerful figures who were inclined to criticize Togliatti as too soft. Far better to fight a minor skirmish with Terracini than to engage in serious conflict with others.

Overall, the Berti and Terracini cases point to one of the basic aspects of Communist strategy, what the Italians have called *doppiezza*, or two-facedness. Togliatti was Janus-like, and so was his party. For those who wished to see tough-minded Stalinism, the face was there; for those who wanted a more moderate profile, or "communism with a human face," it was there as well. The cases cited here are matters of tactics, but there was a strategic dimension to *doppiezza* as well, as seen in the coexistence of the Armed party and the New party side by side for so long. Most students of the PCI have downplayed the covert, paramilitary organizations that always existed in Togliatti's party, or at the least have pretended that they had only a brief existence, and that only because of the activities of some of Togliatti's opponents. Neither hypothesis resists the evidence as we know it today. Togliatti knew of the paramilitary structures, and in fact he commanded them. The conflicts over the role of these organizations were real enough, but regarded specifics and not the *existence* of the armed band. As for the evidence of the Armed party, on one occasion the paramilitary apparatus surfaced, for all to see.

The Attack on Togliatti

On July 14, 1948, a young anti-Communist fired four pistol shots at close range into Togliatti as the secretary general came out of the Chamber of Deputies in Rome. If one can believe the stories, he murmured to Mauro Scoccimaro, "Keep calm, don't do anything crazy," as he lay bleeding in the street. Within hours, following surgery, he repeated the plea to others, and the eruption of the Communist violence that ensued for three days throughout the country occurred without (and in many cases despite) any clear orders from party leaders. In city after city the piazzas filled with workers demanding the downfall of De Gasperi. There were scenes of hand-to-hand fighting, with several presumed enemies of the party killed. In some cities, the secret storehouses were opened, members of clandestine brigades set up control posts, placed machine guns on rooftops, and armed bands paraded through the center of town. In other cities, above all in Venice and Turin, the Armed party took control, usurping almost all the functions of the "official" party leadership.[29]

The Armed party was in the hands of Secchia and Longo, and they immediately established contact with the Soviet embassy in Rome. The Soviet message was clear: whatever happened in Italy, there would be no support from the Russians for violent action. The following morning *l'Unità* printed the text of a telegram from Stalin that made the matter quite explicit: "The Central Committee of the CPSU (Bolshevik) is indignant over the criminal act against the life . . . of our beloved comrade Tolgiatti. The Central Committee is saddened by the fact that the friends of comrade Togliatti were not able to defend him from the cowardly attack."[30] Not only was Stalin not going to support an insurrection, but he even criticized the leadership of the PCI for insufficient security.

The PCI soon found itself trapped between a paramilitary movement that believed the X hour had arrived, and a Soviet overseer who denied assistance and publicly deplored the security breakdown. Togliatti urged calm from his hospital bed, but local Communists—particularly those plugged in to the *Partito Armato,* like Moscatelli—were guiding the insurrection. The American embassy, for example, was told that Secchia dispatched two couriers to the North with orders to intensify action. In Tuscany, in the zone of Monte Amiata, local Communists assaulted the telephone headquarters where the major North-South cable passed (there are different versions regarding the success of the operation; the police maintained that the forces of order never lost control, while many others speak of a short-lived Communist takeover). The same took place in Venice. In Genoa and Turin the armed nuclei within the factories seized the plants, and more than a dozen establishments—those of the greatest importance—had the plant managers taken hostage by the armed bands. The most spectacular of these episodes came at the main Fiat factory, Mirafiore, in Turin, where Vittorio Valletta, the head of Fiat, was held captive for more than a day.[31]

Throughout the country there were signs of an organized plan of action. The Aurelia was blocked at several points, railroad tracks were blown up, the offices of "enemy" organizations were smashed, ranging from the neo-Fascist MSI groups to those of Christian Democrats and Social Democrats. The national trade union movement, the CGIL (*Confederazione Generale Italiana del Lavoro*) proclaimed a general strike, paralyzing the country for a day and a half.

The PCI leaders held their breath. According to a leading Socialist who met with the two on the evening of July 14 and again the following morning, Longo said, "We, the party directorate, have not yet made a move. Let's see how things go. If the protest wave swells, we will let it build, if instead it falls, we will block it."[32] This corresponds to the curiously fragmented situation within the party itself. Comrades from outside Rome tried in vain to obtain orders; the party headquarters did not answer the telephone. The Communist trade union chief, Giuseppe di Vittorio, landed at Ciampino Airport from France a few hours after the shooting and telephoned the party, only to find that the general strike had blocked all communications. At the offices of *l'Unità*, Secchia himself instructed the party to remain calm.

In the meantime, the forces of order proved surprisingly effective. The De Gasperi government had anticipated an armed insurrection for some time, and had been pessimistic about the ability of the police and the army to contain the Communist assault. Yet the government, led by De Gasperi, Interior Minister Scelba, and Defense Minister Pacciardi, moved quickly to stem the violence. By the evening of the second day it was clear that there would be no successful insurrection.[33] Moreover, the CGIL did not hold together. By the fifteenth, the Christian Democrats were threatening to withdraw, thus confronting the Communists with the discouraging prospect of a divided union front, something they had fought against ever since the war. By the third day, the PCI was faced with a defeat of substantial proportions. The government had prevailed, the trade union structure was weakened (and would shortly break), and the party was caught between two enraged groups: those who accused the leadership of having betrayed the revolution, and those who accused the party of having planned a coup d'etat.

In the following months the party analyzed the reasons for the failure and took steps to ensure that there would be no repetition of the spontaneous uprising. There were personnel shifts: Roasio was removed and replaced by Agostino Novella, Berlinguer was put in charge of the youth groups, some of the more violent elements were driven out of the party (this is the period of the emigration of the *Volante Rossa* leaders), and party control was tightened across the board. New guidelines were issued by Secchia. While denying that there was any insurrectionary plan, he insisted that the events of July imposed a reappraisal of the party structures, "piece by piece." And the defects were manifold: "During the course of the (general) strike, in the factories, in the offices, on work sites, strike committees or action committees did not emerge or were not created."[34]

Moreover, some key Communist organizations, such as ANPI (the partisan organization) and the UDI (the women's group) had failed to take charge. And in Bologna, the discussions among party leaders lasted such a long time that others led the strike for a while. Finally, the alliance with the Socialists had not paid off; save for Milan there had been no unity of action.

In his private archives Secchia left a postmortem suggesting that the basis for his criticism was not so much that an insurrection had been attempted, but that it had been so badly done. "Those who fabricate insurrectional possibilities," he wrote, "show that they understand neither the international situation nor the domestic conditions of the time."[35] Insurrections, he continued, require careful planning and rehearsal in order to strike quickly at the enemy's vital organs. In addition, a successful insurrection requires hegemony over the working classes, and also "the presence of vanguard groups in various cities ready to jump into action at the X hour with precise targets. It further presupposes that a part of the adversary's forces have been neutralized, that contacts and connections have been established with certain centers and command posts of the armed forces. All these did not exist."[36]

With Secchia now firmly in charge of the reorganization of the clandestine cadres, it is hard to accept the conventional wisdom, according to which the summer of 1948 marked the end of the Armed party.[37] Having failed its decisive test, it is supposed to have been demobilized, but in reality it almost certainly continued, albeit in a somewhat different form. There is considerable evidence to support this claim. First of all, Secchia's power actually increased in the years immediately following the summer of 1948, and barely two years later it appeared he would replace Togliatti at the top of the PCI. Is it likely that he abandoned his basic goals, or, to put the matter somewhat differently, that the Russians gave up on their Leninist strategy?

At least one detailed report to the American government supports the hypothesis that the Armed party continued after 1948, and that the PCI was restructured in keeping with Secchia's principles: a true vanguard organization, built around small groups of people with demonstrated loyalty and discipline. The restructured party was not to be deprived of its paramilitary capacities. The document in question is a report dated 18 October 1948, and was written by the American Consul in Genoa, Mr. Roger Heacock:

> It has been decided to create cells in the factory and in proximity thereto nuclei of military character for the specific purpose of effective attacks quickly, especially against the forces of order. . . . To establish such nuclei the best men in the factory cells will be selected. . . . Such personnel is enrolled and trained in the greatest secrecy. . . .
>
> The new disposition in connection with Communist military reorganization suggests also that the work of infiltration into the forces of order should be expanded. Furthermore, the activities of SIP (Partisan Information Service) functioning at ANPI under the direction of Avv. Merella should be brought to maximum of efficiency.

The Armed party almost certainly continued to exist at least until the death of Stalin, and some remnant probably continued on into the 1960s and 1970s. The clandestine structures grew smaller, to be sure, but the PCI always kept an elite security force, both to protect the leadership and party property, and to be used for aggressive purposes during emergency.

The real secret of the period, in this specific area as more broadly, was that both the clandestine and the "legal" Communist parties were under Togliatti's control. Thus, while there were certainly differences of opinion, and even fairly heated conflicts between Secchia and Togliatti, there was no disagreement over the necessity for the *Partito Armato*. This being the case, the failure of 1948 was to be laid at Togliatti's feet, and the rise of Secchia's star over the next two years confirms this. Secchia's promotion was actively encouraged by Stalin, and it may be that the Armed party Secchia desired was only established *after* the abortive insurrection. This is only an hypothesis, but the information in the Americans' hands certainly pointed to a drastically changed paramilitary organization. As will be seen, the Americans believed that the numerical strength of the *Partito Armato* actually increased after 1948. And Giorgio Amendola, who succeeded Secchia as head of Organization, has implied in his autobiographical works that he dismantled the paramilitary groups following the removal of Secchia from the apex of the PCI in 1954.

Whatever the truth about the future of the Armed party, the 1948 insurrection certainly removed all doubt about its existence. The embassy in Rome stayed on top of the situation throughout the days of confusion and violence, and drew the proper conclusions. On July 16 Dunn cabled that while there were some within the party who wanted to use the attempted assassination as an excuse for insurrection, the strength of the police was such that the Rome Communist Federation quickly gave instructions to avoid conflict. And Dunn's summary of the affair, sent to Washington on July 21, was exemplary:

> In retrospect it demonstrated that Ital Comms have been awaiting just the moment or excuse for attempt overthrow Govt but since moment of July 14 came unepectedly and hit at very brain of plan, it went off half cocked. Basic outlines were clear: widespread violence fomented by youthful action squads and directed at essential Govt and public institutions; hysterical cacophony of well known propaganda techniques accusing the "opposition," i.e. Govt, of all acts contemplated and effected by the Party; and going through forms of democracy in Parliament by introducing motion of no-confidence.

The party, then, had a mechanism for insurrection, but it may not have had a detailed blueprint for it. In any event, with Togliatti (the "very brain of plan") removed, the PCI lacked coherence and decisiveness. Secchia and Longo were unable to give direction at the critical moment.

Finally, the failed insurrection showed that there was a solid consensus behind De Gasperi, and that the government had sufficient armed strength to cope with a significant level of violence. The Italian government had been quite pessimistic about its chances, but the state held, and performed quite well.

All of this was good news to the Americans, who were by no means mere observers of the events of the summer. For nearly a year and a half the United States had been working, both openly and behind the scenes, in precisely those areas which had been crucial in determining the outcome of the confrontation. The Americans had helped split the Socialist party, thus providing an additional partner (the Social Democrats) for De Gasperi's coalition; they had provided massive support to De Gasperi in the election campaign, helping to produce the national consensus that permitted the government to take firm action; they had supported De Gasperi in his decision to expel the Communists and the Socialists from the coalition in the spring of 1947, thus indicating their belief in the incompatibility between democracy and communism; and they had quietly provided the weapons for use in the event of domestic insurrection.

Notes

1. Gambino, *op. cit.*, 336.
2. Claudin thinks not (*op. cit.*, 466): "Stalin's main battleground ... was Europe, and here he had two closely linked aims: to ensure the invulnerability of the satellites and to prevent the success of the American plan to combine all the Western European countries, including West Germany, into a single bloc led by

Washington."

This sort of view, according to which Stalin was not interested in a revolution in Western Europe, led by the local Communist parties, is shared by Joseph Starobin. Like Claudin, Starobin considers this to have been a Stalinist betrayal of the West European Communists. Cf. Joseph R. Starobin, "Origins of the Cold War: the Communist dimension," in *Foreign Affairs,* July 1969.

3. The CIA described Secchia and Longo as "the two chief contenders for possible future succession to Palmiro Togliatti as titular head of the PCI." According to CIA, "like Longo, Secchia is considered more doctrinaire and 'hard core' in his political approach than is Togliatti."

   These statements come from undated CIA biographies of the two men, released to me under the terms of the Freedom of Information Act.
4. Cf. Michael Ledeen and Claire Sterling, "Italy's Russian Sugar Daddies," in *The New Republic,* 12 February 1976.
5. Giorgio Bocca, *Palmiro Togliatti* (Rome-Bari, 1973), 404-405.
6. *Ibid.,* 405.
7. Bocca, writing in 1973, called it "an anomalous formation" (*ibid.,* 406). But in the light of what is not known about the long history of such groups, the *Volante Rossa* seems rather more traditional than aberrant. Cf., for example, Paolo Mieli, "sul secondo binario c" è un vagone di fucili," in *l'Espresso,* 15 July 1979.
8. Alberto Ronchey and Renato Mieli have both written about the *Volante Rossa* in the *Corriere della Sera* and *il Giornale nuovo,* respectively. But this subject awaits a full analysis; there must be considerable material in the State Archives in Rome.
9. The cable, classified "Confidential," is dated 18 June.
10. In the course of conducting the research for this book, I learned that there is still a considerable body of information in the American archives that is still "properly classified" and hence not subject to release at this time. A good deal of this information deals with the PCI, from its inception to the recent past. Therefore, it is possible that some data of fundamental importance remain to be studied. I trust that future scholars will pursue this information.
11. The "secret" cable was written by Vice Consul Leonard R. Mills, and dated 13 October 1947.
12. The report, number PIR-2819, was dated 22 December 1948. The information came from "a reliable source in contact with inner circles of the PCI organization in Northern Italy and with peripheral party circles."
13. Bocca, *op. cit.,* 620.
14. Cf., for example, Cable #434 from Milan Consulate, 14 August 1947; Cable from Turin Consulate, 20 August 1947; a report from Paris sent to the Rome Embassy on 12 June 1947, by Douglas MacArthur, 2nd; a report to Dunn from Turin Consulate on 5 August 1947; a report to Dunn from the Genoa Consulate on 17 November 1947; a report to Dunn from Milan Consulate on 22 May 1947; and a report to the secretary of state from Milan Consulate on 8 January 1948. These are typical examples of dozens of similar reports that are now declassified; one can only guess at the quantity of classified material, but it is certainly quite large.
15. Milan Consulate to the secretary of state, 14 August 1947.
16. I have obtained three of these alleged intercepts, forwarded by the Milan Consulate on January 7, 10, and 21, 1947.

17. The targetting of Zionists—a well-known Communist obsession—lends some credibility to those interecepts, but I have been unable to either confirm or deny their authenticity.
18. Starting with the earliest days of the Revolution, the Soviets have created ostensibly independent (and sometimes demonstrably hostile) organizations that were actually working for the Kremlin. The first such case was the "Trust," which has recently been one of the major elements in the British television series "Reilly, Ace of Spies." The Trust claimed to be an anti-Bolshevik movement of Russian emigrés, and carried out espionage and assassinations against the Soviets, even though it was a deception run by Soviet intelligence.
19. Milan Consulate to secretary of state, 14 August 1947.
20. The report is dated 30 March 1948.
21. Gianni Corbi, "la parola a Togliatti, Pubblico Ministero," in *l'Espresso*, 18 March 1979.
22. Fondazione Giangiacomo Feltrinelli, *Annali, XIX* (Milan, 1979), 587. This is the "Secchia Archive."
23. Berti is said to have maintained a personal archive as well, but if it exists it has remained a secret. See the interesting obituary of Berti written by Renato Mieli, *il Giornale nuovo*, 20 March 1979, and, by the same author, "Stalinismo all'italiana," in *il Giornale nuovo*, 4 July 1977.
24. Cf. Cable 3399, Dunn to secretary of state, 26 October 1947.
25. *Ibid.*
26. Dunn to secretary of state, 11 November 1947.
27. Renato Mieli, "E Terracini disse: non sono d'accordo," in *il Giornale nuovo*, 30 June 1978.
28. Bocca, *op. cit.*, 486.
29. Cf. Walter Tobagi, *La Rivoluzione impossibile* (Florence, 1978).
30. Bocca, *op. cit.*, 518.
31. Tobagi, *op. cit.*, 12-15, 45. Cf. Cable #3052, from Embassy Rome to secretary of state, 16 July 1948, beginning "there are indications that Communist insurrection may well have been planned to take place throughout Italy following attempted assassination Togliatti."
32. Bocca, *op. cit.*, 517.
33. *Ibid.*, 517-520; Tobagi, *op. cit.*, 41-79.
34. Quoted in Bocca, *op. cit.*, 522.
35. Fondazione Feltrinelli, *Annali, XIX, cit.*, 217.
36. *Ibid.*
37. This is Bocca's thesis, for example, *op. cit.*, 524.

3

The American Response

As has been seen, there was some reluctance on the American side to get deeply involved in internal Italian affairs. This attitude remained fairly constant for the next forty years, with three notable exceptions: the 1947-48 period (when the United States helped block the Communist advance through a variety of means); the 1960-63 period (when the United States encouraged the "Opening to the Left" that brought the Socialists into the Cabinet); and the mid-1970s (when it appeared likely that the "Eurocommunist" PCI might enter the government). In each case, the Americans drafted a program, implemented it, met with considerable success, and then lapsed back into the traditional posture of bemused disinterest.

The American disinterest in early 1947 was compounded by what might be termed a vulgar Marxist theory of the rise of communism. According to this view, communism flourished when people were hungry and miserable, and so if hunger and misery were alleviated, communism lost appeal. The Communist problem in Italy, despite the documented paramilitary and espionage activity of the Soviets and the PCI, was generally treated as a socioeconomic challenge. Hence the Americans concerned with Italian affairs concentrated on providing Italy with grain and credits. In this undertaking they were greatly reinforced by Ambassador Tarchiani and Prime Minister De Gasperi, who constantly used the "communist menace" as a means of prying ever larger quantities of American aid out of a reluctant Truman administration. The published diplomatic documents from 1947-48 show clearly that the overriding interest of both countries lay in the level of economic support Washington would provide Rome.

Despite the keen American awareness that there was a serious Communist threat in Italy, the United States did surprisingly little to suggest that there was great concern in Washington. Indeed, Dunn was often forced to complain about the inaction of his government, and when Marshall finally asked on May 1, 1947, what measures could be taken to ensure the stability of De Gasperi's government, the American ambassador replied in unusually excited tones. Dunn had evidently long awaited the opportunity to advise the secretary of state that something more than economic assistance was required:

> Our practice of holding back from expressing ourselves on ideological views has given all the advantage to the other side, and they have not hesitated to use it and abuse it.
>
> ... We have assumed in the eyes of Italians, a passive role as regards the growth of Italian Communism. The vigor and energy of the Communist Movement in Italy, in particular the efficiency of its organization and propaganda and its penetration of local administrative government ensuring a powerful influence in considerable areas in the distribution of work has contributed to a growing belief among Italians and in many cases, fear that the Italian Communist bandwagon is not seriously opposed by the U.S. and it is the one to board. The embassy is constantly receiving letters from individuals begging the U.S. to take a stand.[1]

Dunn wanted linkage. He wanted to tell the Italians that American assistance would not continue if the country fell to the Communists. He therefore advised Marshall to demonstrate American concern, and show that "we are ready to lend our assistance to the development of an economic life based upon the liberty of the individual and the protection of his political and individual rights."

By May 20 the secretary of state, following discussions with Tarchiani, had formulated a plan of action. "It is evident," he cabled Dunn, "any noncommunist government formed following De Gasperi's resignation must achieve early, visible improvement in economic conditions, and demonstrate Ital people it enjoys Western support if further progress Italy along democratic lines expected." Consequently, if De Gasperi were to form a new Cabinet with greatly reduced Communist participation, or without any Communists altogether, the United States was prepared to make a renewed pledge of support, urge the French and British to extend aid to Italy and take helpful actions in the diplomatic field, provide "every available source economic assistance Italy . . . including post-UNRRA relief," provide military surplus equipment and, finally, take every opportunity to "advertise . . . Ital people U.S. support Italy and U.S. appreciation Italian progress."[2]

In all likelihood it was not Dunn's cable but Italian diplomacy and Marshall's good instincts that had produced the policy shift. De Gasperi had long suspected that the Americans would support an effort to oust the Communists from the three-party coalition that had governed Italy since the parliamentary elections of June 2, 1946. The June elections had given the Christian Democrats 35.2 percent, the Socialists 20.7 percent, and the Communists 19 percent. In addition, the Republic was approved by referendum on the same day, driving the House of Savoy into exile. In this delicate political atmosphere De Gasperi brought the three major parties (and one Republican) into the Cabinet, and awaited further developments.

In November, the Communists advanced in local administrative elections, while the DC and the Socialists lost ground, and the Socialists were further weakened by the defection of Giuseppe Saragat, who formed a new social-democratic party, the PSDI, in December. De Gasperi's January trip thus took place at a time when a stable government without Communist or Socialist participation was possible, thanks to Saragat. The prime minister could therefore sound out Truman about American interest in a non-Communist government in Italy. But if De Gasperi was hoping for strong American encouragement, he was disappointed. Not only was there no ringing statement of support, but the Americans offered only a fraction of the aid they had earmarked for France. Superficially, then, the trip to Washington was not a great success, but it did permit De Gasperi to establish good personal relations with Truman and to discover that the Socialist split had been actively supported by the American Federation of Labor, which had told Saragat that the American labor movement would look with favor on a non-Communist trade union force, and that such a force would not go hungry. De Gasperi had favored the split, and he probably concluded that the PSDI must have had at least the tacit support of the American government.

Italo-American relations in the spring of 1947 were thus somewhat muddled. The Americans clearly preferred an Italian government without the PCI, but repeatedly told De Gasperi that they would understand if he continued to keep the Communists in the Cabinet. For his part, De Gasperi recognized the desirability of a government free of Communist participation (his own party had been demanding it for months), but he was not altogether certain about American support for such a drastic move. He finally decided to force the matter in late April. After consulting with Tarchiani (and perhaps with Dunn as well), De Gasperi sent a personal letter to Truman in late April outside the normal diplomatic channels (Dunn knew of the letter, which was probably transmitted by the Americans).[3] In this letter De Gasperi presented the American president with an alarming picture of the Italian crisis: the country was threatened with starvation, the currency was in real danger of collapse, the majority political party (his own) had no real roots in the country's political traditions and had no real infrastructure, and there was a growing threat to democracy from the Left. Tarchiani repeated these themes when he returned to Washington in early May, when he conveyed a still mysterious message from De Gasperi. What we know about this message is that the Italian prime minister offered to make a private gesture "as a person, as a chief of state, and as a member of his party" that would "demonstrate the loyalty of our country to the supreme canons of international liberty."[4]

We can only guess at the nature of the offer, because Truman said it was unnecessary. The president also told Tarchiani that the United States had made a basic decision about its relations with the U.S.S.R., and with Western Europe as well:

> It is a duty and a necessity for Washington to reorganize Europe economically and politically . . . independently of the U.S.S.R. and, later on, if there were no other solution, against Russia. . . . All this only confirms what I told you here and in Rome: the United States is by now resolved to help only its friends. It is a fact of which we cannot fail to take note.[5]

Tarchiani and De Gasperi had anticipated this response, for by the time Truman's message reached Rome, De Gasperi had resigned and the aged Francesco Nitti was trying to form a government. De Gasperi had risked his prestige to be able to form a government that corresponded to the new international realities. Ten days later he was once again prime minister, and strengthened by his knowledge that the United States would throw its weight behind him, he formed a government composed solely of Christian Democratic ministers.

Many analysts of the period have portrayed this sequence of events as an American-imposed shift, decided in Washington and communicated to Rome. Was it a mere coincidence that both France and Italy expelled the Communists from their respective governments in the same month? And was it a coincidence that the Marshall Plan was announced on the heels of these decisions?

The answer to both questions is probably "yes." There seems to have been no common American initiative to urge the French and the Italians to expel the Communists,[6] and so far as the Marshall Plan is concerned, Thomas A. Bailey has rightly written that "there never was a 'Marshall Plan,' only a 'Marshall proposal.' Presented in this rather vague and offhand way it initially made little splash."[7] The key event in the spring of 1947 was the announcement of the Truman Doctrine, and the American decision to intervene in Greece in place of the British.

In Italy, as has been shown, the initiative came from Rome rather than from Washington, and the change was clear by the end of 1947. The old reluctance to call for more vigorous action in Italy was gone, replaced by a constellation of bright ideas and action programs. The American treasury representative at the time, Henry J. Tasca, submitted a detailed analysis and set of recommendations that typify the changed approach. He began by reviewing the long-term measures to defeat communism:

1. Establishment of minimum standards of living;
2. Development of positive programs for the dissemination of democratic principles;
3. Direct action to neutralize and eradicate the capillary organization and organized action squads of the Communist party; and
4. Creation of opportunities for improvement of position in the social structure or the development of social mobility.

Tasca then turned to an analysis of Communist behavior, in order to better understand the specifics of the required American response. The PCI, he said, had infiltrated both the State administration and the armed forces, so that "the full extent of such penetration will only be known should Communist forces come out in an attempt to seize power." Furthermore, Communist officials had been placed throughout the economic structures (especially the trade unions), and Communist ministers had been used to recruit new members (including the use of amnesty by Togliatti—the minister of justice at the time—to "encourage Fascists to enter the Communist party"). Finally, Communists had been placed within the government and the opposition. Tasca stressed that

> Communist Ministers . . . could propose politically spectacular legislation while opposition in the Communist press over the manner in which such legislation was carried out or the failure to adopt such legislation could be used to safeguard the political position of the Communist party from an electoral point of view, at the same time using the slow rate of recovery to maintain and build up discontent on the part of the workers.[8]

The Communist strategy was thrown into question when the PCI was expelled from the coalition. As Tasca noted, it was then possible for De Gasperi to eliminate many Communists who had "infiltrated into the administrative and state organizations. The ministry of the interior, with its police forces and secret service, could begin to be directed against the Communists." The economy also perked up as the government gained internal coherence.

Tasca then turned to an analysis of American policy, arguing that the United States had to produce action quickly. Thus far, he wrote, the Americans had simply provided economic aid "on the assumption that an improvement in the standard of living would automatically lead the people away from Communism." But the facts had exploded this myth; economic conditions had improved, but so had Communist electoral strength. Tasca's conclusion, as correct today as it was at the time, was that "economic aid cannot constitute other than a premise to further direct action."[9] The action Tasca called for prefigured the electoral campaign of the following spring: increased aid along with a full-blown propaganda campaign stressing the merits of freedom; direct aid to democratic political parties to match the well-financed Communist infrastructure, "counter-intelligence and penetration of Communist organizations," and a special aid program aimed at the lower classes. In addition, Tasca called for a private-sector anti-Communist campaign, support for the non-Communist labor movement and for "fighting democratic movements prepared to engage Communists should violence result."

The electoral campaign that ensued is well known and requires little comment here. Not only did the American government pour millions of dollars into the Christian Democratic campaign (American newspaper accounts put the figure at four million dollars), but Italo-Americans sent money and jewelry back to Italy in a gesture calculated to stress the close links between the two countries (and the cost of breaking the relationship).

Despite the great American effort, not all the money arrived on schedule. On April 6, for example, Dunn complained about delays:

> I am informed that Prime Minister has been given to understand by emissary from Washington that substantial sum approximately $500,000 is being made available. Up to the present (other than the $50,000 reported in my 1353, March 26), funds have not (repeat not) been received. . . . Leaders of Christian Democrats are badly in need of funds and need help.[10]

American financial assistance to the DC was of course encouraged by the knowledge that the PCI had long been on the receiving end of Soviet subsidies. No less a figure than Sumner Welles had made this accusation in the summer of 1947, provoking a heated response from Togliatti, who accused the Americans of having the mentality of a slave trader, wishing to trade Italians like Negroes. This insult, which was widely reported in the United States, helped rally support for the successful American effort.

The Strategic Context

The United States came late to a realization that strong action in Italy was called for, and the evolution of American policy toward Italy was closely tied to the emergence of the "containment" school of geopolitical thinkers in Washington. With the withdrawal of Great Britain from its traditional role in Greece and Turkey, the Americans were forced to design policy for the Mediterranean Basin as a whole, and there was a distinct change in mood between October 1947 and February-March 1948. This can be seen in two successive reports on Italy prepared by the National Security Council (NSC). In the first, the NSC had flatly concluded that the United States should not use its armed forces in the event of an Italian civil war, but by early 1948 this was reconsidered. In this latter document[11] the NSC observed that "the security of the whole Eastern Mediterranean and Middle East would be jeopardized if the Soviet Union should succeed in its efforts to obtain control of . . . Italy, Greece, Turkey, or Iran."

In the Italian case, the NSC envisaged two possible scenarios. In the first case, the Communists might enter the government "legally"; in the second, there would be a Communist-led insurrection ("with their estimated paramilitary organization of 70,000"). In this latter case, the Americans foresaw a partition of the country that would permit support of a legitimate anti-Communist government in the South. Under these circumstances, the United States should be "prepared . . . to deploy forces to government-controlled sections of peninsular Italy," and if the Communists successfully took the entire peninsula, the United States could occupy Sicily and Sardinia. The report suggested that all military action had to be closely coordinated with the British, who would have to assume primary responsibility for the Eastern Mediterranean.

In short, the NSC was prepared to fight the Italian campaign all over again, this time against communism, if the PCI initiated a paramilitary action. The matter was considerably more complex, of course, if the Communists won the elections, and this contingency was addressed with great anxiety in the 1948 NSC document:

> Should the election be held today (March 8), the best result that could be hoped for would be that the People's Bloc would obtain no more than a plurality, which would not of itself prevent the formation of a majority coalition of anti-Communist parties under Christian Democratic leadership. If, however, the current trend continues unchecked until election day, a People's Bloc majority is not improbable. Six weeks remain during which the United States might, by timely aid to the moderate Italian parties, check the current trend or even reverse it. Such aid would be far less onerous and would have greater prospect of success than the measures which might have to be adopted should a People's Bloc victory at the polls result in Communist participation in and eventual control of the Italian government.

This was the basis for the intense propaganda campaign in Italy and for the decision to institute "linkage": American aid would cease if the Communists entered the government. The NSC also recommended that, if the PCI nonetheless gained some ministries, American propaganda in Italy should be "run along the lines of the wartime anti-Nazi program for Italy."

In the meantime, the NSC urged that France and Britain be recruited to bring pressure on Italian political and social forces, particularly the labor movement and the Socialist party. This program was already under way, for the NSC document urged that the United States "*continue* efforts . . . to detach the Italian left-wing socialists from the communists . . ." (the ellipses indicate a still-classified passage in the document, so it is not possible to specify which efforts were to be continued). The Labor party was particularly active in this field, and on March 13, Denis Healey and Morgan Philips, the secretary general and international secretary of the Labor party, respectively, went to Rome to urge Nenni to endorse the Marshall Plan and condemn the Communist coup d'etat in Prague the previous month. The PSI leader refused, and by the end of the year the Italian Socialist party had been drummed out of the Socialist International.

The cooperation between the Americans and European social democrats was a harbinger of things to come, and a further indication that American anticommunism was not a blind endorsement of the status quo or of the conservative political forces, but was viewed by many Americans and Europeans as the best way to avert totalitarianism and to encourage progressive, democratic forces. Western European socialists and social democrats cooperated with the United States in the future to fight communism: during the "Opening to the Left" in Italy in the 1960s, during the Portuguese crisis a decade later, and during the "Eurocommunist" fad a few years later. This cooperation was always based on the tacit assumption that communism was best combatted by parties of the democratic Left and the Center-Left.

This is not to say that there were not those in the American government who favored more violent, unilateral action to forestall the PCI advance in 1948. One of the most eloquent advocates of such intervention was George F. Kennan, who has on occasion claimed that he was misunderstood when he spoke of a policy of containment. Yet a Kennan memorandum to the secretary of state on March 15 suggests that his view of containment in Italy was quite aggressive indeed:

> If Communists were to win election (in Italy) our whole position in Mediterranean, and possibly in western Europe as well, would probably be undermined. I am persuaded Communists could not win without strong factor of intimidation on their side, and it would clearly be better that elections not take place at all than that Communists win in these circumstances.
>
> For these reasons I question whether it would not be preferable for Italian government to outlaw Communist party and take strong action against it before elections. Communists would presumably reply with civil war, which would give us grounds for reoccupation Foggia fields, or any other facilities we would wish. This would admittedly result in much violence and probably

a military division of Italy; but we are getting close to the deadline and I think it might well be preferable to a bloodless election victory, unopposed by ourselves, which would give the Communists the entire peninsula at one coup and send waves of panic to all surrounding areas.[12]

Kennan's extreme solution, which would have sent the American army back into Italy to prevent elections, was rejected by the State Department and the president. But Kennan's views were probably shared by many in the government, and had the Front won the elections Truman would have been under great pressure to intervene.

On the other hand, there were some in the American government who felt the entire Cold War was an unfortunate strategic error based on a misunderstanding of the Soviet Union. If one can take the reminiscences of H. Stuart Hughes as typical, such persons regarded the Americans and the Soviets in the same terms: "As Russians and Americans alike tried to shore up the governments of the countries dependent on them, each act of ideological buttressing was bound to produce a corresponding reaction in the opposing camp."[13]

Hughes left the government in 1947, before the Italian elections, but his attitudes are typical of a fairly large number of individuals. Such persons regretted the conflict between the wartime Allies, and were terribly concerned that the U.S. might find itself allied with reactionary regimes in Western Europe as a result of visceral anticommunism and blind opposition to Soviet hegemony in Eastern Europe. Hughes and his ilk urged acceptance of the "spheres of influence," and called for extension of the Marshall Plan to Eastern Europe and the Soviet Union. They believed that "the readiest way to mitigate the ravages of the incipient Cold War was for our country to keep to its side of the Iron Curtain in the hope that the Soviet Union would oblige us by doing the same."

The trouble with Hughes' approach was that it imposed a false symmetry on the international situation. Even if the United States accepted the "spheres of influence" there would still have been a crisis produced by the totalitarian, anti-American, and pro-Soviet Communist parties in France and Italy, along with a clandestine armed Communist movement in Spain. The Americans intervened at the eleventh hour in Italy precisely because the Soviet Union had meddled in the Western sphere of influence, not only in Italy but also in France and Greece. In Stalin's view of foreign policy, his sphere of influence was his, and ours was also his; only the tactics were different. Hughes' analysis did not reflect the facts.

Despite Hughes' dubious contention that the Marshall Plan was never seriously offered the East, the PCI, along with the Finnish and Czech governments, rejected it on Stalin's orders. American assistance could hardly be accepted by a tyrant who preferred to see the peoples of his empire suffer and starve rather than risk a weakening of his own grip.

As for Hughes' other concern—that the United States might embrace reactionary regimes in order to fight communism—there is little evidence to support the anxiety. In document after document one finds American officials urging that the United States support progressive forces in Western Europe, and promoting the policies of the democratic Left. The State Department professionals were not conservatives; their notion of the Cold War was one of ideological conflict, and they had no doubts about the outcome, provided the struggle was fought on equal terms. But men like James Dunn were frustrated when the American government refused to wage ideological war against communism in Italy, and was slow about making it possible for the Christian Democrats (who were termed "poverty stricken" in the NSC March 8, 1948 document) to campaign on equal terms with the PCI.

Finally, in the early 1950s (when the Korean War was under way) the Americans decided that something might have to be done to combat clandestine Communist activity. In 1948 the NSC estimated the strength of the clandestine paramilitary organization in Italy at 70,000. In 1950 and 1951 the figure was up to 75,000. The NSC accordingly considered some countermeasures. By 1950 the NSC recommended that if the PCI entered the government, or the government "ceases to evidence a determination to oppose communist internal or external threats," the Americans should move:

> The United States should initiate measures . . . designed to prevent communist domination and to review Italian determination to oppose communism. Further, the United States should take military measures in collaboration with other North Atlantic Treaty nations to counter communist actions which would threaten the strategic position of the United States in the Mediterranean.[14]

Such contingencies were never enacted, and were only seriously elaborated at a time when the Americans feared a general Soviet assault against the Western position from Korea to Germany. In 1948, despite the fears of a Communist victory, the election proved to be an easy win for the Christian Democrats. De Gasperi's party gained 48.5 percent of the vote to 31 percent for the PCI-PSI Popular Front. The American effort was crowned with success, with considerable help from two other sources: the Vatican (promising hellfire for those who voted PCI) and the Kremlin (liquidating democracy in Czechoslovakia in February).

The PCI and the U.S.S.R.

For all the cunning and elegance of his tactics, Togliatti failed in both 1946 and 1948. He was decisively defeated in the elections; the party's paramilitary organization was humiliated later in 1948 by the forces of order; and by the end of the year it was evident that there would be no Communist triumph in Italy in the near future. On the other hand the PCI had grown to a mass organization with well over two million members; its prestige and that of Togliatti himself had grown considerably, attracting the cream of the Italian intelligentsia to its fold; and the constant nightmare of every Western Communist leader—that the Socialists might capture the Left—had been greatly reduced.

Togliatti's best chance was for an extended period of relative international calm, with minimum conflict between the superpowers. His position at the time of the *svolta di Salerno* was based on just such an expectation, but with the growing intensity of the U.S.-U.S.S.R. competition Togliatti's position grew more difficult. And his difficulties were not solely the result of the international situation; they were also produced by explicit orders from Moscow.

The occasion for the delivery of this message from Stalin was the founding meeting of the Cominform, held in Szklarska Poreba, Poland, in late September 1947. The PCI was represented by Reale and Longo, the PCF by Duclos, and the Eastern European countries by a variety of distinguished figures (including Kardelj and Djilas from Yugoslavia). The opening speech by Zhdanov indicated that there was a new "line" in the Kremlin. Since the United States was threatening to consolidate Western Europe into an antisocialist unit, the Communist movement had two overriding tasks: first, the institutionalization of Soviet domination of Eastern Europe (the conferees were subjected to lengthy discourses from the East Europeans regarding the methods by which Soviet hegemony was being established); second, fierce struggles against the Americans, and particularly against the Marshall Plan.

By the second day of the conference it was evident that the Western parties were the scapegoats for the tide of American strength. The most ferocious denunciations of the PCF and the PCI came from the Yugoslavs, who accused the French and Italians of having adopted a suicidal strategy of parliamentary methods instead of armed insurrection. The two Western parties were denounced as poorly organized, insufficiently revolutionary, and unduly quiescent. And this despite Longo's opening statement in which he had proudly detailed the preparations by the PCI for armed conflict, the special squads and the quantities and hiding places of well-oiled weapons for the upcoming insurrection.[15]

Duclos vainly attempted a similar defense. The condemnation of the two Latin Communist parties was virtually complete. And when Longo plaintively pointed out that Italy needed Marshall Plan money he was reminded of the sacrifices of the Russians during the war and was lectured on the necessity of sacrifice in the interests of long-term Communist goals.

The last line of defense for Duclos, Longo, and Reale had been proposed before their departure for Poland by Togliatti, and this was to stress that any attempt at insurrection would have simply led to "another Greece."[16] But this sensible claim was swept aside by the Yugoslavs, who acidly observed that such reasoning would have prevented the success of Tito, and some of the East European delegates added that there were better chances for success in France and Italy than in Greece itself.

This meeting has been exhaustively analyzed, with differing conclusions. For Claudin,[17] it was the culmination of Stalin's betrayal of the revolutionary cause in the West. Having ordered the French, Italian, and Yugoslav parties to collaborate with the bourgeoisie, Stalin now elected to use the French and Italians as scapegoats for his own failures. The real question for the Cominform, according to Claudin, was why the Western parties had not taken a more aggressive stance. It may well have been impossible for the PCI and PCF to seize power with American troops on the scene, but this was no excuse for the supine acceptance of and collaboration with the enemy. Claudin argued that the Latin Communists had been outwitted and overpowered by the parties of the Right. Thorez was expelled by Ramadier, Togliatti by De Gasperi. And once placed in the docket by Stalin, the French and Italians could hardly tell the truth (they had simply followed orders). Instead, they had to feign repentance and promise they would be more aggressive in the future.

For Eugenio Reale, on the other hand, the Cominform Conference was designed to lay down a new, ominous line: the extension of Soviet power into Western Europe and the consolidation of Soviet control over the East. Moreover, the internal dynamics of the conference suggested that Stalin deliberately selected the Yugoslavs to play the role of inquisitionists. And once Stalin had made them the vanguard of the attack on the Western parties, he guaranteed PCI and PCF support for the ouster of the Yugoslavs the following spring. If this was his secondary purpose, Stalin fully succeeded, for few attacks on Tito in 1948 were as savage as Togliatti's, and the PCI followed up with action, ordering its satellite party in the Venezia-Giulia region to carry out espionage and acts of violence in Yugoslav territory.

The two analyses dovetail nicely. As Reale observes, Stalin affirmed "the inevitability of a single party dictatorship with all its consequences, the condemnation of the democratic road to socialism, the fight without quarter against the Marshall Plan and the Americans."[18] The standard operating procedure in such cases was to blame someone else for the previous line, and the French and Italians served the purpose. At the same time, as Claudin rightly stresses, the ostensibly aggressive resistance to American efforts in Western Europe had a basically defensive leitmotif, since its goal was "the very utopian one of creating a bourgeois democracy jealous of its national honor and independence in the face of Washington's 'hegemonic' pretensions."[19] Therefore, even though the postconference period saw a return to more aggressive tactics in France and Italy (the autumn was an unusually "hot" one, particularly for the trade unions), there was no public announcement of a new line and no effort to mobilize for insurrection. There was, however, an explicit call from Zhdanov for the Western parties to pass from their awkward role as "parties of government" to the more comfortable one of "parties of opposition."

For Stalin, of course, the Cominform served to reestablish control over the foreign parties. From 1943, when the Comintern was dissolved, to 1947, these contacts had been bilateral, greatly complicating the Kremlin's management of the international movement. Furthermore, the Comintern made it easier for Stalin to play the parties off against each other and prevent the crystallization of any alternative system of alliances between Communist parties and governments. Finally, in keeping with his basically pragmatic cynicism, the Comintern permitted Stalin to keep all his options open. If the Americans showed they were committed to action in Europe, Stalin would wish to consolidate his East European gains and take whatever was available in the West. If, on the other hand, the Americans proved to be paper tigers, he could move ahead with his more ambitious program of launching a broad international action.

There is one other consideration: the American economic offensive in the West was not simply a challenge to Stalin in the Anglo-American sphere of influence; it threatened his prospects in Czechoslovakia (where the Communist party was not expected to do well in the spring elections) as well. With the prospect of more open ideological conflict with the Americans throughout the continent, Stalin had to make a basic choice between the pursuit of a deceptive "moderate" line and a more aggressive ideological assault that would give him greater control over the foreign parties. This point was not lost on those Americans who closely followed Soviet affairs. Less than two weeks after the conference, George Kennan sent to Undersecretary of State Robert A. Lovett a brief but brilliant analysis that pointed to the direction of future American policy:

    1. This is not the top team. As far as we know, Zhdanov was the only one of

the whole group who had a really high position on the Comintern before. While all of these are very high ranking officials . . . this is the level immediately under the top.

2. An effort seems to have been made to have included here
   a. the propaganda chief of each party, and
   b. the official immediately responsible for economic matters.

This brings out the two essential elements of the action, which is one to pull all propaganda stops in a last minute effort to defeat a European recovery program linked to American aid.

3. In at least four or five cases the individuals who set their signatures to these documents were responsible cabinet members. . . . That creates a serious factor affecting our attitude toward the action.

4. In general, this represents the culmination—to date—of a process which has been operating since last spring. Under the policies, the communists are finding themselves subject to a squeeze play which forces them to choose between (1) the retention of their popularity in liberal Western circles with an attendant relaxation of militant discipline of the movement; or (2) a tightening up of the drive for discipline and militancy of the movement at the cost of support in the left-wing liberal world.

Time and again, when constrained to make this choice, they have chosen for the latter. There is evidence that they feel that to relax the militancy of the movement and to appeal to liberal sentiments would be to permit France, Italy, and Czechoslovakia, and eventually others of the satellite countries, to escape from their real control into a series of national-liberal movements with which they would eventually have to come into conflict.

Accordingly, they are constantly sacrificing support in the West in order to strengthen their hold in the East; and they are betting on their ability to seize Czechoslovakia, France, and Italy by strong-arm methods at some time during the coming months.

5. All this indicates that they must have a sense of serious weaknesses and dangers within the communist movement in Europe. We should be able to capitalize effectively in this situation.[20]

All these themes have remained central to American policymaking. Kennan provided a basic insight: a Communist movement that stresses cooperation or detente with the West greatly enhances the popularity of West European Communist parties. Indeed, in all likelihood it is *only* in an atmosphere of detente that such parties can reasonably expect to enter government. But the process of detente necessarily encourages centrifugal tendencies in the international Communist movement, and undermines Soviet control over foreign Communist parties.

For the foreign parties this means that the relationship with the Soviet Union is somewhat ambivalent. A great deal of the support for any Communist party derives from its close linkage to Soviet power. If the Soviet

Union is viewed as benign, the local Communist party can expand its popularity by adopting what Kennan called the "national-liberal" line. But the adoption of this line strains relations with the Kremlin and risks a loss of control over the movement.

In Italy, the national-liberal line taken by Togliatti after the *svolta di Salerno* had shown some signs of becoming centrifugal, the point at issue being the proposed American economic aid. Togliatti and Reale had both hinted in public that the PCI might be willing to accept the money if there were not too many strings attached. This was intolerable to Stalin, for how could Western Communists be permitted to benefit from a Marshall Plan that the Russians had rejected? The violent attacks against the U.S. and against the collaboration of the PCI and the PCF with pro-American parties in their respective governments stemmed at least in part from a desire to maintain a tight rein on the Western Communists.

Having said this, however, it must be stressed that Kennan made an error that would haunt American policy for years to come. The "national-liberal" line did not automatically produce conflict with the Kremlin, and it was the best chance for the Western Communists to enter government. To be sure, this error was evidently shared by Stalin himself, who would brook not the slightest deviation from his wishes, even to the extent of insisting that the Comintern publish its account of the Cominform meeting under the ponderous title *For a Stable Peace, For a Popular Democracy*. When Reale protested to Zhdanov that no Italian workers would enter a bookstore and request something with such a title, the Russian observed that the purpose of a title was to express a concept and a program, and that anyway Stalin himself had telephoned the title that very morning. This closed all discussion.[21]

The joint Soviet and American error of supposing that it was impossible for a Western Communist party to remain loyal to Moscow at the same time it gave voice to national-liberal sentiments greatly complicated Togliatti's life. Togliatti knew better, and also realized that the intensification of the conflict between the U.S. and the Kremlin weakened his own position within the party, to the benefit of Secchia and Longo. On the other hand—to complete the paradoxes of the period—the expulsion of the PCI from the Italian government had probably been a godsend to Togliatti, and this too was a lesson that would have to be relearned by a later generation of Communists. The PCI had been exposed to severe internal tension as a result of its collaboration with the DC.[22] The militant base could not understand why the PCI was working hand-in-glove with its class enemies, instead of trying to destroy them. At the same time, the more moderate elements of the party were quite uncomfortable with the disruptive mass actions led by the party, and may have also been bothered by the clear evidence of Soviet control. We may therefore believe the official theoretician of the "historic compromise" of the 1970s, Franco Rodanò (who in the late forties led a fascinating and still largely unexamined movement of Catholic Communists), who has said that the party was on the verge of internal fission when Togliatti was expelled from the government in 1947.[23]

The lesson, as valid in the 1970s as it was in the 1940s, is that a Western Communist party cannot remain indefinitely in a position halfway between real power and full opposition without paying a large price within the party. A "party of government" inevitably generates frustration at the party's base; a "party of opposition" can rule the Communists, but cannot woo enough moderate support to gain power. A party which is neither one nor the other antagonizes both the Stalinist base and the moderates, and the balancing act required to stay aloft under such circumstances can be performed for a while, but eventually fails.

The niceties of these tactical considerations were of course lost on Stalin, who simply ordered the Western Communists to return to opposition. And in keeping with the dynamics of the new PCI situation, Togliatti found himself under fire from moderates outside the party (frightened by the Stalinist conformity) and from hard-liners within the PCI, encouraged by the support for their own positions from the Kremlin. As word of the Cominform meeting reached Italy, Pietro Secchia believed his moment had come. After all, Secchia had told Togliatti that sterner measures were required, and Secchia had demanded a more effectively organized party.

Togliatti vs. Secchia

The shift to "party of opposition" was duly carried out, the high point of the autumn coming when a Communist squad stormed the Milan prefect's headquarters following the removal of a left-wing prefect. Secchia went to Moscow in December, where he met the Soviet elite, from Stalin to Malenkov and Zhdanov. In preliminary discussions, Secchia stressed that he disagreed with Togliatti on the basic line of the PCI and wanted a more disciplined, mobilized, and aggressive party. The Russians asked him to put it in writing, which he was all too happy to do. The document in question, now published as part of the "Secchia archives,"[24] is at once a profoundly pessimistic document and a highly utopian vision of the possibilities of communism in Italy. Secchia observed that the presence of the American army made the armed seizure of power impossiblle. Moreover, Secchia was disillusioned by the failure of the PCI to react to its expulsion from the government. "There is a great distance between doing nothing and having an insurrection," he noted sadly. "We permitted ourselves to be kicked out of a government without a major mass protest, without a general strike of 24 or 48 hours."

The party was thus too orderly, too passive:

> The gravest defect of our party seems to me to be a great mass of inactive members, who do not do anything. Now, a great mass of inactive members, especially in a period in which we have ceased to be a party of government, represents a danger. . . . A great problem before the Italian Communist party is that of activating the great majority of its members, activating them above all in the struggle.

Secchia recognized that prospects were poor, and that it would probably be a long time before the party could expect to reenter the government. And he made it clear that he did not endorse a drastic shift in strategy: the goal of the party would remain the creation of a progressive, democratic government in Italy. No insurrectionary program should be undertaken. But, and here the divergence from Togliatti was evident, the terrain on which the Communists waged their struggle had to be enlarged. "This struggle cannot be waged only in Parliament," he wrote, rather "it must be waged above all outside Parliament." And if the enemy attempted to block the Communist offensive with force, "we still have a potential force such that we would be able to shatter every violent attempt of theirs, and carry the Italian workers to a decisive success."

This appeal by Secchia for a more vigorous effort, leading in all likelihood to a frontal conflict he believed the PCI might win, was apparently in line with Stalin's orders to the Cominform. But the response of the Soviet dictator was not encouraging: "it is not now possible."[25] Secchia replied that he was not advocating insurrection, but simply asking for a more dynamic mode of behavior. Stalin was not impressed. Such conduct, he observed, leads inevitably to the same end. "Today one can not do it. You must, however, reinforce yourselves, prepare yourselves well, etc."

As always in these situations, Stalin left his petitioner in some doubt about final objectives, but the three elements that emerged from the trip to Moscow were clear enough. First of all, Togliatti's line was Stalin's, so that there was no illusion that the Comintern line was going to be used to weaken the position of the secretary general. Opposition, yes, but not insurrection. The second point was closely related to the first: there was a real possibility that the party would have to fight on nonparliamentary terrain, and the PCI must prepare for it. Finally, the Soviets were impressed with Secchia. Stalin reportedly told him that his continued presence at the head of Organization was ardently desired by the Kremlin. The following year Secchia was elected second vice-secretary of the PCI, despite statutory regulations that made such a post theoretically impossible. The general impression within the party was that the elevation of Secchia was suggested by the Soviets.

Events in 1948 reopened the question of party leadership. With the electoral debacle in April and the abortive uprising in July, Togliatti faced a real crisis. The secretary general had been defeated in Parliament, at the polls, and in the streets. The *Partito Nuovo* had been crushed in the elections by the DC, the Vatican, and the Americans, while the *Partito Armato* had been sent back to its clandestine barracks by the police. Under these circumstances Secchia's critique the previous December appeared prescient, and it was clear that the responsibility for the collapse on all fronts was Togliatti's. While an objective observer would point out that the fundamental errors were Stalin's, this could hardly be said in the context of PCI-CPSU relations; the guilt had to pass further down the chain of command.

Togliatti's biographer has claimed that the Russians decided to remove him in the late 1940s, and only awaited an appropriate moment to carry out their decision.[26] In the meantime, they informed Secchia that they favored his methods and encouraged him to create the kind of party that he favored. The occasion to communicate the news to Togliatti came in 1950, when he was seriously injured in a summer automobile accident, and he accepted Stalin's invitation to come to Moscow for medical care and convalescence.

It was evident that something extraordinary was in the wind, for in city after city he was greeted like a potentate, and once his train entered Soviet territory every station was provided with imposing military force. Such security measures were not usual for the leader of a foreign Communist party, and they indicated that Stalin had something more than rest and recreation in mind for Togliatti. In late December Stalin told Togliatti that Italy was clearly unsafe and that the former Comintern official would be well advised to think of his own security. Why not leave Rome and move either to Moscow or Prague to direct the Cominform?

Stalin's offer was hard to refuse and impossible to accept. Togliatti knew that if he became the head of the Cominform he would serve primarily as a lightening rod, attracting all the complaints of the foreign leaders while having little autonomy. Moreover, even though Stalin promised that Togliatti would remain the secretary general of the PCI, no party could be effectively managed from the other side of the Iron Curtain by a Cominform functionary. Stalin's invitation was an effort to kick Togliatti upstairs. In January 1951, Secchia and Longo were brought to Moscow to discuss the matter, and it was decided to call for a vote of the PCI Directorate.

Togliatti might have hoped for personal loyalty from the Directorate, but it soon became clear that the PCI's basic allegiance was to Stalin. In addition, the party had to decipher the meaning of the invitation to Togliatti. In Secchia's words,

> Was there perhaps someone who thought that Togliatti in Italy was a brake on a policy of a more decisive struggle against American imperialism? Nobody ever raised this problem, but it can be supposed that there was something there, at least from some of the things the old man (Stalin) introduced into the conversation: "Comrade Togliatti has great faith, too much faith in constitutional legality." But this phrase could also have been merely polemical towards Togliatti, who did not share Stalin's opinion that he was in danger in Italy.[27]

The PCI voted overwhelmingly to grant Stalin's request, and Secchia returned yet again to Moscow to bring the secretary general the unwelcome decision of his party. Togliatti was furious, then pleaded with Secchia to help in his hour of need. Together they drafted a letter to Stalin in which the decision to send Togliatti to Prague was accepted, but only after the secretary general had returned to Italy to tidy up his affairs and direct the upcoming Seventh Congress.

That Togliatti's request was accepted by Stalin is a tribute to Togliatti's prestige in the Communist movement, and also to the cynicism with which Stalin conducted his policies. Everyone knew that Togliatti was finished, but it was useful to Stalin to encourage conflict within the PCI leadership. As the case of Tito demonstrated, a united party might pose problems for the Russians, and in Italy the political goal had been accomplished. The Seventh Congress was Secchia's; the PCI was restructured, and the more militant line desired by the Kremlin was carried forward.

It was a pyrrhic victory, for Togliatti was favored by a stroke of luck: shortly after the Congress Secchia suffered a heart attack and retraced Togliatti's steps to Moscow for convalescence. In the interim, Togliatti gained strength within the party, postponed his move to Prague, and hung on long enough to capitalize on the decisive events of 1953 and 1954, first with the death of Stalin, then with a scandal that struck down Secchia.

The death of Stalin and the subsequent power struggle in the Kremlin deprived Secchia of his great protector and gave Togliatti greater room for maneuver. Nonetheless, Secchia still enjoyed enormous power within the PCI until 1954, when his close assistant Giulio Seniga defected from the party with a reported million dollars in secret funds and a considerable quantity of PCI secret documents (an archive he later termed his "life insurance policy"). Seniga had been Secchia's right-hand man for years, carrying documents to Prague and money and instructions back to Rome. Seniga knew the Russians well, and was privy to the most intimate secrets of the party. His defection was thus a mortal blow to Secchia: if his own man turned traitor, he could not possibly lead the party. Secchia was gradually eased out of the Directorate, and was sent to Milan. Year by year his role became less important, and while he often made interesting trips abroad he never again participated at the highest levels of party life.

With Secchia out of the way, Togliatti reassumed his position. And with Stalin dead, and with the shattering revelations of Krushchev at the Twentieth Party Congress of the CPSU in 1956, the rationale for the Armed party slowly disappeared. While the PCI continued to maintain a secret organization, the dream of the X hour had passed away. Henceforth the PCI would dedicate the bulk of its considerable talents to the creation of a mass organization, dedicated to the conquest of power by other means.

Notes

1. *Foreign Relations of the United States*, 1947, Vol. III, 293 ff.
2. *Ibid.*, 908.
3. Gambino, *op. cit.*, 348.
4. *Ibid.*
5. This is from Tarchiani's report to De Gasperi, quoted by Gambino, *op. cit.*, 347-48.
6. See the quotation from Gambino, one of the most intense critics of American foreign policy, then as now, at the beginning of the last chapter.
7. Thomas A. Bailey, *The Marshall Plan*.
8. Tasca's report, "Counter Measures to policies and tactics of the Italian Communist Party," was cabled 27 December 1947, from Rome to Washington.
9. *Ibid.*
10. Dunn to secretary of state, 6 April 1948.
11. "A Report to the National Security Council," 8 March 1948.
12. The Kennan note is reproduced in *Foreign Relations of the United States*, 1948, *cit.*, 848-49.
13. H. Stuart Hughes, "The Second Year of the Cold War," in *Commentary* (August 1969).
14. "Report to the President," 21 April 1950, Reports to the National Security Council, 12 April 1950 and 21 December 1950.
15. For the best treatment of the Cominform meeting, see Eugenio Reale, *Avec Jacques Duclos* (Paris, 1958). Reale published his detailed notes of the meeting after leaving the PCI following the crisis of 1956.
16. According to Reale, Togliatti instructed him and Longo to reply to criticism by saying that the PCI had acted to avoid "another Greece" (interview with Reale).
17. Claudin, *op. cit.*, 381 ff.
18. Reale, *op. cit.*
19. Claudin, *op. cit.*, 474.
20. The untitled note is dated 6 October 1947.
21. Interview with Reale.
22. Gambino, *op. cit.*, 380-81.
23. Cf. Gambino, 380 n.

24. Fondazione Feltrinelli, *Annali XIX, cit.*, 609 ff.
25. *Ibid.*, 426.
26. Bocca, *op. cit.*, 536 ff.
27. Fondazione Feltrinelli, *Annali XIX, cit.*, 230.

4

The Opening to the Left

> *The Socialists underwent in interparty relations the same experience as the Italian nation in the nineteenth century: too weak in resources and structure in the face of the major European countries . . . but too conspicuous to play the role of minor countries.*
> —Alberto Ronchey[1]

The "Opening to the Left," the creation of a governing coalition in Italy with both Christian Democrats (DC) and Socialists, is such a logical idea that one's first reaction is to wonder why it took so long. The DC, irreplaceable keystone of any government since the early postwar period, after 1953 needed coalition partners to govern. Yet until 1963 no working relationship with the Socialists could be achieved. Despite the seemingly irresistible logic of the Center-Left, it was hard to work out.

The difficulties came from all sides. First, came the PSI itself, a party, in the words of a standard Italian witticism, that "does not know what it wants, and wants it immediately." Nenni had been avidly courted by the DC ever since the war's end, but had refused to break his Unity of Action Pact with Togliatti. Nonetheless, De Gasperi continued to propose a Center-Left coalition to the Socialists, only to be rejected on every occasion. Nenni believed that the triumph of communism in Italy (along with that of the Soviet Union in Europe more broadly) was quite likely, and he did not wish to repeat Bukharin's unhappy end. Until the death of Stalin, at the very earliest, Nenni would not seriously consider breaking with the PCI.

Nenni's reluctance may also have been due to more mundane considerations. Nenni personally, and the PSI as a whole, had received substantial financial assistance from Soviet bloc sources. To be sure, there were other sources of funding for the Socialists (unlike the PCI, which received almost all of its money from Soviet and pro-Soviet sources), including some payments from the Americans and the Christian Democrats in the late 1940s, but it would have been highly inconvenient to do without the Soviet subsidies.[2]

In addition, the well-established Soviet method of control over West European Communist parties was replicated by the PCI within the Socialist party. Many Socialists were secretly Communists, placed within the PSI in order to provide Togliatti and the Russians with intelligence, help manipulate the Socialists, and organize factions within the PSI that could both weaken the leadership and threaten the party with schisms should political events require.[3] Nenni was never in complete control, and the Action Pact with the Communists was a reflection of the real state of affairs within the PSI. It is not known how many Socialists were under Communist control, but the sequence of suicidal political decisions in the late forties—leading first to the loss of Saragat and his followers in 1947, and then to the presentation of a single PSI-PCI list in the catastrophic election campaign of 1948—may have been due in part to the actions of the clandestine Communists.

Finally, of course, came Nenni's own convictions. Like so many Italian and French Socialists, he was impressed and intimidated by the superior organization of the Communist party. In the shared exile with the Communists in Paris during the war, Nenni saw firsthand the great strength the Communists derived from their Moscow connection. He saw the imposing discipline of the PCI, and he saw—and shared in—the steady flow of money from the Comintern. As dozens of Italians and Americans have confirmed, Nenni's party received money from the PCI, and for quite a long time this subvention could have had only one source: the Kremlin. In addition, Nenni was himself a victim of the Stalin myth, omnipresent among the leaders of the postwar European Left.

Thus, the PSI was hardly an attractive candidate for alliance with a Christian Democratic party that based much of its electoral appeal on anticommunism and support for the Atlantic Alliance. At best, the Socialists were questionable allies; at worst, they were a Communist Trojan horse. Most members of the DC regarded the prospect of a Center-Left government with deep suspicion, as did most of the leaders of other NATO nations. Yet other, more farsighted Christian Democrats realized that in the long run it was in the interests of the country, and the DC, to attempt to absorb the Socialists for a second time, following the model of Giolitti earlier in the century. But the operation required patience, along with the good will of a significant part of the PSI. Throughout the forties and early fifties, this latter ingredient was lacking; the Socialists opposed NATO, aligned themselves with the U.S.S.R. on most foreign policy questions, worked hand-in-glove with the Communists in the trade union field, and condemned "American imperialism" in violent terms.

Yet political logic pointed unerringly toward an "Opening to the Left," especially after 1953, when the DC just barely failed to gain a majority of the popular vote that, under the terms of an electoral law passed especially for the occasion, would have awarded the Christian Democrats a substantial bonus in Parliament. The DC failed by a tiny percentage, thanks to a savage attack against the so-called fraudulent law from the Left, and various questionable maneuvers during the voting by the Right.[4] The result was the end of Christian Democratic domination of Italian politics, and the beginning of a decade of uncertainty. Henceforth the DC had to make ever greater concessions to its coalition partners, and since neither the PSI nor the PCI was acceptable, this meant a steady procession of centrist and Center-Right coalitions. As the decade passed, the DC paid in two ways for accommodating to this necessity: it steadily lost votes to the Right, and it virtually abandoned any effort at equitable structural reform of Italian society. Since this, in turn, meant that the gains from the spectacular Italian "economic miracle" of the late 1950s were distributed inequitably, the DC found itself increasingly under attack from the Left on quite reasonable grounds: the government was not meeting the just demands of the working classes and the lower middle classes.

Thus, the Christian Democrats sought other partners. Indeed, De Gasperi himself pleaded with Nenni to create a Center-Left immediately after the 1953 elections, but the PSI leader again refused. For although there was a compelling domestic argument for such a coalition, the domestic and international requirements for such a government made it very difficult for the Socialists to come to terms. In essence, the Socialists would have had to break with the PCI in a forthright and decisive manner and endorse the Atlantic Alliance. This was impossible at that time, for not only was the PSI financially dependent upon the Communists (and their Soviet paymasters), but also the Socialists were a prime example of the success of the Togliatti-Gramsci strategy of cultural hegemony.[5] The Communists dominated the political culture of the country, and, in keeping with Gramsci's dictum that communism in Italy would eventually triumph as a result of such cultural domination, the PCI assiduously recruited intellectuals from all fields, ensuring that there would be no intellectually respectable resistance to their efforts to manipulate Italian public opinion. The most distinguished victim of this brilliant strategem was the Italian Socialist party.

The Gramscian Strategy

That Antonio Gramsci should have become the court philosopher of Italian communism must be counted among the more bizarre developments of the postwar period, for Gramsci himself was hardly a model party member. In open conflict with Togliatti and the Comintern over the *svolta*, and in almost total isolation from his other party comrades in prison (where Communist cells functioned without interruption throughout the Fascist era), Gramsci seemed destined to be remembered as a victim of the PCI rather than one of its contributing geniuses. Indeed, at least one occasion his comrades attempted to injure him, when they hurled snowballs with rocks inside. And there is reason to believe that by the end of his life, Gramsci had decided to leave the party. He had certainly little patience with the complete subordination of the interests of the party to those of the Soviet Union, and had he lived Gramsci might well have suffered the same sort of humiliation to which Umberto Terracini was subjected at the end of the war.

Despite the very real disagreements that had separated him from the party, Gramsci was elevated to the level of party philosopher by Togliatti upon the latter's return from Moscow because, in the elegant words of George Lichtheim, "from the prison cell in which he had been sealed by Mussolini, Gramsci elaborated a doctrine more totalitarian than that of his gaolers."[6] This theory was ideally suited to the needs and the personality of the secretary general of the PCI, and Togliatti quickly made it his own, as well as that of the party.

Traditionally, Communists tended to denigrate intellectuals, whose mental labors were held to be inferior to the physical exertions of the working class, but Gramsci realized that a Communist revolution in the West could only take place after converting public opinion, and not as a result of a proletarian uprising. This conversion depended upon the intellectuals, the modern "princes," and Gramsci argued that once they had become good Communists, it would be a relatively simple matter to seize the levers of institutional power. Indeed, if Communist cultural hegemony were properly achieved, the institutions would be quite irrelevant, for most everyone would be in accord with Communist goals.

The Gramscian vision of revolution[7] was the reverse of Lenin's. Instead of first seizing the central organs of the state and then imposing the will of the party upon the masses, the party was first to capture the minds and hearts of the masses and then—in the final stages of the revolution—capture the state. Gramsci has often been compared with the Jesuits, who stressed the importance of early instruction in religious tenets, but the more proper ideological context in which to understand Gramsci is that of fascism, the system that incarcerated him and took his life in 1937. For Gramsci fully appreciated the success with which Mussolini created a genuine and dynamic consensus in Italy around himself and his regime. And Gramsci also realized that Mussolini's efforts were not thoroughly successful, and Italian fascism was "an incomplete totalitarianism." Gramsci's own utopia would be more thorough-going. One can almost sense the envy in Gramsci's account of the medieval Church: "The Roman church was always the most tenacious in the struggle to prevent the 'official' formation of two religions, one for the intellectuals, and another for the 'simple souls.'"[8]

Gramsci's vision of totalitarianism and his new strategy for the conquest of power in a modern society were many years in advance of developments, for one of the strengths of Gramsci's theory is that it lends itself perfectly to the technology of the mass media. If the theory of the "new prince" made sense when intellectuals had only the printed word, the movie screen, and the radio at their disposal, it was even more effective with the vastly more powerful methods of mass manipulation that were developed in the following forty years.

As Enzo Bettiza has written, the Gramscian focus on cultural hegemony has often diverted attention from the exquisitely totalitarian essence of the doctrine. "If," in Bettiza's words, "Catholic totalitarianism has successfully moved from the Inquisition to the pedagogical domain without losing its unitary connotation, why could not a sophisticated communism repeat the same steps in more absolute and efficacious terms?"[9] In other words, the PCI, by adopting Gramsci's strategy, manages to appear the spirit of sweet reasonableness by stressing its desire to achieve a degree of national harmony (the so-called policy of national unity) while all the while deferring the final revolutionary triumph. As Bettiza puts it,

> The renunciation of the immediate revolution can cast the Eurocommunist parties as normal social-reformist parties; while the aspiration for a complete totalitarianism, always deferred until the fullness of tomorrow, can make them seem downright utopian. Instead, they are neither one of these.[10]

The Gramscian goal—fully adopted by the PCI—is the domination of the political culture of Italy, to gut the system from the inside in order to restructure it in keeping with Communist precepts. In concrete terms this means that the Communists aimed at control of the instruments of popular culture: schools, radio and television, newspapers, movies, and publishing houses. And anyone who has studied the cultural strategy of the PCI cannot help but be impressed with the diligence, skill, and tenacity with which the strategy has been pursued.[11] In this context, the tactic of the "historic compromise" in the mid-seventies was only logical, for it emphasized the unity of the major political forces in the country. If ever achieved, the Communists would hope to manipulate the new government to their own ends. But whereas a traditional Leninist would call for the destruction, say, of the Catholic forces, the Gramscians urge consensus, agreement, and unity. Instead of attacking frontally, the PCI seeks to convince, soothe, and eventually control.

It was accordingly quite understandable that Togliatti should disembark at Salerno and call for national reconciliation rather than open conflict. With occasional exceptions (generally dictated by international events, or by the needs of the Soviet Union) this strategy lay at the heart of the PCI's behavior throughout the postwar period. And it was quite successful indeed; on at least two occasions it appeared that the party was on the verge of establishing virtual cultural hegemony, only to be thwarted by external events: the catastrophes of 1956 (the Khrushchev secret speech at the Twentieth Congress of the Soviet Communist Party, and the invasion of Hungary in the fall), and the assassination of Aldo Moro by the Red Brigades in 1978. Coincidentally, both occasions served to catalyze the process of PSI rupture with the Communists.

The triumph of Communist "culture" in Italy in the forties and fifties has been well described, and hardly needs detailed analysis here. So far as the Socialists were concerned, there was precious little to distinguish the PSI from the PCI in formal ideological terms, and Togliatti always acted in such a way as to minimize differences between himself and Nenni, even shifting his own position when called for. This strategy was known to Italians as the "quail jump," and its classic description came in a remark by Togliatti to R.H. Crossman in June 1953:

> (De Gasperi) cannot drive a wedge between the PSI and the Communists, because if Nenni moves to the Right, I jump over his head and move even further to the Right . . . De Gasperi knows this perfectly well from his experiences in 1944 and again in 1945.

Not that any masterful political skill was called for to guarantee that the Socialists would remain within the PCI orbit; as Giorgio Amendola has wryly observed, throughout the forties and early fifties, the Socialists were frequently more Stalinist than the Communists (a phenomenon that was repeated throughout the postwar period with a variety of non-Communist forces on the Left, for they felt compelled to demonstrate the purity of their left-wing credentials). This was the case, for example, with the trade union movement, where the Socialists (and, even more so, the Christian Democratic trade union leaders) often made more outrageous demands than the Communists.

To be sure, there were exceptions, and there were distinguished intellectuals and party leaders within the PSI, like Norberto Bobbio and Luciano Pellicani, who challenged the "democratic" claims of the PCI and urged the Socialists to take a more explicitly Western, democratic course. But they were a small minority until the late 1970s, and their ideas were too close to those of the Social Democratic schismatics to gain acceptance by the PSI leadership and the rank-and-file. Communist hegemony rarely was effectively challenged from within the Socialist party.

Finally, the threat from the Communists was not purely political, and the Socialists had at hand several examples of what happend to more moderate forces on the Left once the Communists took power. They had lived through the establishment of Soviet control over Eastern Europe, and they had watched the quite nasty campaign of espionage, sabotage, and intimidation that the PCI conducted against Tito from Trieste in the late forties and early fifties. With such lessons so near in time and space, the PCI leaders would have needed considerable courage to open a fissure between themselves and the Communists.

The Development of the Rupture

Despite everything that tied the Socialists to the PCI, and notwithstanding the brilliance of the Gramscian strategy, there were still many Socialists who preferred the West to the Soviet bloc; at worst, they advocated a kind of benign neutralism for Italy. And even though the PSI had tried briefly to establish democratic centralism in the late 1950s (when Nenni became a minority figure for a while), it never altogether lost its more democratic tradition that made a genuine conversion to democracy possible. Stalin was a great PSI hero, but there was always an anti-Stalinist wing of the party; the Soviet Union was held to be a great model of socialism, but there were always many Socialists who found the U.S.S.R. repugnant; the party invariably condemned the United States as an "imperialist" power, and generally tilted toward the Soviet position in East-West disputes, but there were many who did not share Soviet goals and who dreaded Soviet expansionism.

Lastly, there were domestic considerations. There was always hope that the PSI would eventually realize that so long as they played leitmotifs to the Communists' main theme, the PSI would eventually become irrelevant. The same logic could be applied to the trade union field, where the Socialists steadfastly refused to break with the Communist CGIL. In the long run this strategy was suicidal, but there were very few signs of a meaningful change in the early and mid-fifties.

Yet the desire that the PSI split with the Communists was so strong that many observers insisted that, despite the overwhelming evidence to the contrary, it was imminent. An official American document from 1955 described this wishful thinking in some detail:

> There is . . . a strong opinion that the Communists could not long support a reformist government even for the tactical purpose of penetrating it or influencing it in favor of a pro-Soviet foreign policy. The Communists, according to a theory held by (President) Gronchi and shared by some Christian Democrats and moderate left politicians, would thus sooner or later try to force the Socialists to quit their collaboration with the Center, and the Socialists, being moderates and essentially democratically minded, would refuse to do so. A battle between the Socialists and the Communists would then take place, according to this theory, and the Socialists would eventually emerge as the party of the Left, since the Communists no longer represent the wave of the future to Italian workers and peasants.[12]

I have cited this theory at length, because it became an integral part of the theology of the Opening to the Left. For despite the lack of evidence to support this theory, many Italians and Americans came to believe not only that the participation of the PSI in the government might stabilize the political situation and help some Socialists move away from Communist domination, but also that the creation of a Center-Left government would seal off the PCI from power in Italy. Furthermore, according to this belief, the Socialists—suddenly transmuted into a democratic, relatively pro-Western party by its elevation to the Cabinet—would subsequently dominate the Italian Left.

This theory received some feeble support from Nenni's efforts to find a small patch of political turf between Togliatti and the DC. Nenni moderated the party's opposition to NATO (provided that the country moved toward a more neutralist position overall and rejected many American military proposals), supported some of the economic policies proposed by the progressive wing of the DC, and hinted broadly that he might be willing to cooperate with the DC in governing the country if the circumstances were right. These moves came in 1953 and again in 1955, but they took place against a background of very close coordination with the Communists, to the point where the State Department's Office of Intelligence and Research concluded a discussion of Italy in 1955 with the observation that, from the PCI's standpoint,

> The only realistic way of undermining Italy's position in the Western Alliance appears to be through a Socialist party, whose free-wheeling actions offer hope to non-Communist Italians that it may eventually break from the PCI but whose Communist ties are, however, sufficiently in evidence that its acceptance, as even a limited partner in an Italian government, is likely to be rejected by the NATO powers and to cause splits in the center parties. Togliatti appears quite willing to risk the consequences of an eventual break with the PSI if in the meantime the PSI can provoke the appropriate chain of reactions which will lead to the neutralization of Italy.[13]

These hypotheses were not tested, because the following year saw the first real break between the parties of the Left since the Nazi-Soviet Pact of 1939-41. The break of 1956, like that of 1939, was produced by the actions of the U.S.S.R., first in Moscow and then in Budapest.

The first great event was the Twentieth Party Congress of the CPSU in Moscow, at which Khrushchev presented his account and denunciation of Stalin's crimes. While the Khrushchev secret speech to a closed session of the Congress has often been portrayed as a bolt from the blue skies of the international Communist movement, the European Communists had been given ample warning. The PCI was the first Italian party to get advance notice, when Secchia brought back reports of the catalogue of Stalin's crimes—and of the intentions of the new Soviet leaders to describe and condemn them—shortly after the dictator's death in 1953.[14] But Togliatti was hardly interested in opening such a discussion within the PCI (not least of all because of his own complicity), and the question was swept aside for the moment.

Nenni, too, had been warned, by Khrushchev himself in the summer of 1955 (oddly, in the published version of his diaries,[15] Nenni does not mention a discussion of this subject when he met with Khrushchev in Yalta). Yet, like Togliatti, Nenni avoided a full discussion of the issue within his party. Like Togliatti, Nenni fully expected that the matter would remain sealed within the Kremlin walls, even if bits and pieces of the truth filtered out to "fraternal parties." But when Israeli intelligence officials came into possession of the Khrushchev text and passed it to CIA counterintelligence chief James Angleton for worldwide publication, the question could no longer be avoided.

Before the publication of Khrushchev's text by the *New York Times,* Nenni had hailed the work of the Congress as a vindication of his own mildly critical position in the twenties and thirties, and he had gone on to praise the Soviet Union for its "creative force" and its willingness to indulge in self-criticism to the point of undertaking a "revolution of liberal tendency." But once the text was published he changed his emphasis (although, in his diary, Nenni bemoaned the speech, suggesting that some scholarly books and articles would have been more useful).[16] Under attack from the Social Democrats, who correctly stressed that the speech had vindicated *their* position, not Nenni's, he first claimed that he had known the truth all along, and then criticized the Congress for having failed to provide a sufficiently Marxist analysis of their problems. In a lengthy analysis published in late March in *Mondoperaio,* Nenni said that the basic questions had not been faced: how had the dictatorship been made possible? How had collective leadership been transformed into a cult of personality? These were indeed devastating questions, but Nenni followed them up by criticizing the likes of Walter Ulbricht—for jumping on the anti-Stalin bandwagon with indecent haste.[17]

There was not the slightest suggestion that Nenni regretted his Action Pact with the Communists, and indeed he reserved great praise for Togliatti, who was said to have "well understood the positive character" of the Congress. After all, Togliatti had often spoken of the need for a "new party" and for the "Italian road to socialism." Thus, there was no reason to abandon the alliance simply because the truth about Stalinism had been revealed.

The fact of the matter was that neither Nenni nor Togliatti was enthusiastic about Khrushchev. Nenni rather liked him personally, but was alarmed by his policies; Togliatti disliked him on both grounds; both believed that Khrushchev would soon be removed by the old guard. Togliatti was the first person in Italy to have the text of the secret speech, for the KGB had arranged to have a copy delivered to him on the day Khrushchev spoke in Moscow, but he chose to downplay its significance. But as time passed, Togliatti found himself in the midst of a genuine internal party crisis, caught between an elite that was profoundly disturbed and that demanded an extended discussion of the errors of Stalinism, and a base that bitterly resented the attacks against *il baffone* and considered Khrushchev terribly disruptive, if not a traitor.

Togliatti's reaction to the crisis was embodied in one of the most famous documents of the PCI, an interview in *Nuovi argomenti*[18] that is often cited as the starting point for Eurocommunism. The interview came in dramatic circumstances. By the summer of 1956 the PCI had closed ranks behind the Soviet Union and had rejected any suggestion that the revelations of Khrushchev necessitated a complete reappraisal of the Soviet system. So loyal were the Italians that Ilya Ehrenburg, the famous Russian novelist and poet, noted the irony that while Soviet intellectuals were full of enthusiasm for serious analyses of the crimes of Stalin, the Western Communists were trying to keep at least part of the Stalin myth intact.[19]

Togliatti's interview was one of his most brilliant performances. In quick succession he criticized Stalin (for his "errors"), Western critics of Stalinism (for their "apologies for Western civilization," their dilettantish criticism, and their "habitual reactionary idiocies"), and, above all, the "bureaucratic degenerations" that characterized the Stalinist epoch. Thus, in the words of one of the most careful scholars of the period,

> If everything cannot be blamed on Stalin as an individual, and if on the other hand the foundations of the regime remain solid—that is, nothing can be blamed on socialism—there must be something in between that has degenerated: and it is, according to Togliatti, the bureaucratic apparatus.[20]

It was a political tour de force; Togliatti came close to transforming the disaster of the Twentieth Congress into a triumph of morale for the party, and if other events had not intervened in the autumn, he might well have coopted the anti-Stalinist campaign. But it was not to be.

In the first place, the shock to the Communist intellectuals was quite deep, and led to challenges to Togliatti's leadership. As Fabrizio Onofri wrote in *Rinascita* that summer, the revelations about Stalin seemed to suggest that the PCI had failed to pursue an "Italian path towards socialism." If this were a serious objective, was it not necessary to transform the party itself?[21]

Togliatti's response was worthy of *il baffone*: such suggestions, he said, smacked of "the enemy." But the worst was yet to come, first in Poland (with the brutal Polish and Soviet response to the Poznan workers' demonstrations) and then in Hungary. This sequence of events cost the PCI hundreds of thousands of members, the cream of the Italian intelligentsia, and the Action Pact with the Socialists.

The Ruptures of 1956

Nenni's mild dissent with the U.S.S.R. and the PCI following the secret speech was sufficient to open discussions with the Social Democrats about the possibility of reunification of the two parties. Fusion was discussed between Nenni and Saragat in mid-summer, and by the time that the Soviet tanks entered Budapest reunification was taken for granted. Logic dictated that the Action Pact would be a fatality of the new strategy, even though Nenni acted as if that was not necessarily so. But logic prevailed once the repression of the Hungarian uprising began.

The Hungarian drama shattered the hopes of those who had seen in Khrushchev's denunciation of Stalin, and in the brief cultural "thaw" that accompanied it, the beginning of the long-awaited and oft-predicted liberalization of the Soviet empire. Not only did the events of the summer and fall of 1956 drive a wedge between the PCI and the PSI, but it produced a major exodus from the Communist party. If one looks at the list of intellectuals who left the party in the two years following Budapest, one finds a "who's who" of Italian cultural life in the sixties and seventies. The party never fully recovered from this trauma; membership dropped from nearly two million to 1,700,000, and has never again approached the two million mark. Worse still, 1956 marked a major setback to the Gramscian strategy; first the Twentieth Party Congress unmasked Stalinism, then Poland and Hungary demonstrated that Soviet power would be ruthlessly deployed against attempts to democratize the Soviet empire.

The exodus was not limited to intellectuals and rank-and-file; leaders such as Eugenio Reale and Antonio Giolitti forced the party to expel them for their ourspoken attacks against the Stalinism of the PCI. Both went over to the Socialists and Social Democrats, and Reale, who had been one of the organizers of the PCI's complex system of financing through the Soviet bloc, revealed some of the most embarrassing activities of Communist leaders.[22] Scholars, artists, musicians, journalists, and party apparatchiks all left, taking with them an enhanced understanding of the basic principles of the Communist party. The uncompromising defense of the Soviet Union presented by Togliatti and those who remained within the party left no room for equivocation; and while many who deplored the actions in Poland and Hungary remained, their faith was shaken. It was only a matter of time before a second exodus took place—the *Manifesto* group in the 1960s—including several figures who had criticized the Hungarian invasion.

There was thus a double schism: that of the Action Pact with the PSI, and that of 300,000 of its own members. The two were closely linked, for many of the defectors joined the PSI, where they found a mixed reception. Nenni, for the most part, encouraged the ex-Communists to join him, while the more radical wing of the party (dubbed the "Tank Faction" because of their support for the Soviet invasion of Hungary) treated the new arrivals with considerable animosity.

The Unity of Action Pact was terminated in the autumn, and talks with Saragat went on apace. Yet, although the events were dramatic, there was no similarly dramatic shift in the Socialists' positions. Nenni's rather grudging acceptance of the Atlantic Alliance took precisely the same form as that of Enrico Berlinguer a decade later: NATO was a reality that one had to recognize, and all in all one would try to live with it. To quote one of Nenni's most ardent American admirers, Arthur M. Schlesinger, Jr.:

> By 1969 no one could doubt Nenni's break with the Communists . . . by ingenious reinterpretation, Nenni had defined his party's traditional neutralism as meaning the preservation of the existing European equilibrium: since Italian withdrawal from NATO would threaten that equilibrium, Nenni explicitly opposed such a withdrawal as an unneutral act.[23]

This is about the best face that could be placed upon Pietro Nenni's "conversion" to Atlanticism. There was no endorsement of the importance of defending Western Europe against the Soviet Union, little recognition that communism threatened freedom, and no concern about Soviet expansionism or Communist efforts to destabilize Italy. Instead, there was a grudging acceptance of the status quo in the name of stability. Finally, at no point was there any indication of Socialist desires to challenge the PCI's hegemony over the trade union movement. On the contrary, Nenni insisted that the PSI would continue to support "working class unity," which in practice meant continued Communist domination. Nenni's split with the PCI on the poitical level was not followed through on the level of trade unionism.

None of this prevented the "progressive wing" of the Christian Democratic party—above all, Amintore Fanfani and Aldo Moro—from pushing for the creation of a Center-Left. But the moment was not yet appropriate, and in addition to the purely Italian political forces, the Americans had to think through the implications of such a development.

The United States

As has been seen, many American experts on Italy, in the government and out, had emerged from the Second World War with what might be termed "progressive" expectations and desires. By and large, these Americans preferred liberal and social-democratic governments to conservative ones, and there was a built-in sympathy for the European Left after the joint struggle against fascism and nazism.

At the same time that the American government encouraged the emergence of "progressive" governments in Western Europe, the American trade union movement was engaged in similar efforts vis-à-vis their European counterparts. In particular, the American Federation of Labor, recognizing that any effective Communist takeover in Western Europe depended upon strong working class support, encouraged the anti-Communist trade unions in countries like France, Italy, and Germany. The three central figures in these operations were Jay Lovestone (a former Communist leader and union organizer and head of the AFL's international office who turned violently anti-Communist), Irving Brown (a close friend of Lovestone, and the head of the AFL's European office in Brussels), and David Dubinsky (the head of the ILGWU in New York, and a leader of the Jewish Labor Committee). Knowing that the Communists had a great advantage in organizational skills and financial assistance from the Soviet Union, these three men felt it urgent to get similar help to the democratic trade unions. The story of *Force Ouvrière* in France provides one example of the sort of operation the AFL could carry off, and similar efforts were made in Italy.

As in France, the key to the AFL's operations was the almost complete domination of the central union organizations, the CGIL, by the Communist party. While maintaining the fiction of "unity" between Communist and Socialist elements, the policies of the CGIL were generally determined by President Giuseppe di Vittorio, a talented man of liberal instincts but strong Communist discipline. The Socialist leader in the

CGIL, Oreste Lizzadri, had already learned what could happen to him if he failed to respect Communist wishes, and there was little challenge from that quarter.

The AFL therefore focussed its early attentions on the Catholic trade unions, while establishing contacts with the elements within the Socialist party that would later split with the party leadership to form the PSDI. When Saragat broke with Nenni in 1947, he received support not only from the American government, but also from the AFL.[24] And although Saragat's allies in the trade unions did not immediately leave the CGIL, Irving Brown—backed by the political and financial resources of Lovestone, Dubinsky, and their friends back in the United States—was able to protect them from the Communist and Socialist efforts to cut them off from sources of income. Once the CGIL split in 1948, the AFL was able to take an even more active role in supporting the free unions.

For years there has been a great debate over the origin of the money that Irving Brown contributed to the free trade unions in Italy in the postwar period. Some—largely hostile to the operation—have claimed that the bulk of the money came from the CIA; others—above all Brown himself—have vigorously denied the accusation. While the full story will not be known for many years (and in all probability, many aspects of this courageous undertaking on the part of the AFL will never be known), some tentative conclusions can be stated with considerable confidence.

First, the bulk of the money, and perhaps all of it, came from sources other than CIA. An examination of dozens of letters between Brown and Lovestone[25] demonstrates that the funds were transferred from New York to Switzerland by the Jewish Labor Committee. This money was raised by Dubinsky and others, in part from some of the wealthy American families (like the Harrimans, the Lovetts, and the Forrestals) who agreed with the AFL's goals.

Second, once the Marshall Plan got going, the United States government was able to transfer "unvouchered funds" for trade union purposes (these transfers were approved by the European governments in question).

Finally, as in France, the actual sums involved were not large; for the most part the AFL provided money for operating expenses, typewriters, mimeograph machines, and paper for propaganda and organization. Brown and Lovestone were worried about the nuts and bolts of the unions' fight against the Communists, and not with "buying" the leadership.

Some have suggested that these activities were only part of a much broader American initiative. While it is impossible to demonstate that something did *not* exist, it can be confidently stated that if there was a close working relationship with the American government, it only concerned small aspects of the overall AFL program in Europe. For example, Brown was often consulted about the selection of labor attaches at American embassies, and Lovestone was pumped for his intimate knowledge of Communist organizational and espionage methods.[26] Finally, the AFL was involved in the administration of the Marshall Plan itself. But the American union leaders were hardly inclined to place themselves under CIA control, especially because some attempts at collaboration had turned out badly. When some AFL sources in China came to Hong Kong in the early fifties to meet with a CIA representative, it resulted in their cover being blown, and they disappeared shortly thereafter. This put a chill on future attempts at joint efforts.

Furthermore, there was the inevitable frustration of dealing with the American governmental bureaucracy. Brown often complained that the Americans in Europe did not understand the urgency of the situation, were taken in by the elegant language and pro-American protestations of unionists looking for easy money, and failed to distinguish between the real leaders and political opportunists. But the AFL defended American diplomats who were smeared in the press, such as when Jefferson Caffery, our ambassador to Paris, was tarred by the thick brush of Drew Pearson.

Brown discovered that Italy was a difficult place for clean and easy solutions. In the first place, the Socialists, even Giuseppe Saragat's PSDI, were reluctant to have anything to do with the Catholics. Brown wanted to see the CISL (Catholic) and the UIL (lay) unions unite to make more effective common cause against the Communists, but this was a virtual impossibility.

Matters were made even more difficult by problems on the American side. After an initial period of cooperation, the AFL was undermined by the CIO, as their conflict was projected onto Europe from the United States. The conflicts were often personalized and hence exaggerated; Walter Reuther, fresh from an intense struggle against Communists within the CIO, tended to agree with Lovestone, Brown, and Dubinsky. But others in the CIO disagreed, and the likes of Philip Murray and Victor Reuther strove to keep the non-Communists within the umbrella organizations (like the CGIL). This was a part of the CIO's overall strategy of fighting the Communists from within the big organizations, rather than trying to split off the non-Communists and form competing organizations. The CIO stayed in the WFTU until the bitter end, when even the British TUC had withdrawn from the blatantly pro-Communist organization.[27]

This rivalry between the two American federations had unfortunate consequences, especially in Italy where the local trade unionists were quick to take advantage of the situation. The Italians played the Americans off against each other, often ensuring double funding while postponing painful decisions. If, as often happened, Brown and his associates (from Vanni

Montana to Harry Goldberg) insisted that there be a clean split with the Communists before full cooperation (and funding) could be established, the Italians could often find a sympathetic ear among the CIO people.

Paradoxically, the success of the Italian Social Democrats in retaining a separate union, the UIL, while apparently a triumph for their independence of both the Communists and the Catholics, actually guaranteed that Saragat would not be able to count on a mass organization. For the Social Democrats had both history and sociology against them. There was no traditional "base" for such an organization, and no prospect for a lay, moderate anti-Communist mass movement. The Italian spoils system was polarized between Catholics and Communists. And since the lack of a mass organization enfeebled the PSDI at the polls as well as in the social arena, this meant—as Brown and Lovestone fully realized—that Saragat was doomed to play the role of a philosophically and morally correct leader with no army. Had it been possible to convince the democratic trade unions in Italy of the necessity for a common front against the CGIL, the PCI might have been faced with a dilemma without a good solution: either moderate its behavior or find itself isolated. Alas, the test did not come before the 1980s.

The AFL strategy in Italy failed, after its initial success in the immediate postwar period. To be sure, the anti-Communist unions managed to guarantee the arrival of Marshall Plan shipments. (And of course, it must be said that Togliatti never went all out to block their arrival, realizing full well that such behavior would have been extremely unpopular. He therefore attacked the Marshall Plan verbally but stopped short of waging an effective action campaign against it.) But the democratic trade unionists were unable to sustain an alternative to the CGIL in the long term. The primary cause of this failure, as of the overall failure of the non-Communist progressive forces in Italy, lies with Nenni and the PSI. The Socialist party was too firmly under Communist influence (and its own suicidal mythology) to serve as an effective rallying point for a non-Communist mass movement. Over time, the PSI withered away as a working-class party, and became increasingly a "party of opinion," supported by white-collar voters and intellectuals. And on the other end of the spectrum, the Catholic unions were little better, for they came from an anticapitalist tradition centuries old and were even less interested in a reformist strategy than were the Socialists.

Nonetheless, it might still have been possible to achieve a progressive reformist policy if the Christian Democratic party had been reasonably united behind this goal, but the DC was divided into many currents, some of which (especially within the CISL) took extremely radical positions, even when a DC-led government defended business interests. Each of these various conflicting and competing interests found (and finds today) support within the party, and each was institutionalized in a "current" complete with a leader (or group of leaders), staff, fund-raising apparatus, public relations organization, and spoils system. The diversity of interests that the DC had to defend, along with the corruption attendant on the proportional representation system, eventually made of the DC an almost totally incoherent political body, more a bundle of power centers than an efficient organization. This process was well under way by the mid-sixties.

The DC could not play the paladin's role, but since the DC was the only alternative to the Communists, the United States was doomed to support a political organization it did not generally admire. And the obvious necessity of this arrangement was galling to many Americans. Since the PCI was luxuriously looked after by its "sugar daddy" in the Kremlin, the Americans helped keep the DC competitive by helping to meet party expenses. It might be thought that this would have increased American leverage, but in practice the Christian Democrats were quite resistant to American pressure. They knew full well that there was no acceptable alternative to their rule from the American point of view. Between a disappointingly conservative and unimaginative party that supported NATO, and a Communist party that was solidly in the Soviet camp, the American choice was automatic.

This did not mean, however, that the Americans were resigned to supporting the DC forever, and from time to time there were efforts to engineer some sort of breakthrough. The AFL on at least two occasions (once in the fifties and again in the mid-sixties) believed it had reached an agreement with the non-Communist trade union leaders that would have produced a democratic trade union movement capable of challenging the CGIL. Both times the Italians backed out at the eleventh hour. And in the second half of the fifties, the embassy in Rome was convinced that an heir to De Gasperi had been found, in the miniature form of Amintore Fanfani. This, too, proved an illusion, but this one was linked to an even greater dream about the Opening to the Left.

The Americans and the *Apertura a Sinistra*

Accounts vary considerably about American enthusiasm for the Opening to the Left in the early and mid-fifties. It was difficult for State Department officials to take an overtly pro-Socialist position in this period, because in the McCarthyite atmosphere of the time such advocacy was tantamount to politial suicide. With the department under constant surveillance by anti-Communist zealots in Washington, the foreign service officers generally kept a low profile and hewed to the official line of fighting

Communists—and the Communists' Socialist allies—on all fronts. Yet some Italian hands believed that the solution to the Italian problem could only be achieved through the PSI, and they found support from some of their counterparts in the Central Intelligence Agency.

The CIA was sheltered from McCarthy by Allen Dulles, and therefore throughout the fifties and into the sixties, the agency offered sanctuary for liberals who might otherwise have faced early retirement and multiple blacklists. In addition, the CIA was best suited for carrying on clandestine contacts with the Socialists in Europe, for such conversations could be held without compromising American policy and without embarrassing the Socialists themselves. As in the case of the Communists in the seventies, the discussions with the Socialists were almost always conducted at relatively low levels (Nenni, for example, was not a regular contact, and most information about his thinking came from third parties such as travelling American scholars and journalists, in addition to the normal Italian sources). Finally, there were some important officials of the CIA who believed that the time had come to swing American covert support firmly behind the Socialists. This was the view of William Colby, who arrived in the Rome station for a five-year stint in 1953 to conduct, in his own words, "the CIA's largest covert political-action program undertaken until then, or, indeed, since—an unparalleled opportunity to demonstrate that secret aid could help our friends and frustrate our foes without the use of force or violence."[28] His responsibilities included funding "center forces," anti-Communist propaganda, and the creation of viable democratic institutions in all areas of activity.

From the very start, Colby was one of the most vigorous advocates of the Opening to the Left, and he took this position even though he knew that "the web of (Nenni's) supporting organization in labor, cooperatives, and elsewhere were under Communist control and would be used against an independent Socialist Party."[29]

Colby hoped that by splitting the Socialist party (or a significant part of it) from the PCI, and replacing the Communists (and the Soviet Union) as the Socialists' primary source of external funds, the Communists "would be reduced at one blow to a mere 20 percent of the Italian electorate, and a very minor threat to the Western alliance." Consequently, Colby proposed that the United States promote the Opening to the Left both politically and financially:

> It was apparent that one of the inhibitions to a clean break . . . was where (the Socialists') future financial and political support would come from. But if this could be assured by a combination of an outgoing attitude among the center democratic forces . . . *and* an assurance of a continuing source of financial support from unspecified and understanding "friends" in America, then the

inhibitions might be eliminated and the Socialists might take the step that would end American concern over the slim majority that stood for Western democracy in Italy.[30]

With minor variations, this was the vision that would prevail in the sixties. It was a peculiar vision, for on Colby's own account, there was no reason to believe that by bringing the PSI into the government, "the slim majority that stood for Western democracy" would have been greatly strengthened. This was a matter of the convictions of the participants, and not merely a question of who paid the bills. Simply transferring the PSI from Moscow to Langley could not change the nature of the Socialist party. As Brown and Lovestone had learned to their sorrow, Italian Socialists were quite capable of making promises, obtaining money, and then continuing on as before; surely the CIA was aware of this. Then there was the problem of the Communist infiltration of the PSI, another subject that had long occupied the Rome station of the agency; how could one be sure that the "Socialists" brought into the government were not actually Communists?

Even if one could somehow be convinced that the PSI was "really" independent and democratic in its heart of hearts, there were still two powerful political objections to the Opening. First was the possibility that the promotion of the PSI from opposition to government might actually favor the Communists. This was particularly worrisome if Nenni were supported prior to an open break with the Communists on such basic questions as NATO. Should the Americans support a "neutralist" party? Was it not more prudent—and better politics—to insist upon an ideological quid for the rather substantial political and economic quo the Socialists would obtain? Was it not necessary to insist upon a transformation of the PSI before granting it full legitimacy, in order to avoid setting a dangerous precedent that might come back to haunt Italy and the United States in later years?

Finally, there was the question of the continuing Action Pact, which was in full force in 1953. The theory of Colby and the others who supported the *Apertura* was that, once in the Cabinet, the Socialists would end their ties to the PCI. Aside from the profound cynicism of this view (suggesting that the Socialists acted not out of conviction but out of sheer opportunism), there was a crucial lesson from the forties and early fifties that suggested the Americans should be more reticent. The example of Saragat had shown that anti-Communist parties of the Left were inevitably forced to fight an unequal battle if they did not have the support of a mass organization. Put bluntly, this meant that a successful schism had to involve the unions. Nenni would be isolated if he left the Action Pact without taking a substantial part of the CGIL with him. Indeed, he risked achieving the unenviable position of participating in a reformist government (at best) while a large part of the Socialist base continued to militate in a maximalist union. On purely pragmatic grounds, the PSI had to achieve a full break with the PCI and the CGIL if a reformist government were to have a fighting chance of achieving its objectives.

Colby was cognizant of these objectives, but was unmoved by them. In his view, the Communist problem was political, and it had a political solution: the *Apertura*. Once the Socialists were in the government, the Communists would be isolated, and the process initiated by the *Apertura* would inevitably strengthen the Socialists. He continued to hold these opinions even after the reservations over the strategy were amply supported by events. In 1979 he still argued that the only reason the *Apertura* failed was that it took place ten years too late.

Colby's views must be regarded as part of a more general internal discussion of the proper role for the CIA in Italy. In keeping with the strict compartmentalization of roles that characterized the agency, Colby had very little to do with the Communists, and was also generally out of touch with many of the covert agents that the agency was "running" at the time. For those members of the CIA who were involved in counterintelligence work in Italy—a program initiated by James Angleton and continued on the spot until 1956 by his hand-picked successor Ray Rocca—the problem was considerably more complex. Such people realized that the "Communist problem" went deeper than the purely political manifestations of the PCI. They knew, for example, that the Communists, thanks to their close ties to the Kremlin, were in possession of great quantities of extremely damaging information about Socialist leaders that could be produced at the first sign of a dangerous split. They also knew that the PCI was only in part a national party.

When Anatoli Golitzyn defected from the First General Directorate of the KGB to the United States in 1961,[31] he brought with him snippets of information from files he had read in preparation for his leap from the Soviet Union. Among these was one excerpt from a file on Italy that was to tantalize the CIA for many years. Golitzyn claimed to have read a document that dealt with a key KGB agent in Italy code-named "Felix." This very important agent was said to be in place at a high level within the PCI, where he reportedly ran a substantial *apparat*. "Felix" was in turn under the control of an official in the Soviet embassy in Rome, thus giving the Russians a direct operational chain of command over at least a portion of the Italian Communist party.

Golitzyn's information referred to the late forties and early fifties, and he did not know if "Felix" still existed, nor the identity of this key agent. So far as is known, the CIA was unable to establish Felix's identity, although there were many theories. But if Golitzyn told the truth (and, as is often the case with information from defectors, this was open to considerable challenge), then the system of control typified by the Fried group in Paris[32] also existed in Rome. Moreover, it was not known whether this KGB operation extended to the Socialist party as well.

Colby was not privy to all this information, and he was uncomfortable in the presence of several operations that were run totally outside the control of the station, and that on some occasions were in direct contact with top-level officials in Washington. Colby believed in a more bureaucratic method, was hostile to the more covert preferences of Angleton and Rocca, and—as he said in exaggerated and somewhat misleading form in his autobiography—tried to cut back on some of the more free-wheeling operations that were under way at the time.

In a certain sense, the CIA in Italy was living off previously accumulated capital throughout the fifties. Despite his reputation for conspiratorial machinations, Angleton had great respect for close cooperation with Allied intelligence services, and insisted on establishing an intimate liaison with the Italian agencies. He realized that independent CIA operations in Italy would, if discovered, strain relations with Italy, and he consequently worked to maintain excellent connections with the Italians while keeping American initiatives to a minimum. This inevitably meant that the CIA was heavily dependent upon the Italians, and required that the agency representatives in Italy have a profound understanding of the country and its people. Angleton himself certainly met these requirements, but with the passage of time, many of his successors have lacked such qualities.

Colby's view of the Opening to the Left typified this sort of development, and the battle between Colby's view of the country and that of Angleton presaged the more intense and damaging battle between the two that culminated in the mid-1970s with Angleton's departure from the CIA after Colby released damaging information about him to the *New York Times*.

It is hard to gauge the extent of support for Colby's views; it was certainly a minority position, but it had some powerful endorsements, not least of all from Ambassador Claire Boothe Luce, at least for a brief period. Like every American ambassador before and since, she recognized that the policies of the Italian government were insufficiently progressive, that Italian industrialists were quite backward, and that an Italian "New Deal" was desirable. But like every ambassador, she came up against the maddening reality of Italian politics: the DC was hard to move, and no pressure could be effectively brought to bear on the DC without risking a Communist advance. After a brief flirtation with the idea of supporting the PSI, Mrs. Luce thought better of it and decided it was too risky.

Nonetheless, there was evidently enough support for the *Apertura* in the mid-fifties to provoke a heated condemnation from the State Department's Bureau of Intelligence and Research in October 1955. The bureau agreed that if the Socialists truly broke with the PCI and adopted a reformist position, it "would be the most devastating blow dealt the Communists during the postwar period." But the report rejected the notion that such a change had taken place:

> There is no basic policy difference between the Nenni Socialists and the Communists, and . . . the Socialists are insisting on the "Opening to the Left" in order to extricate the Communists from their political isolation . . . the non-Communist Left . . . no longer demands that Nenni break with the Communists as a precondition for collaboration with him. It now hopes that collaboration will spark the autonomous forces of the Nenni Socialists into an open break with the Communists. However, the opposite is more likely to happen . . . the non-Communist Left is more likely to be converted to Nenni's idea that Communist support is necessary for the achievement of economic and social reforms.[33]

The bureau argued that American support for the *Apertura* should await a true conversion by the Socialists. This remained the basis of American policy until the administration of John F. Kennedy.

The Kennedy Initiatives

For the Kennedy administration, the Italian situation was translated into American categories, and the *Apertura* was supported by analogy: the Christian Democrats were like the American Republican party, while the Nenni Socialists were like the Kennedy Democrats. Thus, the DC were considered a bit slow intellectually and somewhat reactionary. The Nenni Socialists, on the other hand, were considered the main agents of social reform, and, in the words of White House advisor Arthur Schlesinger, "A progressive administration in Washington should certainly not be in the position of discouraging progressive policies in Rome, especially when social reform was required to isolate the Communists, eliminate the conditions which bred them, and begin the reclamation of the working class for democracy."[34]

Schlesinger had accepted the vulgar materialist theory for Communist success, and the theory was false. Communist electoral strength had risen throughout the fifties, the period of the Italian "economic miracle," and had not even been fatally weakened by the disasters of 1956. In a secret CIA analysis dated 12 January 1962[35] the agency's weekly summary noted that the steady growth alongside increasing prosperity "indicates that economic discontent is not the major basis for Communist electoral strength." Much of the strength of the PCI was due to its power and its abilities to deliver favors and rewards. Thus, the *Apertura* could not possibly isolate the Communists.

But people like Schlesinger distrusted the CIA's analyses, and believed the simpler proposition that political problems had political solutions, and like William Colby before him, Arthur Schlesinger believed that Pietro Nenni was the solution to Italy's problems. Early in March, Ambassador at Large Averell Harriman went on a fact-finding tour to Rome. According to a recent account, Harriman "came away . . . convinced that effective economic and social reforms in Italy were impossible without bringing the Socialists into the government coalition. He also concluded that U.S. support for the Socialists would likely take the PSI out of the PCI's orbit, hence weakening—and perhaps isolating—the Communists."[36]

Harriman reportedly urged that the American government support the Opening in his briefings in Washington at the end of March. This picture of Harriman's role is supported by Victor Reuther, another committed advocate of the *Apertura*.

Yet the official documents dealing with Harriman's mission provide a different picture of things. Only a few fragments of the documents have been declassified, but those fragments run strongly counter to the conventional wisdom and to Harriman's own subsequent comments. For example, in a March 9 conversation with President Gronchi,

> Mr. Harriman said that his impression was that Nenni was still just as much in bed with Togliatti as ever. . . .
>
> Mr. Harriman said he had high hopes that, terrible as the Hungarian episode was, it might have served to speed up the detachment of the Italian Socialists from the Communists, and he had been disappointed in this respect . . . Mr. Harriman commented that probably Nenni could not take the whole party with him.[37]

On March 11, Harriman met with Giuseppe Saragat:

> Mr. Harriman said he agreed with Saragat, for it was difficult to trust a man like Nenni, who had worked so long with the Communists.

And later on the same day, Harriman met with Fanfani at the Viminale Palace:

> Mr. Harriman said that he feared Nenni had been too closely associated with Togliatti for too long and that attempts should be made to win over the Socialist electorate, rather than Nenni himself.

Was Harriman simply provoking his Italian interlocutors, or was he reflecting what they were privately saying to him? All three of the Italians were ostensibly in favor of the *Apertura*; why should Harriman have repeatedly stressed his own lack of confidence in Nenni?

Whatever one makes of this, it is clear that one must rethink the role of Harriman in the entire affair. For whatever support he may have given to the Opening to the Left, he must have reported that there were problems: Nenni was not entirely reliable, and the PSI had not evolved into a pro-Western, moderate party. The Americans might wish to encourage the continued evolution of the PSI, but they should be careful not to take any active steps to promote Nenni's advance.

In fact, this was official policy. In June, Fanfani came to Washington where he was told by Kennedy that "we would watch developments with sympathy" if he favored the *Apertura*, but there was no active encouragement. And in November, the State Department provided our diplomats with guidelines[38] concerning an Italian government "dependent on PSI support." They were supposed to tell Christian Democrats that while the United States fully appreciated the possible advantages of gaining PSI support for the Italian government, this was so "provided, however, that this could be accomplished without any compromise whatsoever with PSI on foreign policy." And in conversation with the Socialists, American diplomats were instructed to duck any questions about American attitudes toward a Center-Left government, and to stress American concern over "and disagreement with current PSI foreign policy positions and our hope that party will move to wiser positions in the future."

This measured, prudent policy was also Kennedy's. In a conversation with our ambassador to Italy, Frederick Reinhardt, the following year, the president was told that "there were . . . people around the President who were pursuing, or endeavoring to pursue a policy which was more aggressive. It was their view, apparently, that the United States ought to be pushing and working actively and openly for such a political development in Italy. I certainly didn't share this."[39] Kennedy said he agreed with Reinhardt, but if so, he did little to rein in those people working in the White House who were promoting the Center-Left. The individual most active was Arthur M. Schlesinger, Jr., supported by Robert Komer, who had moved from CIA to the staff of the National Security Council. Schlesinger was not content just to write letters encouraging Italians to support Nenni's increased participation or urging Kennedy to be sympathetic to the *Apertura* in his meeting with Fanfani; he even went in for secret diplomacy. In September 1961 or February 1962, Schlesinger went to Rome

where, without the knowledge of the Embassy, he met with Pietro Nenni, Ugo

> La Malfa . . . and Giuseppe Saragat. . . . In subsequent talks with Italian leaders travelling in the United States, Schlesinger made the same point, frequently expressing fervent sympathy for the *Apertura* movement.[40]

Ambassadors always dread the use of "back channels" to leaders in their country, and Schlesinger's activities were particularly outrageous to Reinhardt (and DCM Outerbridge Horsey), because Schlesinger "had no mandate to do this; it was not his field of responsibility." In addition to this conflict over "turf," there was a real political disagreement.

Schlesinger has encouraged the belief that he, Komer, and Harriman fought a political battle with the State Department's anti-Communists in order to permit events in Italy to take their normal course. But his role was far more active than that, for Schlesinger supported covert activity to favor the *Apertura*. He encouraged covert aid to the PSI (to replace the Communist money that would be lost), and to democratic elements in the trade unions. The first program was carried out by the CIA, the second by leaders in the American union movement, including the Reuthers. Their actual dimensions are still unknown.[41]

These efforts were violently resisted by Reinhardt and Horsey, for they felt that Schlesinger's activities represented a distinct change in policy. They were prepared to accept, or even mildly encourage, the Opening to the Left, but not to pay for it. To pay the bill for Nenni's entry into the Italian government was foolish, for it put the Americans in a poor position no matter how the experiment turned out. If it succeeded, the Americans would be expected to pay the PSI for the foreseeable future, while if it failed, they risked the wrath of a frustrated Socialist party. Moreover, since the basic convictions of the PSI were at issue in the whole debate over the *Apertura*, it seemed unwise to attempt to buy off the Socialists. It would have been more prudent, according to Reinhardt and Horsey, to require the PSI to take clear positions first, and then and only then try to help the party out of its financial straits.

The supporters of the clandestine programs saw things differently, of course: the Socialists needed money, having broken with the Communists, and the failure of the United States to take up the slack would have driven the PSI back towards the Communists. But opposition to the program was strong enough that Schlesinger and his associates could not drive it through in blanket form.[42] In the end, a compromise was reached: the CIA-administered funds would go to select members of the PSI, and not to the party itself, and this practice continued until the scandals in the seventies led to a termination of all support of democratic forces in Italy.

On the trade union side, there was a substantial effort to encourage the democratic elements of the CGIL, CISL, and UIL to work together in a clear anti-Communist context, but despite the expenditure of a considerable amount of money, nothing came of the initiative.

Postmortem

In the end, the Opening to the Left was carried out with substantial American financial support. And just as American assistance to the Christian Democrats failed to produce any substantial control, so the aid to the Socialists had little real effect in terms of American leverage. American money may have encouraged the independence of at least some Socialists, but this is questionable.

The Center-Left turned out just about as one should have expected: the PSI split, with the far Left creating a new party (that eventually was absorbed into the PCI). At the same time, the Socialists searched for a gesture to show that their entry into the government represented a new era in social policy. The symbolic act was the nationalization of the electrical industry, which led to a drop in popular support for the DC, and a drastic fall in the number of stockholders and in the value of common stock. This occurred in 1962, when a Fanfani-led government received parliamentary support from the PSI. When a Center-Left coalition was formed by Aldo Moro in 1963, his strategy of moving as slowly as possible at all times guaranteed that the Center-Left would not represent a major turning-point in Italian history. In other words, the PSI was coopted by the DC. No serious changes took place as a result of Socialist participation.

The Opening also failed on the international front, where the PSI's lackluster "conversion" to the Atlantic Alliance (accepted with strong neutralist overtones in the first few months of the Center-Left) dissatisfied most everyone. As a result, within a few years the Communists could claim to be the only legitimate party for those Italians who wanted real structural change. And the Socialists found themselves in a quandary from which they only began to emerge in the second half of the seventies, when Bettino Craxi took charge of the PSI and gave it a solidly pro-Western foreign policy and a firmly rational reformist domestic policy. But following the Center-Left, having been tarnished by their association with the DC, the Socialists felt compelled to outflank the PCI on the left on domestic questions (thus often making the Communists appear moderate), and having failed to embrace the Atlantic Alliance with enthusiasm, the Socialists were in a poor position to challenge the PCI on foreign policy. Not surprisingly, prior to Craxi the PSI saw its share of the electorate steadily diminish.

To what extent was this an American failure? It was certainly a failure by those who had seen the Socialists as the harbingers of a new political and social order in Italy. On the other hand, it is unfair to view the Opening as primarily an American initiative. The Italians themselves wanted it, and the Americans simply accelerated the movement. But in adding impetus to the trend, the United States may well have altered the final reality. For so long as American support was in doubt, Nenni was under constant pressure to demonstrate his true loyalties, and to change his positions. By encouraging the DC to accept the PSI as it was, the Americans may have put a premature end to the evolution of the Socialist party in the 1960s.

The strategy of supporting an independent Socialist party in Italy was excellent, but the problem with American behavior during the debate over the *Apertura* was that it was based on an unduly simplified picture of Italian politics. The DC was not as reactionary as many Americans believed, and the PSI was not capable of playing the role assigned to it. Nenni's party simply could not shore up an anti-Communist barricade; too many Socialists were too closely associated with the PCI for such a plan to work. Under these circumstances, one must agree with Reinhardt and Horsey: it was a mistake to finance the participation of the PSI in the government.

The failure of the American vision is even clearer when one turns to the question of the trade union movement. For there could be no serious challenge to the PCI unless that challenge extended to the trade unions. To believe that one could fight the PCI on the purely political level meant that the lesson of 1947-48 had not been learned. Saragat's example showed that without a mass base, the Communists could not be defeated, and thus if the United States wished to support Nenni's entry into the government, it was necessary to link the *Apertura* to a major effort in the trade unions.[43]

Schlesinger appears to have understood this, but there is no indication that the action program undertaken was commensurate to the demands of the situation. None of the key American figures (from Schlesinger, Komer, and Harriman to the Reuther brothers, Arthur Goldberg, and Robert Kennedy) had the experience and understanding of the Italian problem needed to deal with the actual problems. In fact, Communist control over the unions may have been so secure that no program could have succeeded. But if that is true, then the Americans should have known that the *Apertura* could not possibly have produced the results predicted for it.

In the end, the failure of the *Apertura* must be laid at the feet of Pietro Nenni himself. Awed by the myth of Stalin, financed in part by the Russians, convinced that the future of Europe was likely to be painted in red, Nenni refused to make a decisive choice of the Western camp. In his heart of hearts Nenni might have been a true man of the West, but he lacked the courage to commit himself in that direction. Even after his one great moment—the break with the PCI and the U.S.S.R. after the Hungarian repression—Nenni permitted the Socialist trade unions to remain allied with the Communists, and he continued to support local alliances with the PCI. And even immediately after Hungary, he unendingly denounced "American imperialism," making it impossible to make the Center-Left a rallying-post for pro-Western forces. Nenni was the only Socialist with sufficient prestige to challenge Togliatti, and he failed to seize his historic opportunity.

Notes

1. Alberto Ronchey, *Accade in Italia, 1968-1977* (Milan, 1977), 164.
2. Since much of this chapter rests on confidential sources, a few words of explanation are in order. I have discussed aspects of these questions with most of the CIA station chiefs in Rome from the creation of the CIA to the present, with top officials of OSS and CIA counterintelligence, and with several directors of Central Intelligence, and with several deputy directors. In addition, I have spoken at length with leading trade unionists in both Italy and the United States, with Italian intelligence officials, with leading officials of the Communist, Socialist, and Christian Democratic parties, and with leading Socialists in several other European countries. So while there may well be errors in this account, they do not depend upon a single source.
3. This was known to Nenni and some of his top assistants, and further details arrived after the 1956 PCI crisis, when knowledgeable Communists joined the PCI and informed Nenni of these matters. Significantly, some of these ex-Communists eventually came to advise Bettino Craxi in the 1970s and 1980s, thus providing Craxi with an insight into the nature of the PCI and its activities within his own party that few other Italians could match.
4. See Michael Ledeen, *Italy in Crisis* (Beverly Hills and London, 1971), 13.
5. See Massimo Salvadori, "Gramsci e il PCI: due concezioni dell'egemonia," in *Monodoperaio* (11 November 1976).
6. George Lichtheim, *Marxism* (New York and London, 1963), 368.
7. *Ibid.*, 368-70.
8. From Antonio Gramsci, *Quaderni: il materialismo storico e la filosofia di Beneedetto Croce*, quoted in Enzo Bettiza, *Il Comunismo Europeo* (Milan, 1978), 100.
9. Bettiza, *op. cit.*, 102.
10. *Ibid.*
11. See, for example, the courageous book by Lucio Lami, *La scuola del plagio* (Rome, 1977).
12. Department of State, Office of Intelligence Research, *International Communism, 1955* (December 1955), 24. I have obtained these detailed studies through the terms of the Freedom of Information Act.
13. *Ibid.*, 25.
14. Fondazione Feltrinelli, *Annali, XIX, cit.*, 239-40.
15. Pietro Nenni, *Tempo di Guerra Fredda; Diari 1943-1956* (Milan, 1981).
16. *Ibid.*, 738-41.
17. Pietro Nenni, "Luci e ombre del XX Congresso," in *l'Avanti!*, 26 March 1956, and reprinted in *Mondo operaio*, March 1956.
18. "9 domande sullo stalinismo: Palmiro Togliatti," in *Nuovi argomenti* (May-June 1956).

19. Ilya Ehrenberg, "Un bilancio del disgelo," in *Il Contemporaneo*, 22 March 1957.
20. Cf. Nello Ajello, *Gli intelletuali e il PCI* (Rome and Bari, 1979), 382.
21. Fabrizio Onofri, "Un inammisibile attacco alla politica del Partito comunista italiano," in *Rinascita* (July 1956). Togliatti replied in the same issue: "La realtà dei fatti e la nostra azione rintuzza l'irresponsabile disfattismo."
22. Reale published an exceptionally interesting magazine for 13 years afterwards, entitled *Corrispondenza Socialista*.
23. A.M. Schlesinger, Jr., *A Thousand Days: John Fitzgerald Kennedy in the White House* (Boston, 1965), 876.
24. The details of the AFL's actions are to be found in the still-private correspondance between Jay Lovestone and Irving Brown. Many of my conclusions in this chapter are based on those documents, which I have read but have agreed not to quote explicitly. Cf. also Roy Godson, *American Labor and European Politics* (New York, 1976).
25. The correspondence is in the possession of the AFL-CIO in Washington, D.C.
26. Lovestone was on intimate terms with William Donovan, the head of OSS, with Allen Dulles of the CIA, and with James Angleton, among many others. He remained a significant influence on American foreign policy well into the 1980s.
27. The best study of the Italian unions is Daniel L. Horowitz, *The Italian Labor Movement* (Cambridge, Mass., 1963).
28. William Colby, *Honorable Men* (New York, 1978), 109.
29. *Ibid.*, 125.
30. *Ibid.*, 126-27.
31. While Golitzyn is one of the most controversial Soviet defectors (he believes the Sino-Soviet split was a deception, for example), his information on actual Soviet espionage operations proved extremely accurate.
32. The Fried case in France showed that the Soviets had installed a series of their own East European agents within the French Communist party, in order to keep the PCF under near-total control on all serious questions. One good account is provided by Philippe Robrieux, *Maurice Thorez; vie secrete e vie publique* (Paris, 1975). The biography of Eugen Fried provides a good outline of the sort of thing that went on. Born in Slovakia, Fried served as a sort of liaison between Bela Kun and the international Communist movement during the Hungarian Communist revolution of 1919. He worked with Gottwald and Slanski in the twenties, was condemned by the Comintern for "deviation" and summoned to Moscow in 1931, where he went to work for the Comintern. At the end of the spring or early summer of 1931, he was named the head of the "college de direction" of the French Communist party (in other words, the real head of the PCF). He moved to France, where he remained until the outbreak of the Second World War. He was killed in Brussels in 1943, "officially by the Gestapo, more likely by the Russian secret services" (Robrieux, 649-650).
33. Department of State, Office of Intelligence Research, *International Communism* (October 1955), 18.
34. Schlesinger, *op. cit.*, 877.
35. This basic point was often overlooked by the likes of Colby, Schlesinger, and the Reuthers: political, not economic considerations, were paramount (as they are today).
36. Alan Platt, "U.S. Policy toward the Opening to the Left" (Ph.D. diss., Columbia University, 1976).

37. The documents, untitled, were released to me under the terms of the Freedom of Information Act.
38. Rusk to Rome, 8 November 1961. Cf. also, Department of State, *Guidelines for policy and operations: Italy* (1962).
39. Reinhardt's memorandum is in the Kennedy Library at Harvard. His account is corroborated by William E. Knight, "U.S. Policy in the Opening to the Left: The View from the State Department," in Austin Ranney and Giovanni Sartori, eds., *Eurocommunism: the Italian Case* (Washington, D.C., 1978), and by Roger Hilsman, "U.S. Policy in the Opening to the Left: The Role of the President's Advisers," in the same volume. I have confirmed this basic account through dozens of additional interviews.
40. See the Reinhardt memorandum, and Knight, *op. cit.*
41. There is a hand-written note among Arthur Schlesinger's papers that mentions that Nenni was prepared to "make public statement of the fact that the American Labor Unions have helped his Party." The note is dated Paris, 12 December 1961. I cannot make out the signature, but the author had spoken with Moro, Nenni, and Gronchi. As for the CIA money, Colby discusses it at length in his book.
42. The debate was nicely summarized in a typewritten draft note, apparently by Schlesinger:
"At present, it should be noted, the PSI receives covert assistance from the Italian Government through state economic organizations."
As for (e), Ambassador Reinhardt in his letter dated 22 June expresses his doubts about the advisability of assistance to the PSI.

"Pro and con on assistance to the PSI
"Ambassador Reinhardt argues (1) that the autonomist wing of the PSI is doing well on its own and does not need further external assistance; (2) that future PSI gains will be at the expense of the CD and PSDI parties, not of the Communists; (3) that, as the PSI grows stronger, its competition with the Communists for working class support will compel it to press the Italian Government to ever more radical positions; (4) that the center-left experiment, far from isolating the Communists, is at present giving them new respectability and producing a popular-front mentality; (5) that our support should be conditioned on 'a fairly clean break with the PCI or a split of the PSI.'
"The opposite argument would be that it is to the US interest to seek out the PSI rather than to wait for them to come to us—that the more we can implicate them, the more we bind them to the west. Moreover, the PSI provides us what we have not had up to this point—a means of broad contact with the Italian working class through which we can reach the Italian masses and intensify the polemics between the PCI and PSI. It is a serious question, for example, whether a split in the PSI would be to our advantage—whether it might not turn Nenni into another Saragat and delivery the *carristi* to the PCI.
"Ambassador Reinhardt's points 2, 3, and 4, are matters of which Fanfani, Moro, and Saragat are presumably the best [two pages are missing from the released material].
"One other point must be taken into account. If we should go ahead on a policy of aid to the PSI, we will face a problem within the American labor movement. The Reuthers are strongly in favor of such a policy. The Meany group . . . is opposed to assistance at present. . . . So long as the PSI continues to favor fighting the Communists within the CGIL instead of reinforcing the CISL and

The Opening to the Left 101

the UIL, the Meany group will probably be unhappy about assistance to the PSI.

"In short, I don't think we know enough for a final decision. Since our policy is to strengthen constitutional democracy in Italy, surely we should know whether the defenders of Italian democracy believe that aid to the PSI would strengthen or injure their cause."

Schlesinger eventually decided that the aid should be given.

43. By 1969, the Center-Left could be declared a substantial failure, at least in the messianic political terms in which it had originally been cast. This was reflected in the CIA's *National Intelligence Estimate 24-69: The Center-Left Experiment in Italy, Accomplishments, Shortcomings and Prospects:*

"The center-left coalition has failed to achieve one of its major objectives—that of bringing into the political life of the national major groups of Italians who had for years felt themselves estranged from their government. The two major governing parties are still beset by dissensions and rivalries; the political appeal of the Communists continues high; and large segments of the Italian public seems to remain alienated from their rulers.

"The coalition has so far failed to enact the basic reforms in its program. Even without basic reforms, however, the present Catholic-Socialist political formula can probably go on quite a while before the Italians decide it won't work any longer and before the government's accomplishments fall so far behind what is needed that a political crisis emerges. During this time the Communists will increase their influence and political role, and they appear to many Italians to be changing in a way which will make them acceptable partners in a new government formula. All things considered, the situation may develop to the point where the Communists could enter the government in the 1970s; this would be more likely to occur in the latter than in the earlier part of the decade. But there are so many imponderables that we can make no confident estimate on this point. What we can say is that the chances of such a contingency are greater than they were a few years ago."

So the Center-Left had increased, rather than decreasing, the chances of Communist entry into the government in Italy.

5

The Italian Communist Party

The Communist party of Italy (PCI) is unique in the Western world. Communist parties have virtually disappeared in Northern Europe, Canada, and the United States, their ideological appeal lost along with the vanished myth of Soviet "socialism." Communist parties in Western Europe really count only in the Latin countries: Portugal, Spain, France, and Italy. In the first three, the Communists are overshadowed by stronger Socialist parties. In Italy alone the Communist party dominates the Left, just as only the PCI seems at all likely to enter the government in the reasonably near future.

The success of the PCI is due in part to the traditional skill of its leaders, particularly compared to those of the various Socialist parties that have contested it for the leadership of the Italian Left prior to the late 1970s, when Bettino Craxi, to the great consternation of the Communists, took charge of the PSI. It may well be that Italy's Communist leaders benefit from comparison with most other Italian politicians in the postwar period, but men such as Luigi Longo, Palmiro Togliatti, and Enrico Berlinguer are impressive figures by any standard, and they have been well served by a distinguished supporting cast of trade union leaders, intellectuals, newspaper editors and publishers, and second-level party officials. Until quite recently, the PCI was able to pursue its long-term strategy without a sustained challenge from the Socialists, permitting the Communists to appear to be the sole effective representatives of "progressive" forces in Italy. Had the PSI been able to achieve unity and coherence in the forties or fifties, the Communists would almost certainly have had greater difficulty. During those brief periods when the Socialists challenged the PCI on the obvious grounds of ties to the Soviet Union, lack of internal democracy, and a basically totalitarian vision of society, the Communists inevitably suffered. But such periods have never lasted, at least in the past.

The Christian Democratic party (DC), the other major force in Italian politics, has not produced a series of leaders who could rival those of the

PCI. Yet it has proven remarkably durable. The DC is not a modern political party; rather it is a loose bundle of different interests, closer to a federation of small principalities than to a well-structured and disciplined political machine. This contrast between a highly efficient Communist party and a visibly disjointed DC has worked to Communist advantage at critical moments, when the country seemed to need strong action. But at other times, voters have been reassured by the DC's lack of clear direction and its tendency toward pragmatic compromise, even at the cost of sloppiness, corruption, and inefficiency. The DC's fumbling and easy-going ways were generally preferred to the often threatening discipline and rigor of the PCI. Nevertheless, there has been fairly steady growth in Communist strength, particularly at the local and regional levels, where the electorate demonstrated a willingness to experiment with Communist participation in government, without having to make a possibly fatal commitment to granting the PCI access to the levers of national power.

But the attraction of the PCI does not rest only on its superior leadership and more efficient and disciplined structure; the steady advance of the PCI over the past three decades makes plain that more and more Italians have become convinced that the risks associated with Communist entry into the national goverment have diminished. Ever since the great anti-Communist vote of 1948, the Communists have worked relentlessly and effectively to convince Italians that the PCI is just like the other Italian political parties. Moreover, party leaders have changed the positions of the PCI on some critical issues: the method for achieving political power, the rationale for its international policies, the "model" for a future Italian society, and its attitude toward European integration. In moving toward Western positions and away from Soviet dogma in the mid-1970s, many outside observers concluded that an historic transformation had taken place.

By the end of the decade, however, the Communist bandwagon had failed to reach its objective of attaining at least a share of national political power. Despite its great electoral triumphs in 1975 and 1976, and despite the willingness of some of the most powerful Christian Democrats to support its entry into the government, the PCI did not achieve the breakthrough called for by Enrico Berlinguer in 1973: the creation of a national government based on an "historic compromise" between the PCI and the DC. Its failure was all the more notable because a series of significant developments—economic, social, and political—were working in favor of such a breakthrough. The PCI had achieved a large measure of control over Italian popular culture; at the same time, a wave of scandals damaged the Christian Democrats and their American allies; a domestic economic crisis of dramatic proportions erupted; and the continued failure of the PSI to offer any viable alternative to Communist domination of the Left, the visible erosion in the power and prestige of the United States, and the success of detente all worked in the Communists' favor. Finally, there was the catalyzing element of the terrorist wave that swept the country during the second half of the decade, which lent support to the Communist claim that Italy would remain ungovernable so long as the PCI was excluded from the Cabinet. Why did the Communists fail?

The Problem of the Historic Compromise

Unlike the elite "vanguard of the proletariat" described in the revolutionary tracts of the early twentieth century, the PCI opted for the strategy of the mass party relatively early in its history. The Gramscian doctrine called for the achievement of "cultural hegemony"[1] over the country in order to establish a mass base for the PCI's conquest of political power, and from the moment of Togliatti's return at the end of the Second World War, the PCI pursued this vision with single-minded intensity. By the mid-seventies there was good reason to believe that the Communists were on the verge of succeeding. The mass media were largely pro-Communist, as was the film industry, which had been a major DC stronghold for years. The Communists were increasingly successful in shaping the television and radio broadcasts, and there had been a dramatic change in the printed media: *Panorama* and *l'Espresso*, the two major weekly "news" magazines, vied with each other for left-wing credentials; several major columnists became open advocates of the *compromesso storico*, and major newspapers that had held to an anti-Communist line switched abruptly in the 1970s, the most dramatic example being that of Milan's *Corriere della Sera*, perhaps the country's most influential daily. The shift in the *Corriere*'s "line" was so sharp that a group of the newspaper's journalists left in order to found a new anti-Communist paper, *il Giornale nuovo*.[2] But no similar breakaway movement took place in Rome when *il Messagero* moved to the Left (and moved so quickly that the paper's ownership was taken by surprise; this was demonstrated in the mid-seventies when the internal groups at *il Messagero* rejected the nomination of the liberal anti-Communist Luigi Barzini as editor-in-chief).

Not only were people like Barzini excluded from the newspapers by the so-called *comitati di redazione* (workers' groups organized by the Communist trade unions, or by groups to the left of the PCI) but the editorial committees increasingly assumed control over the content of the newspaper, the language of its headlines, and the subject matter discussed. A few examples suffice to illustrate this important and alarming phenomenon.

First, at the height of the Portuguese crisis in the mid-seventies, the Lisbon correspondent for the *Corriere della Sera* filed a story about the

Communist-led closing of the Socialist newspaper *Republica*. The editorial committee censored part of the article and rewrote the headline in order to change its tone by downplaying the seriousness of the episode and the role of the Portuguese Communists. The Italian journalist resigned in protest.

Second, in November 1976 another *Corriere* journalist wrote a story about conflicts between Communist trade union leaders and the rank-and-file at a meeting at an Alfa Romeo plant; the *comitato di redazione* attempted to spike the story. When that failed, the *comitato* called a 24-hour strike at the newspaper in protest.

Third, when the *New Republic* published a story in 1976 about the finances of the PCI, *La Stampa* of Turin bought the Italan rights, promising to publish the story immediately. But it was first delayed, then spiked altogether. At the end of the week a story appeared, written by the paper's Washington correspondent, claiming that the *New Republic* article had been orchestrated by the American government, most notably by the CIA.

Most journalists quickly learned that anti-Communist articles generally led to unpleasant conflicts with the *comitati di redazione*, and for the most part they were unwilling to fight such battles daily. And even the most courageous and strong-willed Italian correspondents were forced to concede that the committees attained increasing power throughout the second half of the 1970s.

A similar pattern held in the schools, where textbooks—which in Italy are adopted on a national basis, and not district by district—increasingly conformed to the Communist world view.[3] Orthodox Communist language about "Western imperialism," Zionism, socialism, racism, the Soviet Union, and the Third World made its way into the texts, and on those occasions when challenges were made, the challengers were portrayed as antidemocratic or worse. There was a notorious case in 1976, when the author of a textbook found that his account of modern history had been altered by left-wing editors without his permission. He was compelled to fight a long and costly legal battle before winning his right to have his own ideas in his book. The case was not unique.

Finally, the universities became battlegrounds. So-called reactionary professors were verbally and physically abused, and Communist-led or supported student groups and trade unions advanced schemes that would have given the control over scholarly research and teaching to collective organizations that were easy prey for the Left. Had these proposals been adopted, they would have led to the "Sovietization" of the universities. But even though the most extreme of their measures failed, it is fair to say that most of the professors in the mid- to late seventies were forced to make some sort of accommodation with the Communists.[4] The mood on the campuses was distinctly "red," driving several of the country's leading intellectuals (including former Communist philosopher Lucio Colletti and left-wing professor of architecture Bruno Zevi, both of the University of Rome) out of Italian universities.

Perhaps the high point of Communist cultural domination came in this period, at the very moment that the PCI achieved its greatest political successes. Yet the Communist party found it difficult to exploit its dual triumph. For while "cultural hegemony" was a splendid strategy so long as the PCI knew precisely the nature of the "culture" it was to enforce, the strategy broke down at a time when the party was forced to offer drastically different faces to different audiences. And in the mid-seventies, the political requirements of the PCI were changing, just as the party itself was undergoing a considerable internal turmoil.

The New Face of the PCI

In the past, both voters and card-carrying members knew what they were getting when they supported the Communist party. Prior to the early seventies, the PCI's major internal problems came from members more pro-Western than the party leaders. Such persons either left the PCI—notably after the trauma of 1956—or were expelled, as in the case of the *Manifesto* group a decade later. But this changed with the announcement of the *compromesso storico*.[5]

Ever since the failure of Togliatti's "national unity" approach in the 1940s, the Communists had driven for power as the sole legitimate representative of the Left, with a program that would move the country toward the PCI's version of socialism. Berlinguer now declared his desire to form a government with the DC—the historic compromise. Although the notion was quite similar to Togliatti's position in the immediate postwar period, prior to the Cominform shift, the announcement came as a shock to many, particularly to those Communists who had viewed the DC as the class enemy of the revolution, and the tool of American imperialism in Italy. Their anxiety was increased by Berlinguer's attempt to resurrect the old idea of "Cathocommunism" by proposing a dialogue on communism and Catholicism with the bishop of Ivrea.[6] Thus, for the first time, the PCI leadership was faced with the possibility of defections from the Stalinist wing of the party.

It was not immediately apparent that the tactic of the historic compromise would subject the PCI to terrible internal stresses, for it was originally justified on purely pragmatic grounds. Berlinguer observed that the PCI could not expect to govern the country effectively without an impossibly large majority. If the PCI obtained, say, 51 percent of the popular vote, it would find itself in a situation similar to that of Allende in Chile—compelled to attempt to carry out its Communist program because of its tradition and its promises to its supporters, yet unable to carry it out because of the existence of a large opposition force. Therefore, the PCI called upon the DC to join with it in the creation of a government whose majority would be so great that it would be irresistible.

The argument certainly rested on a solid enough base: the Chilean, and later the Portuguese, cases indicated that it was very difficult for Communist or pro-Communist governments to endure in the West, where international pressure could be brought against them. On the Western side of the Yalta line, it seemed necessary to shelter such governments from pressure, whether in the form of strong domestic hostility or of antagonism from powerful foreign countries. The *compromesso storico* seemed to meet these requirements, since it would either leave only a handful of tiny parties in opposition or sweep them up in a grand coalition. Moreover, the *compromesso* would help shield the PCI from American, French, British, and (possibly) German pressure: a PCI-led government would inevitably come under foreign attack, but it would be difficult for the Americans or Germans to unleash an assault against a government that included the DC.

Moreover, the notion of the historic compromise intermeshed nicely with the Soviet approach to detente. Indeed, it may be said that the *compromesso storico* was simply the Italian version of the detente theory. If Nixon and Kissinger could sit down with Brezhnev and Gromyko to discuss and perhaps even resolve their differences (and, in the Italian view of things, establish a superpower "condominium" over the rest of the world), why could not Berlinguer and Moro do the same with the Italian peninsula? And just as the Soviets were surprised at the favorable reception given its call for detente and peaceful coexistence (permitting them to increase trade while continuing their military buildup, all the while bringing pressure on Western countries to cut military spending and be nicer to the Soviet bloc), so the Italian Communists were surprised at the favorable reception that their own version received among the DC.[7]

But detente turned out to carry its own problems, and both the U.S.S.R. and the PCI discovered that some of these problems had not been easy to foresee. For the Soviet Union, for example, the Helsinki Final Acts were supposed to legitimize their hegemony over Eastern Europe once and for all, but it also raised the terribly embarrassing and threatening question of human rights within the Soviet empire, thus giving the Kremlin's enemies a new and powerful ideological weapon.

Similarly, the PCI advanced the idea of the historic compromise at least in part to achieve legitimacy within the Italian political universe and thereby lay the groundwork for an extension of Communist power. While this objective was accomplished, at least superficially, it carried a considerable price: the PCI was now led up against a Western, democratic yardstick. The Communists now had to demonstrate that they were reliable partners, rather than revolutionary alternatives, and this struck at the heart of the entire theory of the organization of the party. For if discipline were maintained through democratic centralism, then the PCI would be revealed to be antidemocratic; while if democratic centralism were abandoned, the party leaders would lose control. In the end, the campaign for the *compromesso storico* had the totally unanticipated result of demonstrating that it was a contradiction in terms unless the PCI underwent a drastic change. The Communists were incapable of achieving that transformation, even though some leading members were clearly willing to try.

The Mass Party and its Enemies

The mass party desired by Togliatti and his successors was difficult to control, and required highly professional leadership. A traditional, Soviet-style "vanguard" party would have been easier to manage, both because of its smaller size and because of its more limited activities (notably the absence of the drive to achieve control over the popular culture), and a party like the other Italian parties would have been far more chaotic than the organization Togliatti desired. The *Partito Nuovo* was therefore new not only because it was different from other communist parties; it was something quite new in Italy: an organization managed and represented largely by professional politicians, men and women trained within the structures of the PCI to perform the tasks required of them by the party. Professor Giuseppe Are of the University of Pisa undertook a detailed study of the actual makeup of the PCI as of the early 1970s, and the tendencies he describes appear to have intensified in the intervening decade and a half:

> In 1972, 80 percent of the PCI national leaders were professional politicians (that is, party, trade union, or cooperative officials) and 8.6 percent were journalists, who in the PCI are merely a different variety of party official, while only 2.2 percent came from the professions. At the provincial level, 60 percent of the officials were professional politicians, 2.2 percent were journalists, and 5 percent were from the professions, while the others came from various other walks of life. . . .
>
> There was also a close connection between the extent of the PCI's political importance in any given area of the country and the degree to which the party organization was run by professionals in that area. Where the party had obtained more than 40 percent of the vote in 1969, for example, professional politicians or party officials accounted for 69 percent of the local leaders, while in places where the Communists got only 20 percent of the votes, only 43 percent were professionals (note, however, how high even this figure is!). Further, the party officials held all the vital posts; 35.4 percent of them

occupied two or three positions per head inside the party and they held all the offices of Provincial Secretary and Vice-secretary, which are the real keystones. . . . Finally, 83 percent of the professional politicians held public office in the boroughs and provinces. In the PCI you do not become a leader because you manage to get a good personal following among the electorate; rather, you are elected to public office only if you have control over, or at least the consent and approval of, the leaders in the party.[8]

The PCI also maintained rigorous control over the selection of candidates. In the period analyzed by Are, there was a much higher turnover among PCI representatives than in the DC—many more Communist deputies and senators were sent away from Montecitorio and Palazzo Madama to undertake other party tasks. And this high turnover was *not* the result of voter dissatisfaction with individual Communists, as is demonstrated by the fact that over 80 percent of those who failed to return simply did not run for reelection. So the turnover was determined at the top of the party hierarchy, not through the electoral process.

This rigid control over party lists made it possible for the PCI to offer political plums to its new recruits. I have seen letters on PCI stationery guaranteeing that certain persons would be elected to Parliament if they agreed to run on the PCI ticket. No other party in Italy made such guarantees to its candidates; if such offers were made there would be rebellion among the incumbents. But the PCI carried off such operations without a whimper from the rank-and-file.

The Communists achieve such internal discipline thanks to the traditional method of "democratic centralism": the Politburo decides, and the rest of the members fall into line. To be sure, the PCI is now so large that a certain amount of dissent emerges when particularly difficult changes in policy are announced; but the dissenters are generally brought under control in relatively short order. For example, there was a brief explosion at the Fifteenth Party Congress, held in Rome in late March-early April 1979, when Giorgio Amendola implored the party to abandon some of the mindless social slogans of the past and face the grave structural challenges confronting the country. "This party must stop demanding everything and the opposite of everything," he declared, calling for an open debate on PCI economic and social policies. In particular, Amendola insisted that the trade union movement would have to accept some serious austerity measures (possibly even including limitations on the national escalator clause built into every national contract—a key feature of the so-called labor charter that has long been one of the untouchable conquests of the Italian Left). As the controversy threatened to dominate the congress, Berlinguer announced that it would not be productive to continue discussion on the matter, and all debate quickly ended.[9]

In the foreign policy field, the PCI generally manages to move in tandem with the Soviet Union without serious internal disruption. When, in 1977, the Russians suddenly shifted their attention and alliance from Somalia to Ethiopia, the PCI—long one of the most steadfast supporters of the Eritrean Liberation Movement that was fighting against the central government of Ethiopia—did the same, without protest from within.[10] In 1979, when the question of the modernization of NATO's theater nuclear forces (the so-called INF) was debated, the PCI echoed the violent Soviet attacks against the deployment of American Cruise and Pershing missiles in Italy, even though the Communists' recently formed foreign policy "think tank" had taken a far more open position. Again, few Communist voices called for support of the NATO position.

The most difficult problems came when the leadership took positions different from those of the Soviet Union, as in 1956 (Hungary and Poland), 1968 (Czechoslovakia), 1979-80 (Afghanistan), and 1980-81 (Poland). All were provoked by Soviet military (or, in the case of Poland, Soviet-guided military) action, and all led to varying degrees of criticism from the PCI. Yet in each case, there were indications that the faithful were not as upset as some of the leaders; the rank-and-file seemed to remain loyal to the U.S.S.R. even in the winter of 1979-80, when the Kremlin moved its armies to attack outside the bloc for the first time since World War II.

Berlinguer's call for a grand coalition with the DC exposed him and his comrades to pressure from the two sources most likely to cause them severe difficulties: the Soviets and the pro-Soviet PCI base. Neither of these forces would quietly accept a major shift in the PCI's foreign policy position, and neither would accept a drastic change in the model of society espoused by the party. Yet Berlinguer knew that he could not achieve his goal without both a substantial increase in support from the more moderate middle classes and at least a certain degree of legitimization from the Christian Democrats and the Americans. In other words, he needed to change just enough to woo the opposition, without changing so much that he would lose his pro-Soviet base, or provoke an open conflict with the Soviets.

Finally, the entire process had to be tightly controlled, both because midcourse corrections might be necessary and because there was some risk of elements within the mass party getting out of hand. There were dangers on both sides: years of demanding a total transformation of Italian society had produced elements in the trade union movement that would not stop short of major restructuring. Communist efforts to moderate the unions ran the risk of alienating the activists in both the party and the union, and driving them into the arms of the so-called extra-Parliamentary Left that ranged from the autonomists to the Red Brigades. In foreign policy, there was the dual problem of the pro-Soviet base and an increasingly "European" group that talked more and more as if it were actually possible to switch from the Eastern to the Western camp. Each of these tendencies was dangerous, for if the PCI moved too close to the Soviet position, or to an extremist position even on domestic questions, it would lose moderate votes; while if it shifted too far toward the Atlantic, it risked an internal split.

To be sure, this had been a problem from the beginning of the postwar era, but the stakes were higher, and there was an urgency that had not been felt for nearly three decades. Berlinguer faced two deadlines: the first was dictated by the tempo of Soviet response, the second by the reaction from below.

This was a difficult balancing act, and it was rendered even more difficult by the fact that if Berlinguer were unable to deliver positive results within a reasonable length of time, there would be great pressure on him to return to a more traditional strategy. Under the circumstances, his performance was extraordinary. Through a series of carefully modulated positions, Berlinguer and his comrades weaved their way through the political obstacles of the mid-seventies. Aided by a growing domestic bandwagon and by a fascinated and rarely critical international press, the Communist leaders achieved their greatest results in the national political elections on June 20, 1976. It was during that campaign that Berlinguer made his famous "endorsement" of NATO. It took place in an interview in the *Corriere della Sera* just before election day, and both the interview and Berlinguer's follow-up point out the difficulties of the moment:

> Q: You, then, feel more tranquil precisely because you are in the Western area.
>
> A: I feel that, not belonging to the Warsaw Pact, from this point of view there is an absolute certainty that we can follow the Italian road to socialism without any conditioning (from the Soviet Union). But this does not mean that there are no problems in the Western bloc: indeed, it is true that we see ourselves forced to demand, within the Atlantic Pact, a pact that we do not place in question, Italy's right to decide its own destiny in an autonomous manner.
>
> Q: In short, the Atlantic Pact can also be a useful shield in order to construct socialism in liberty. . . .
>
> A: I want Italy to remain in the Atlantic Alliance also for this reason, and not just because our exit would upset the international equilibrium. I feel more secure over here, but I see that there are serious efforts to limit our autonomy here as well.[11]

This remarkable statement turned out to be somewhat less significant than one might have hoped. In the first place, when the official party newspaper *l'Unità* published the text, the crucial paragraphs were deleted

(PCI spokesmen claimed it was a technical error!). And once the electoral campaign was over, Berlinguer told an interviewer from the French Socialist weekly *Le Nouvel Observateur* that "I have never maintained the thesis, which would be truly paradoxical, that the 'forces of NATO' would guarantee socialism in the West."[12]

Such behavior smacked of the 1940s, when PCI leaders told their own followers one thing and outside observers something different. Undoubtedly the party faithful interpreted Berlinguer's words much as they had interpreted Togliatti's following the *svolta di Salerno*: phrases designed to deceive the enemy. As in the forties and fifties, the leadership of the PCI was widely believed to be speaking in code.[13]

Given such conflicting statements, it was only natural that a goodly number of people began to wonder about Berlinguer's "real" beliefs. While the question was understandable, it was—as it almost always is in politics—irrelevant to a sound analysis of the situation. The central question was, what could be expected of the PCI and its leader? The response was not encouraging.

For one thing, Berlinguer's statement about NATO was repeated word for word in the same *Corriere della Sera* in 1979, once again just before a critical election. And once again, the pro-NATO exchange was omitted from *l'Unità*'s version. Meanwhile, less than a year after the original interview, *l'Unità* printed a front-page editorial by Alberto Jacoviello, stating that it was "unthinkable" that the PCI could accept NATO "as it actually is," and arguing that "the relations between the countries of Western Europe and the two superpowers must be rediscussed."[14] Why the need for such an agonizing reappraisal? Because, in the words of the editorialist, NATO was "one of the principal instruments for American manipulation of the politics and economy of our country and of Western Europe."

American policy, then, was seen as threatening to Western Europe; what of the Soviet Union's? In the same campaign that brought forth Berlinguer's endorsement of the pro-Socialist NATO shield, he gave his complete support for what he called "the peace policies of the Soviet Union." Aside from the PCI's occasional dismay at the Kremlin's military actions, the PCI was in total agreement with the foreign policies of the U.S.S.R. In the words of Professor Giuseppe Are,

> The PCI is very clearly using two different propaganda stratagems, not simply adapted to circumstances but as the outcome of cold calculation. In the fellow-travelling press, aimed at the general, predominantly middle-class public (which the PCI influences either directly or through editorial boards), the party enlarges upon the few, vague signs of independence towards Moscow which it has shown so far and praises them to the point of mystification. At the same time, however, it makes an effort to get this same general

public to appreciate the wisdom of its decision to never really break with Russia and to recognize that Moscow's foreign policy is a good one.[15]

The PCI has adopted the Kremlin's basic line on international affairs. The Soviet Union is portrayed as a peace-loving country, forced to arm and to take action to defend itself against the threat of imperialism, embodied in the policies of the United States. Advances in American weaponry are portrayed by the Communist media as terribly threatening to world peace, while Soviet advances are not given anything remotely approaching the same tones of alarm. Typical of this lopsided approach was the PCI's reaction to the American call for the modernization of European-based theater nuclear forces in the fall and winter of 1979-80. The United States called for deployment of Cruise and Pershing-II missiles in Europe in response to the deployment of hundreds of Soviet SS-20s. As the moment for a European decision drew closer, the Italian press generally recognized that the balance of power on the continent had been destabilized, and that a NATO response was reasonable. When the Cossiga government decided to accept the missiles on Italian territory there was a clear majority, both in Parliament and among the public at large, in favor of this decision.

The PCI went all-out to block deployment. While leaving open the question of whether the Soviet deployment had indeed destabilized the strategic balance, the PCI portrayed the American plan as a threat to world peace. They called upon the government to reject the plan, and urged acceptance of a Soviet call for a European arms-limitation conference to discuss the matter (a conference that would have greatly assisted Soviet efforts to drive a wedge between the United States and Western Europe). At a minimum, this would have given the Russians another six months to add to their growing arsenal of SS-20s without any Western response, and might have led to an even longer delay, or to a rejection of the proposal.

Parliament voted against the PCI, but the campaign continued apace. The NATO modernization was put on par with the Soviets' invasion of Afghanistan and was berated as a fundamental cause for the breakdown of detente. On January 9, 1980, for example, *Paese Sera*, the Communist evening paper in Rome, reported a parliamentary interrogation signed by a group of Communist deputies under the misleading headline, "PCI Deputies call for the withdrawal of Soviet Troops from Afghanistan." The story reported that the group had expressed its "full reprobation of the Soviet military intervention in Afghanistan, which constitutes a violation of the principle of independence and national sovereignty." It then went on:

(The deputies wish to know) how the government intends to assume its own position within the Atlantic Alliance in order that a line of negotiations and detente prevails in the face of the risks stemming from the military intervention of the U.S.S.R. and the measures of retaliation and worsening of relations announced and adopted by the U.S., so that Soviet troops will be withdrawn from Afghanistan and that understandings and accords will be achieved for the control and reduction of armaments, and for guarantees of reciprocal security and peace.[16]

The intent of the PCI's parliamentary maneuver was evidently threefold: first, to put the Soviet invasion and the American missile modernization on an equal footing; second, to oppose the American position within NATO; and finally, to insist that *both sides* were responsible for the breakdown of detente. Both sides would therefore have to make concessions.

Compare this with the language used at the time of the Chinese invasion of Vietnam a year earlier. During the Vietnamese attack upon Cambodia that preceded the Sino-Vietnamese hostilities, the PCI had strained to maintain the fiction that the Vietnamese had only supported an indigenous movement to overthrow Pol Pot. There was no condemnation of the Vietnamese. But the Chinese attack was roundly denounced, albeit in tones of sadness regarding a "revolutionary" country. There was no suggestion that Vietnam had contributed to an erosion of detente or to a heightening of tensions in the region, nor was there any suggestion that the Vietnamese would have to make some concession if a peaceful solution were to be found.[17]

In short, when the Soviet Union or a Soviet ally invaded a neighboring country, every effort was made to find mitigating factors, but when the United States moved to reestablish a strategic equilibrium in Europe, its actions were termed dangerous and destabilizing. When the Soviets built and installed missiles aimed at Western Europe, it was held to be a subject for detached discussion, but the Western response was firmly condemned.

To be sure, on occasion the PCI had to retreat in the face of dramatic facts, as in the case of the armed conflicts in Southeast Asia. The fighting there showed that war was as likely between "socialist" countries as between others, thereby demonstrating in a single stroke the nonsense of nearly thirty years of Communist rhetoric, predicting an end to war once the revolution had triumphed everywhere. The PCI, of course, tried to explain this away by claiming that only an incomplete transformation of Asian societies had been accomplished, and that the fighting represented a legacy of American (and even French) imperialism. Communist leaders were saddened by the spectacle, but they certainly did not criticize it in the terms reserved, for example, for the abortive American rescue mission in Iran in April 1980. There were good reasons for caution: not only would the Soviets have been angry at a condemnation of their Vietnamese allies, but the members of the PCI itself would not have tolerated open condemnation.

The Institute of Educational Sciences at the University of Bologna conducted a detailed analysis of the PCI base in the spring of 1979,[18] and found that the rank-and-file had not followed Berlinguer toward a more pro-NATO position. Indeed, of those Communists polled, a majority believed that there was greater democracy in the Soviet Union than in Italy. Moreover, although there was ostensible support for the *compromesso storico*, this proved to be largely superficial, since no less than 40 percent of the party base believed that nothing in Italy would change so long as the Catholic church existed.

Moreover, the team at the Institute of Educational Sciences found that the attitude of party members toward the Soviet Union was closer to Lenin than to "Eurocommunism." Eighty percent termed the U.S.S.R. a Socialist country, and a majority felt that there was greater democracy in the Soviet Union than in Italy. Finally, a full decade after the invasion of Czechoslovakia, a third of the members unconditionally approved the action, despite the condemnation on the part of the leadership.

All this shows that while the formal positions of PCI leaders may have changed, the great mass of party members had remained in their previous positions. And it became increasingly clear that the faithful were opposed to any meaningful transformation of PCI doctrine that would move it closer to democratic socialism or, in international affairs, to the Atlantic Alliance. This point was apparently well understood in Moscow, for a pro-Communist columnist for *l'Espresso* who travelled there early in 1978 was told by "two Soviet journalists in charge of foreign policy reporting on one of the two major national dailies," that

> (Berlinguer's words to the *Corriere della Sera*) constituted a rather strange move on the part of a Communist leader. We are convinced that the Italian Communists do not agree with them. . . . The PCI grassroots do not share Berlinguer's opinions and fears . . . anti-Sovietism has never profited anyone.[19]

In other words, whatever conflicts may develop from time to time between the PCI and the U.S.S.R. at the level of the party elite, the Soviets can count on the support of the PCI's rank-and-file. This means that the PCI leaders are limited in their efforts to move in a pro-Western direction, whatever their own sentiments may be (and there are certainly some PCI leaders who would prefer to move closer to the West). The effect of this fundamental loyalty to the Soviet Union is seen most clearly in foreign policy matters, as Robert Legvold sadly observed during the great debate over Eurocommunism:

Most analysts are fascinated by the ideological restlessness of the West European Communist parties rather than by their foreign policy constancy. Our attention is fastened on the challenges to "proletarian internationalism" and orthodox Marxism-Leninism and not on the essential similarity in the way most Communist parties—East or West—approach international affairs.[20]

The Rules of the Game: the PCI and the U.S.S.R.

The conflicts between Berlinguer and the Soviet Union over Eurocommunism will be discussed separately in a later chapter. For the moment, it is necessary to look at the relationship between the PCI and the U.S.S.R. over the past several decades.

Clearly, the PCI in the late seventies and eighties has operated with considerably greater possibilities for autonomy than previously. During the Comintern, and well into the postwar period, all foreign Communist parties were kept in line by the Kremlin. There was a general demand that foreign parties remain faithful to the Soviet line, and the Russians gave advance notice of the most serious changes so that their foreign comrades would have time to prepare the apparatus for the shift. There was also an important financial linkage: at the end of the war, the PCI, like all other Communist parties, was heavily dependent upon direct Soviet financing, which arrived in large part in cash (generally American dollars) through Soviet and satellite embassies in Italy. Over time, the quantity of direct subsidies diminished, being replaced by commissions and payoffs derived from trade between Italy and the Socialist bloc, whether in Eastern Europe or the Third World. Thanks to the Soviet connection, the PCI was and is able to offer its good offices to private entrepreneurs and governmental organizations eager to engage in commerce with Socialist and pro-Soviet countries. The Italian Communists have been well rewarded for this economic work, earning as much as 7 percent commission on the importation of meat from Eastern Europe.[21]

The evolution of this commerce meant that the PCI was less dependent upon direct subsidies, and it also greatly increased the party's income, but it did not thereby automatically loosen the bonds between the Kremlin and *via delle botteghe oscure* in Rome. For the income from the commercial activities was just as closely linked to the Politburo as were the satchels of hundred-dollar bills that had arrived regularly in Rome some years earlier. The Russians had arranged the business, and the Russians could cancel it. On some occasions, the spigots to the PCI were tightened, and even closed, to signify Soviet displeasure with PCI activities.

On the other hand, the Soviet leverage was certainly not absolute, and the PCI could sometimes prepare to defend its autonomy—but at a price.

In 1968, for example, prior to condemning the Soviet invasion of Czechoslovakia, the party leaders prepared an emergency austerity budget that would have been put into effect if, as was widely feared, the Soviets cut off the clandestine financing. The contingency budget demonstrates that Longo, Berlinguer, and company recognized the linkage between Soviet-organized financing and the PCI's political behavior. But it also demonstrates that under certain circumstances, the party was prepared to cope without the funds.

In addition to the political and economic control, the Kremlin exercised clandestine control through the KGB and the GRU. At least until the death of Stalin, the Soviet Union maintained "control groups" within the foreign Communist parties, using agents of the Soviet security agencies within the foreign parties. The best-documented case is France, where the control group headed by Eugene Fried constantly guided the PCF during the 1930s and 1940s.[22] It was not possible to have a group of precisely the same sort in Italy during this period, because the PCI itself was a clandestine organization, and control was accordingly carried out through the Comintern under the direction of Moskvin.[23]

After the war, the old methods survived for at least some time. The Soviets kept loyal men within the leadership of foreign Communist parties, and even had groups similar to that of Fried "in place" in the late forties and early fifties. At least this was the claim of some of the Soviet defectors to the West who were in a position to know, and the same claim has been reiterated by one of the best informed and most balanced of the Italian ex-Communists, Renato Mieli:

> In fact, the relations between the leadership groups within the Communist parties and the U.S.S.R. did not undergo any substantial changes after the death of Stalin. That invisible component within the Communist parties that welded them to Soviet secret services had certainly not disappeared along with the various edifices of the Communist International. It had, of course, changed with the times, first adjusting to the requirements of Khrushchev's policies, and then to those of Brezhnev, but it had remained throughout, invisible and decisive as in the past.[24]

Nonetheless, the operational relationship between PCI leaders and the Kremlin has changed considerably since Togliatti's day. So long as Togliatti was in charge (and through part of Longo's tenure as well), the general secretary was kept informed about many of the clandestine activities of the KGB and its sister East European services in Italy. But beginning in the second half of the 1960s, the leadership of the PCI was no longer advised. This change in operational procedure took place before the invasion of Czechoslovakia and is not attributable to the PCI's reaction to that event.

In fact, it may well be the other way around: the PCI fears that the Russians were going to cease the clandestine financing of the party may have been motivated at least in part by the shift in operational procedures.

Of course, the existence of such methods demonstrated that the Soviets didn't trust the leaders of the Western Communist parties, and the testimony of former European Communists and of Soviet defectors coincides on this point. Both sets of sources indicate that the Kremlin never fully trusted the European Communist leaders, and was particularly suspicious of the Italians. Togliatti was an exception, because he had been so fully compromised by his murderous activities on behalf of the Comintern. But the Russians were still shocked by his reflections on "polycentrism," and apparently decided that even Stalin's old henchman couldn't be fully trusted. The situation became more delicate after Togliatti died, such as when the Soviets tape-recorded a one-on-one meeting between Tito and Longo, in which the Italian secretary general was quite supportive of the Yugoslav.[25] This was not good for Longo's image in the Kremlin, and the Soviets' view of the PCI became even worse with the accession of Berlinguer.

The Kremlin's biggest objection to the PCI was that the party violated the basic Leninist rules. The PCI was not an elite vanguard, but rather a mass organization, and hence not subject to the sort of strict, hierarchical control that the Soviet Communist party leadership preferred. The Soviet reaction was to create a reliable organization within the PCI, one that could transmit Soviet orders, carry out instructions, and, should the PCI ever achieve power in Italy, eliminate the suspect elements and take control of the party and the country. The Soviets were so suspicious of Berlinguer and his friends that they instructed Czech intelligence to conduct hostile operations against the PCI. The details of these operations were revealed to American intelligence officers by the Czech General Jan Sejna, following his defection in Trieste in early 1968. The most famous of these was the creation of a "Nazi-Maoist" group in the second half of the sixties.[26] This group, under Czech control, was to have achieved three objectives for the Soviet Union: first, it made it possible for the Kremlin to identify the pro-Chinese elements within the PCI, for they came forward to help the "Maoist" movement; second, it permitted the Soviets to gauge Chinese intentions, for the "Maoists" asked Peking for instructions; finally, it permitted the Soviets to go to Berlinguer and say to him, "Look, the Chinese cause trouble for you; they create factions within your party. We don't do such things. Aren't you better off with us?"

But paradoxically these policies are more a testimony to Soviet shortsightedness than to the rebelliousness of the PCI. There was never any real possibility that the PCI would break with the Soviet Union, because the rank-and-file would never stand for it. If there were going to be a real rupture between the U.S.S.R. and the PCI, it would be the result of a Soviet excommunication, and not the product of an Italian defection. The rank-and-file is the greatest guarantee the Soviets have of the loyalty of the party, because no party leader will walk away from the Kremlin so long as he knows that if he does so, he will have very few people walking with him.

When the PCI condemned the Soviet invasion of Afghanistan, letters to *l'Unità* ran five-to-one against Berlinguer's position. The case is particularly instructive, since the leadership of the PCI had no real political alternative to condemning the invasion. To have endorsed it—as the French Communist party did, for example—would have alienated so many moderate voters that Berlinguer would have had to abandon all reasonable expectation of getting into the government in the near term. But even though the party's condemnation was wrapped in the more carefully modulated rhetorical blanket, and even though some of the PCI's most charismatic figures—including Giorgio Amendola, widely considered the most moderate of the party leaders—refused to condemn the Soviets, the reaction from the base was overwhelming.

Furthermore, the leadership was itself divided over Afghanistan, as it is on many questions. The *compromesso storico* was always somewhat controversial at the highest levels of the party, since it required an accommodation with the Catholic church—a bitter pill for some Communists to swallow. And this split is not a clean "East-West" division, for some of those (like Amendola) who support the most "Western" policies on domestic questions, and on issues like Italy's participation in the Common Market, turn out to be spokesmen for Soviet policies in international affairs (Amendola endorsed the Afghan invasion). On the other hand, some of those who hold very tough positions on domestic issues (like Pietro Ingrao) are in the forefront of the condemnation of Soviet policies such as the Afghan invasion or the suppression of Solidarity in Poland.

This internal division among the leadership parallels that between the rank-and-file and the moderate voters, and is subject to Soviet exploitation. The Kremlin knows that it can rely both upon the rank-and-file and upon a certain number of leaders. For the rest, the Soviets can afford to be patient, weighing in whenever circumstances require.

Above all, it is important to remember that there seems to be little chance that the party will make a definitive commitment to the Western camp, or for that matter that it will alter its internal structure and end democratic centralism. Thus, the Soviets do not have to fear a decisive break, although there are certainly limits to their toleration of imaginative political strategies by foreign Communist parties. This was the case of the *compromesso storico*.

The Failure of the Historic Compromise

The general elections of June 1976 were the last in which the PCI made any effective gains for half a decade. Berlinguer found himself trapped halfway to his objective; while not yet a party of government, no longer a party of opposition. The PCI now had to accommodate mutually exclusive demands from its supporters. On the one hand, having entered several local and regional governments, the party had to show that it could govern better than the other parties. But three decades of Communist activity had helped make the country extremely difficult to govern, for the DC had not dealt effectively with the challenges from the radicalized working classes and the suddenly active radical bourgeoisie. And, of course, if the PCI took steps toward more effective government—for example, by bringing the unions under greater control, or demanding more orderly behavior from the radicalized judiciary—it would thereby antagonize its own activists, who expected Communist political advances to produce fundamental transformations of Italian society—along the lines of the Soviet model.

But if the PCI followed the call of its own rank-and-file, it risked frightening those middle-class voters who had supported Berlinguer as a last resort. They were willing to take a risk with the PCI, provided that the Communists gave them law and order, a better business environment, and a promise of future stability. None of this was delivered, even though the PCI participated in a record number of local and regional governments and, in March 1977, joined a so-called programmatic majority in Parliament that installed a new Andreotti government. At that time, it appeared the PCI was on the verge of reaching its goal: having achieved a new degree of legitimacy, with a great deal of political momentum and their Christian Democratic opponents in disarray, the situation clearly favored the Communists.

But the Communists failed. On the very day the new government won its approval in Parliament, its major architect, Aldo Moro, was kidnapped by the Red Brigades, and after nearly two months in a "people's prison," he was murdered. Shortly thereafter came the local elections that, for the first time since 1948, produced stunning setbacks for the PCI. The electorate evidently held the Communists responsible to some degree for the tragedy, even though they had been extremely supportive of the government's refusal to negotiate with the terrorists. The party has yet to recover its lost momentum, although there was a brief forward surge in 1984 following the death of Berlinguer. Once the "long march through the institutions" was interrupted, the mood of the country shifted, and the electorate delivered enough votes to the lay, non-Communist parties to enable first Giovanni Spadolini and then Bettino Craxi to serve as prime minister.

In retrospect, the *compromesso storico* could only have succeeded if the Communists had been able to move quickly into the government. For the longer they remained stuck between government and opposition, the more telling became the blows from both Left and Right. Finally, as they sat halfway along the path to power, the Communists saw a marked deterioration in the international field. With the abrupt shattering of detente under the assault of Soviet activities in Asia and Africa, and then with the election of Ronald Reagan in the United States, another necessary precondition to Communist success in Italy was removed. By the mid-eighties the Communists were forced to abandon the call for an historic compromise.

The greatest irony of the Communist failure was that the most telling blow against the historic compromise was delivered by the Red Brigades, who—in the words of an eloquent ex-PCI member—had come right out of the party's "family album." At a time when the PCI was claiming to have embraced Western values, and to have abandoned much, if not all, of its Leninist heritage, the Red Brigades reminded the Italian electorate of the Leninist roots of the party and of the intimate ties between the Communist party and the strategy of armed insurrection that the Red Brigades so well embody.

The Red Brigades

Despite the enormous quantity of information that has been acquired about the Red Brigades, this subject still awaits its historian. Still, enough is known to attempt a first, somewhat tentative approximation. Alberto Ronchey, one of the finest contemporary Italian journalists, claimed in mid-1979 that the PCI had direct responsibility for the terrorist organization: "The party raised it, nourished it within its own ideological obsessions, and finally discovered it had produced a problem child."[27] At the time, Ronchey intuited a connection that has since become better documented. He remembered the old days of the *Partito Armato*, when Pietro Secchia and his friends were in charge of the clandestine paramilitary apparatus of the PCI, when the party's archives were kept in Prague, where Italian Communists in trouble could find sanctuary. Ronchey realized that there was an historic connection between the first generation of Red Brigadiers and Prague: Renato Curcio, the first leader of the terrorist organization, had repeatedly visited Prague, as had both his close associate Alberto Franceschini and the "godfather" of Italian terrorism, Giangiacomo Feltrinelli. Ronchey also knew that the PCI's Czech connection had never really ended. Prague remains one of the busiest centers of PCI commercial activity; Radio Prague has been a haven for PCI members under indictment since the end of the war, and when several members of the party were expelled from Czechoslovakia in 1975, Berlinguer himself made a speech expressing concern about the "status of our people in Prague."

Ronchey perhaps did not know that several among the first generation of Red Brigades were actually trained in Czechoslovakia by Soviet military intelligence—a fact that was revealed for the first time in the late seventies in the United States by General Jan Sejna, a Czech defector who had kept the books for these GRU-run training operations. Sejna's information was originally challenged, but with the passage of time it has received striking confirmation: some of the persons Sejna said had been trained in Czechoslovakia (names that were totally unknown at the time he provided them) have since proven to have been very important terrorist leaders. Furthermore, there was a biographical continuity between the Secchia-led groups of the 1940s and early 1950s, and the Red Brigades some twenty years later.[28]

The red thread that connects Secchia's Armed party with the Red Brigades passed through Rome, Prague, and Havana. This oft-repeated itinerary is symbolized by the person of Feltrinelli, the millionaire radical publisher who achieved great fame with his publication of Che Guevara's diaries. Feltrinelli also embodies the relationship of the terrorist movement with the PCI. A party member in the early 1950s, Feltrinelli was one of the handful of persons who had safes in their homes in Italy for the deposit of the clandestine funds that came from the East. But Feltrinelli was not simply a party activist and "banker"; like many wealthy individuals with a taste for radical politics, he was attracted to the violent revolutionary doctrines of the period. After several trips to Latin America in the 1960s, Feltrinelli undertook to organize an urban guerrilla movement in Italy along the lines advocated by Che and Regis Debray, his French publicist. This activity was evidently agreeable to someone in Czechoslovakia, for between December 1969 and the time of his death in March 1972, Feltrinelli's passport had been filled with twenty-two Czech visas.

Feltrinelli's Czech connection was of great interest to Italian intelligence, and as early as October 1950, the top secret division of *Affari Riservati* of the Interior Ministry sent a telegram in cipher to the Italian border guards at Udine, asking them to stop Feltrinelli and his wife en route to Prague, and search for documents related to possible military espionage. It is not known whether any evidence was found, but the Italian security forces were well avised to watch Feltrinelli. According to Sejna, and in the view of Italian security officials at the time, by the second half of the 1960s, he had become a Soviet agent, trained in the most advanced techniques of paramilitary operations by Soviet military intelligence, the GRU. The training was done at a camp in Doupov, near Prague, where there were terrorist recruits from all over the world. At least a dozen Italians, including Franceschini, passed through the Doupov camp.

Feltrinelli had contacts with other Communists who shared his taste for travelling to Cuba and other Latin American countries. In his efforts to create a guerrilla movement in Italy, Feltrinelli worked closely with Giovanni Battista Lazagna, a PCI official himself, an intimate friend of Curcio, and a former associate of Secchia. In addition, Aristo Ciruzzi, a noted Genovese architect, who was a member of the foreign section of the PCI Central Committee, was close to Feltrinelli. Ciruzzi and Lazagna were arrested in Genoa in 1972 along with Vittorio Togliatti (Palmiro's nephew) and Marisa Calimodio, former wife of Vittorio Togliatti and at the time the mistress of Ciruzzi. The group was charged with criminal conspiracy and terrorist activities.

The Genoa group had been under observation for years, and the Italian authorities had gathered a formidable dossier on them (much of which was never used in their trial). According to high-ranking Italian officials, the Ciruzzi group had established a vast network of terrorist contacts ranging from Latin America to Eastern Europe. All of this was done under cover of a Catholic benevolent association, the Columbianum Institute. Nearly ten years before the arrests, one of the leading members of the Columbianum had undertaken missions to Prague and Havana. Ciruzzi often travelled to South America (where he met with Feltrinelli) and Eastern Europe. He was also in touch with Alessandro Beltramini, a Milanese doctor arrested in Caracas in April 1965, with $270,000 in his luggage, apparently destined for Venezuelan revolutionaries.

Ciruzzi's activities in Genoa were of a piece with his international connections. He was in frequent contact with the Cuban Consul, with Swiss and Latin American revolutionaries, and with Lazagna and Feltrinelli. Lazagna later achieved notoriety as the man who had introduced Red Brigades leader Curcio to a radical Italian priest who had spent years in Latin America. Nicknamed "father machinegun," the priest betrayed Curcio to Italian authorities. At the time of his arrest, Lazagna, along with others in the group, had been involved in efforts to negotiate a merger of Italian left-wing terrorist groups, including the Red Brigades.

As Mario Pirani, a leading Italian journalist and editor, put it, "It is an error to think that the Red Brigades are merely the fruit of 1968 and of the most extremist currents of the 'autonomist' movement. They come from further back . . . Stalin was always their prophet and revolutionary violence was their word."[29]

This is not to suggest that the Red Brigades were protected or otherwise encouraged by Berlinguer and his comrades in the Politburo of the PCI. On the contrary, there is a reason to believe that the Red Brigades were and are hostile to the party's leadership, viewing Berlinguer as too moderate for their tastes. The ideological tracts of the Red Brigades denounced Berlinguer, and in the early spring of 1978 Communist activists found a Red Brigades banner locked in a storeroom in the Rinascita bookstore, within the party headquarters. Since that building had perhaps the best security in Rome, the provocative placement of the flag sent a clear message to Berlinguer: the Red Brigades are here, in your midst. They can come and go as they wish. Indeed, one member of the PCI Central Committee told me that it had become a game to try to guess the identities of leading PCI members who were also involved in the Brigades.

Sejna claims that many of the Italians sent to Doupov and other training centers in Czechoslovakia were selected by pro-Soviet elements of the PCI, but he stresses that Berlinguer was not informed of the training center, nor was he necessarily aware of the recruitment program. But the PCI has an historic tie to the Brigades: the language of the terrorists is right out of the PCI's lexicon, and while it does not fit well with Eurocommunism, its lineage can hardly be challenged. Moreover, the international connections, from Prague to Havana (and to Luanda and Tripoli as well), that are apparently involved in the ideological and material training of Italian terrorists are those long since established by emissaries of the PCI. Even if many of the youngsters who threw themselves into terrorism in the seventies were not party members, their activities were often encouraged by the party.

> Delegations from extra-parliamentary groups went to Luanda to gather, in the victory of Agostino Neto, the testimony that imperialism can be defeated through armed struggle. And how many youngsters (including those from the PCI) have enthusiastically participated in the sugar cane harvest of Fidel Castro alongside those mililtiamen who today fight under Soviet orders against Somalis and Eritrean patriots?[30]

To which one might add, how many youngsters now participate in activities in Nicaragua, alongside the 40-odd members of the Red Brigades that Prime Minister Craxi announced had found safe haven with the Sandinistas?

To be sure, there was certainly another strand in the Red Brigades, one that drew its ideological vitality from a Catholic tradition. Curcio himself was never a member of the PCI, never participated in PCI activities, and can hardly be termed a product of Communist culture. Instead, Curcio, and many like him, came from a radical Catholic background that gave his anticapitalism and anti-Americanism a particular intensity. The organizational history of the Red Brigades passes not only through Prague and Havana, it also lies through Trent, and its Catholic University. It was there that many of the first generation of Red Brigadiers studied and plotted, eventually to merge with the Communist component to create the terrorist version of the *compromesso storico*. Not for nothing did Indro Montanelli, perhaps the greatest wordsmith of the postwar period, write that he dreaded the historic compromise, not least of all because the Red Brigades would be in charge of law and order, the KGB of the new society.[31]

While Berlinguer was generally outspoken in his denunciation of terrorism in Italy, it took quite a while before he and the others were willing to grant that the Red Brigades were truly an organization of the extreme Left. Prior to 1978, for example, he had argued that terrorism was always "fascist," and that anything that suggested that terrorists were from the Left was simply a hoax. But even later, there was considerable ambiguity in the PCI's position, and during the Moro affair several party leaders suggested that the United States was behind the operation.

The same ambivalence characterized the PCI's collaboration with Italian authorities in the antiterrorist campaign. Given the history of the Red Brigades, and the fact that many of their leaders were recruited from Communist organizations, or from other groups that had received assistance from the PCI, the party was in a good position to identify both members and sources of recruitment. But PCI support was minimal; during the Moro affair they offered the names of 100 persons to the police, but none of these leads panned out. And on at least one occasion, Berlinguer learned something quite interesting about the Red Brigades, but failed to communicate it to Italian authorities.

During the Moro operation, Berlinguer quietly asked Rumanian dictator Ceausescu if he could help locate the Red Brigades' "prison," and the Rumanian secret service was put to work on the case. Moro was never found, but the Rumanians did discover that some members of the Red Brigades had been trained in Bulgaria, where there was an ongoing training operation. This vital information did not reach Italian counter-terrorist authorities at the time (and it was only learned by American intelligence a few years later).[32] In short, the PCI never provided the sort of full and enthusiastic cooperation that Italian security forces desired. The Italian electorate was therefore justified in worrying about the first word in the name of the terrorist organization. The brigades are, after all, Red. And their objectives are the historic objectives of the PCI: the creation of a Communist state in Italy. While the Brigadiers themselves are the first to grant that the leadership of the PCI is now reformist, the ambivalence of the PCI on Red terrorism, like its ambivalence on the democratization of the party itself, suggests that there is still a strong Leninist heritage at work within the party. This is perhaps the most enduring problem for those citizens of the West, from Rome to Washington, who contemplate the PCI as a potential element in the Italian government.

The Question of Leninism

Henry Kissinger once observed that the problem with the Eurocommunists was not how pro-Soviet they were, but how Communist.[33] In the end, he argued, such parties threatened the security of the United States because they would inevitably attempt to install a totalitarian regime, incompatible with American democratic ideals. The spread of such regimes would leave the United States isolated and without sufficient resources to survive with democracy intact.

Kissinger was correct. Quite aside from the matter of the PCI's ongoing pro-Sovietism and its various connections with left-wing terrorism, it remains a fundamentally antidemocratic organization. This is particularly evident in its continued allegiance to the principle of democratic centralism, as it is in the party's antidemocratic efforts in the field of culture, particularly regarding free and open access to the mass media.

Communist leaders are understandably defensive about the internal organization of the PCI, and from time to time the more Western-oriented among them have suggested that greater internal democracy should be instituted. Unique among Italian political parties, the PCI has no formal internal divisions, no "currents" tied to leading figures or institutions. There is no provision for an institutionalized dissent from official positions; once a decision is made at the top, all are expected to abide by it.

Observers of this impressive political machine inevitably ask how the PCI can be expected to protect political pluralism, if the party itself permits very little of it. What reason is there to believe that the PCI will suddenly transform itself in power, when it has not done so in opposition? These questions are particularly important when it is recalled that every other Communist leader promised full respect for and defense of political freedom prior to the seizure of power; but no Communist state has ever permitted such freedom once the Communist elite had taken over. For the past several years, the more liberal members of the PCI leadership have suggested that a structural change was required, and there was some expectation that a step in that direction would be taken at a meeting of the Central Committee at the end of 1976.

Indeed, there was an attempt. A motion for a revision of "democratic centralism" was introduced by Cervetti, but Armando Cossutta, one of the most outspoken pro-Soviet hardliners in the party, delivered a broadside against the proposal, which was quickly defeated. Despite occasional rumors (like the one suggesting that "Leninism" would be abandoned at the 1979 Party Congress) no further steps have been taken; indeed there has been a marked regression in the official statements of party leaders ever since the failure of the Cervetti initiative. At the *l'Unità* festival in Genoa in the autumn of 1978, for example, Berlinguer claimed that democratic liberties were more threatened in capitalist countries than in the Soviet Union. In the former, he said, freedom was menaced by a system that tended to limit and ultimately destroy democracy. But in the Soviet Union, despite "errors and repressions," the revolution had initiated "a process of liberation of the masses and of oppressed peoples."[34] This suggested that the PCI's concept of democracy was closer to the Kremlin's than to that of most of the democratic West.

The same disappointing themes are heard when the party speaks of pluralism. First of all, PCI spokesmen say repeatedly that pluralism is a "means, and not an end unto itself." And nothing in the practice of the party suggests anything different. Certain aspects of Communist behavior (far more revealing than any exegesis of official texts) suggest that there are distinctly Stalinist elements at work. For example, during the 1976 electoral campaign, the young Radical party attempted to get its slate first on the ballot in several voting districts, so that they could steal the PCI's favorite slogan, "vote high on the Left" (you can vote for the entire party list in an Italian election by marking the party symbol on the ballot; this is particularly common in areas of low literacy). Since the position on the ballot is determined by the order in which the parties submit their lists, the Radicals lined up ostentatiously in front of the electoral offices several days before the filing date. But on the night before filing, gangs of Communist thugs took to the streets, beat up the Radicals, removed them from their position in front of the electoral offices, and then took their places. The PCI symbol was again first on the ballot.

Moreover, the PCI is quite intolerant of ideas critical of its own. In recent years the most successful anti-Communist group in the country has been that around the daily newspaper, *il Giornale nuovo* in Milan, created in 1974 by journalists who had left the increasingly left-leaning *il Corriere della Sera*. By the time of the 1976 elections, the *Giornale* was so influential that it was widely credited with having prevented the Communists from becoming the most popular party in the country. At the beginning of that year, the *Giornale* group began running the evening news broadcast (in Italian) on Telemontecarlo, a small television station that covered much of the country thanks to a series of relay towers from Milan to south of Rome. While the news broadcast was quite rudimentary—a single camera transmitting in black and white—the point of view was so refreshing that the show achieved an amazing success, with an estimated 6-7 million viewers at its peak in 1976.

This threatened the PCI's Gramscian strategy, and party leaders accordingly demanded that Telemontecarlo be suppressed. Just a year before, the Communists had taken the opposite position on the general question of foreign television broadcasting to Italy. At that time, the Christian Democratic minister for telecommunications had been accused of "fascism" when he dutifully instructed that foreign broadcasts be jammed (the Italian Constitution giving a monopoly on all broadcasting to the government). To the cheers of the PCI and the rest of the Italian Left, the Constitutional

Court ruled that the minister had acted improperly. But this campaign against Christian Democratic "fascism" did not prevent the PCI from taking the same position regarding Telemontecarlo.

The pretext adopted by the PCI to justify its position was that it was legitimate for foreign commercials to be jammed or otherwise blocked, even though actual programs could not be. The practical effect, of course, would have been the same, for *il Giornale* could hardly buy air time every night without some commercial sponsorship, but it was noteworthy that the PCI never asked for the suppression of commercials broadcast on Radio Montecarlo (one of the most popular pop music stations in the Mediterranean area), or of television shows from Istria (which the director of Telemontecarlo termed "the chosen tribune of the Italian Communists," in an interview with a *Le Monde* correspondent), or for that matter of Italian-language television and radio broadcasts from Switzerland.

Telemontecarlo was a different matter, and was treated as a major threat by the PCI. One party senator told the French Communist newspaper *l'Humanité* that Telemontecarlo seemed part of a "war of the airwaves by encirclement, rather like that which was done to Allende's Chile."[35]

The PCI failed to shut down the evening news on Telemontecarlo, but the campaign demonstrated that the PCI's notion of pluralism did not extend to ideas they considered politically unacceptable. The normal PCI tactic was, of course, to attempt to extend their "hegemony" over all the media. As has been seen, the Communists aimed at penetration of the media through a campaign of "Sovietization"; all decisions would have to be ratified by assemblies that could be controlled by Communist propaganda and organizers.

It may be objected that there are few political leaders in Italy today, of whatever political party, who share American notions of freedom of the press and pluralism. Moreover, many Communist leaders are imbued with democratic passions as intense as one could wish. True enough, but the other political leaders do not command a Leninist organization, and the question of the personal desires of individual Communist leaders is irrelevant to the political future of the country. One must examine their political possibilities, and the real political parameters on their actions. Sentiments, even powerfully democratic ones, cannot change the physiognomy of the party itself.

Today, there are undoubtedly more Communists with genuine pro-Western and democratic sentiments than at any other time in the past, and one must therefore wonder whether some real change may be possible in the future. The most balanced judgment comes from one such person, who left the PCI in the 1950s, Renato Mieli:

> The internal labor pains within the PCI are . . . more serious than might

appear on the surface. It can not proceed along the path of complete emancipation from the U.S.S.R. because the most vital element of the party will not permit it. Indeed, the PCI has been compelled to backtrack in order to maintain party stability and the efficiency of its very operational structure. But the party must also limit its retreat, for if it goes back too far, it may lose the power and the influence it has carved out for itself within Italian society. Thus, at least for the moment, it must muddle along, waiting for more favorable conditions that may permit it to overcome the blocked position in which it finds itself today.[36]

Notes

1. The literature on Gramsci is vast, but three fairly recent works will give a good insight into the way in which Gramsci's thought was integrated into the overall strategy of the PCI. The most thorough treatment is in Luciano Pellicani, *Gramsci e la questione Comunista* (Firenze, 1976), which begins with the key to the whole issue:

    > The theme on which Gramsci meditated in prison with greatest attention, and which became the principal object of his theoretical reflection, is that of the conquest and administration of power by an emerging historical force that intends to create a new kind of civilization. Exactly the problem that Lenin had raised: sustain, organize and direct those energies not only to destroy the existing order, but also and above all to build a new order. . . .

    In addition, it is useful to read Enzo Bettiza, *il Comunismo Europo* (Milano, 1978) and Nello Ajello, *Intellettuali e PCI* (Rome & Bari, 1979).
2. *Il Giornale Nuovo* was for several years one of the most interesting Italian newspapers, boasting of such distinguished names as Indro Montanelli, Enzo Bettiza, Lucio Lami, Frane Barbieri, Rosario Romeo, Renza de Felice, Luigi Barzini, and Francesco D'Amato. By the mid-1980s, however, the original zeal had died down and many of its best journalists and contributors had moved elsewhere.
3. Cf. Lucio Lami, *La Scuola del Plagio* (Rome, 1977). The case cited below is that of the historian Armando Saitta; his book was published and altered—without his approval or knowledge—by the Nuova Italia publishing house in Florence. But again, this is simply an extreme case (of which there are many, ranging from the publishing houses to the radio and television networks, to the movie producers and the teachers).
4. The intimidation of intellectuals was not merely a matter of verbal violence; professors were assaulted physically at the universities, and some were actually murdered. It thus took physical as well as moral courage to take a different line in the mid-seventies; those who did so had to be prepared for violence of all sorts (for an example of cultural terrorism, Cf. Michael A. Ledeen, "Renzo De Felice and the Controversy over Italian Fascism" in *International Fascism; New Thoughts and New Approaches* [London and Beverly Hills, 1979], which discusses the Communist attack on De Felice after the publication of his *Intervista sul fascismo* in the summer of 1975).
5. Cf. Enrico Berlinguer, "Riflessioni sull'Italia dopo i fatti del Chile," in

Rinascita, 28 September, 5 October, 9 October, 1973. This is where the expression "compromesso storico" first appeared.
6. Cf. Domenico Settembrini, *La Chiesa nella politica italiana (1944-1963)*, (Milan, 1977), 72-78, Carlo Falconi, *La Chiesa e le organizzazioni cattoliche in Italia* (Torino, 1956), 500 ff. This fascinating and important phenomenon still awaits its historian.
7. Kissinger's primary motive for detente was to attempt to remove the United States as a divisive issue in European politics. At the time, the streets of virtually every European capital were full of demonstrators against U.S. policy in Chile, Vietnam, and the Middle East. He did not anticipate that detente would serve to increase the strength of European communism; but even if he had been so prescient, he might well have judged it worth the risk.
8. Giuseppe Are, *Eurocommunism: Implications for East and West* (Typescript, 1977). A more detailed analysis appeared in his book, *Radiografia di un Partito* (Milano, 1980).
9. Every five years, it seems, there is an episode of this sort; Amendola's fate was repeated by Lama in 1986.
10. This sort of shift was rarely commented upon by those who insisted that the PCI was quite independent of the Kremlin.
11. *Corriere della Sera*, 13 June 1976. The interviewer, Giampaolo Pansa, sent Berlinguer the text for approval prior to publication . . . and Berlinguer approved it. Thus all talk of technical errors and the like is false.
12. On 30 June, Berlinguer told a press conference in East Berlin, "a Marxist cannot consider NATO a shield in the fight for socialism." Cf. *il Giornale nuovo*, 1 July 1976. Finally, there is the statement by Lucio Lombardo Radice (*Encounter*, April 1977), that if there were an East-West war, the PCI would support the Soviet Union: "in the unlikely event of a showdown, we as a Party could not be expected to work against the general interests of the Soviet Union, and by 'interests' I mean the historic achievements of socialism, which we don't want to see destroyed or diminished. . . ."
13. In this manner, it didn't matter *what* the PCI leaders said; Italians could believe whatever they wished. This sort of double-think was symptomatic not only of the methods of the Communists, but also of the fear they had inspired in many quarters in Italy. For the willingness to indulge in such wishful thinking (believe what you want, don't bother checking your beliefs against the actual statements of the Communists) is a clear sign that the Communists' intimidation was having some degree of success.
14. Jacoviello's article appeared 1 March 1976. For a more detailed discussion of the PCI's habit of saying quite different things to different audiences, Cf. Michael Ledeen, "Italian Communism: the Soviet Connection," in *Commentary* (November 1976).
15. Are, ms. *cit.*
16. *Paese Sera*, 9 January 1980.
17. This theme was repeated several times in articles in *l'Unità* and *Rinascita*, as well as in public statements by Pajetta, Bufalini, and Berlinguer.
18. Cf. Marzio Barbagli and Piergiorgio Corbetta, "Una tattica e due strategie. Inchiesta sulla base del PCI," in *il Mulino* (November-December 1978).
19. Antonio Gambino in *l'Espresso*, 22 January 1978.
20. This is from a paper prepared by Dr. Legvold while at the Council on Foreign Relations in 1978: "The Soviet Union and West European Communism," in Rudolf L. Tokes, ed., *Eurocommunism and Detente* (New York, 1978), 351.

21. Cf. Ledeen and Sterling, "Italy's Russian Sugar Daddies," *cit.*
22. On Fried, in addition to the material cited in note 32, Chapter Four, Cf. Roland Gaucher, *histoire secrete du Parti Communiste Francais* (Paris, 1974), 224-239, and Philipe Robrieux, *Notre Generation Communiste* (Paris, 1977), 234 ff.
23. Moskvin was the *nom de guerre* of Trilisser, who was the head of the NKVD for Western Europe. Cf. Renato Mieli, "Stalinismo all'italiana," in *il Giornale nuovo*, 4 July 1980.
24. *Ibid.* Indeed, if the KGB ceased to operate within the PCI it would constitute a real revolution.
25. This characterization of Longo is confirmed by General Jan Sejna, *We Will Bury You* (London, 1982), 137: "President Novotny told me, in some disgust, that Luigi Longo . . . had revealed that he and the PCI Politburo were unanimous in agreeing that not a single adviser from the Soviet Union would be accepted after they came to power."
26. This was called the *lotta del popolo*.
27. Cf. Alberto Ronchey, *Libro Bianco sull'ultima generazione* (Milano, 1978), 92. In the same essay Ronchey quotes an elegant line from Giuseppe Are. Are suggested that the terrorists could well respond to PCI critics of their actions with the words, "hypocrite censeur, mon semblable, mon frere."
28. I was apparently the first person to whom Sejna told his account of the training of Italian (and other) terrorists by the GRU in Czechoslovakia. When he gave me a (phonetically spelled) list of names of Italians he believed were trained in his country, I passed the list on to Francesco Cossiga, then the Prime Minister, and to Claire Sterling, who had just begun work on her book, *The Terror Network*. It was not until several years later that we could appreciate the accuracy of what Sejna had told us, for some of the names he had given—which were totally unknown to any of the experts who worked on Italian terrorism—turned out to be involved in the *Hyperion* institute in Paris, which served as a control base for the Red Brigades, and a liaison with KGB and other intelligence officials.
29. Mario Pirani, in *la Republica*, 26 April 1978.
30. Mario Pirani, in *la Republica*, (n.d., but 1977 or 1978).
31. Montanelli sent these remarks to the conference on Italy and Eurocommunism sponsored by the American Enterprise Institute in Washington, D.C., 8-9 June 1977.
32. The information came from Ion Mihai Pacepa, the deputy director of the Rumanian Secret Intelligence Service and President Ceausescu's personal adviser. Pacepa defected in 1978, after the death of Aldo Moro.
33. See Kissinger's speech to the conference on Italy and Eurocommunism, delivered 9 June 1977. The Italian translation (a very good one) was published in Rome by Circolo Stato e Libertà.
34. It is virtually impossible to find any top Italian Communist official who admits that there is greater freedom in the West than the East. They are willing to say that the Soviet Union has made various "errors," but they generally follow that up with a long list of Western sins.
35. The most complete account of the Telemontecarlo affair is Enzo Bettiza, "Les debuts de la terreur communiste en Italie: vers la suppression des moyens d'expression independant," in *Est & Ouest* (Paris, 1-15 March, 1977).
36. Renato Mieli, "The autonomy of the PCI," in *The Washington Quarterly*, (Washington, Autumn, 1979).

6

The Myth of Eurocommunism

> *Take into your hands the banner of all the bourgeois liberties, and transform them into the instrument for the final victory of socialism and communism.*
> —Stalin, 1953, to West European Communists

The strategies of the West European Communist parties in the 1970s were so similar to those of the immediate postwar period that one is inevitably drawn to Marx's wry remark that revolutionary movements imitate anachronistic models, thereby turning tragedy into farce. Just as the Paris Commune produced a disproportionate reaction from both supporters and opponents, so the claims of the Spanish, Italian, and French Communists in the seventies to have broken with the past and embraced a democratic Western tradition, evoked distorted responses from both sides of the political spectrum and both sides of the Iron Curtain. In the debate over Eurocommunism it was rarely noted that the efforts of the Communists to convince the electorates of their countries that European communism was different from the Soviet variety were at least three decades old. If Togliatti could execute the *svolta di Salerno* in 1944, there was little reason to be astonished at Berlinguer's endorsement of the international order of the mid-1970s or at Carrillo's about-face on the monarchy, the constitution, and the church in Spain in 1977. After all, Togliatti had led the PCI through the same rhetorical shifts three decades earlier. In short, the flexibility demonstrated by the Eurocommunists had long been a feature of at least some Communist parties in Western Europe (and, of course, of Eastern European communism prior to the seizure of power and the fall of the Iron Curtain).

When Henry Kissinger reminded his listeners in the spring of 1977[1] that every Communist leader from Lenin to Gottwald had promised national integrity, personal freedom, and democracy, he was only echoing the warnings of others who had lived through the triumph of communism in previously democratic countries like Czechoslovakia. One such participant, Vaclav Pelisek, had the same reaction to the slogans of the West European Communists in 1977:

> I cannot forget the important role played by certain sophisms dear to Eurocommunism in the conquest of power (in Czechoslovakia in 1948). Only now do I understand the tactical importance of the ban on using terms like "dictatorship of the proletariat," "Sovietization," and "collectivization" in the press and in all the party schools. Gottwald himself requested it in 1946, thirty years before Mr. Marchais.[2]

Given such precedents, and given the frequent use of systematic deception as a method of the Communist movement, the claims of Berlinguer, Marchais, and Carrillo should have been greeted with scepticism in the United States. Instead, by mid-1977 the bulk of the American intellectual establishment had concluded that West European Communists had reached a point of no return in their relations with the Soviet Union. The Eurocommunist parties of Spain, France, and Italy were held to be well advanced along the road toward independence from the Kremlin, as well as toward true democracy and even a pro-Western identification. It was generally supposed that there would be a rupture with Moscow, just as the positions of Tito in the fifties and Mao in the sixties had led to their expulsion from the world Communist movement.

The widespread adoption of the term "Eurocommunism" as a positive concept was one of the ironies of the seventies, for its original meaning was thereby debased. The word was coined in June 1975, by a Yugoslav correspondent for an Italian newspaper, and both the correspondent (Frane Barbieri) and the paper (*il Giornale nuovo*) were strongly critical of the phenomenon. In fact, Barbieri chose the word to suggest that there was little ideological coherence or political consistency between the French, Spanish, and Italian Communists. He believed that the three shared a common geographical position and a commitment to communism, but that aside from this generic linkage, the ideas of Carrillo, Marchais, and Berlinguer were so vague as to elude serious analysis. He thus chose "Eurocommunism," rather than "neocommunism," to stress the intellectual shallowness of the three leaders. Barbieri's own articles are among the best ever written on the subject, and his reflections on it are particularly useful from the vantage point of the present:

> Precisely because it was unclear just exactly what it was, I wondered and still wonder if a European community dominated by Eurocommunism would manage to keep intact its own significance and the international framework in which it was conceived. . . . The Eurocommunists themselves claim to

desire the independence of Western Europe from the United States and the Soviet Union. If we look at the programme presented by Carrillo to the Eighth Congress of the Spanish Communist Party in 1972 we could actually ascribe to him the intention of promoting the Europeanization of the Soviet system from the outside. But this is an illusion. If anything, the reverse would occur: a Eurocommunist Europe would undoubtedly mean the Sovietization of Europe.[3]

Barbieri realized that the Communists of Western Europe had neither the ideological tools nor the institutional integrity to embrace the West. While they might differ with the Soviet Union on various questions, and while none of them desired to repeat the destiny of Alexander Dubcek, there was no serious possibility that the Eurocommunists would initiate a rupture with the Kremlin. If this were to occur, it would be the result of a Soviet excommunication, and not from a European Communist initiative. Furthermore, even as the Eurocommunists proclaimed their independence from Moscow, the importance of the Soviet connection continued to be demonstrated.

To be sure, the notion that some Communist parties wished to be independent from Moscow was neither new nor controversial, although the consequences for the West of a rupture were not altogether clear. The cases of Tito and Mao showed that genuine splits were possible, and while the regimes of China and Yugoslavia were undemocratic, they offered the United States the possibility of a foreign policy more flexible than those of the bloc countries. Alliances of convenience were available, as the Chinese case showed. Signs of tension between the Eurocommunists and the Kremlin might therefore have been welcomed on the grounds of realpolitik: Washington might hope to exploit the conflicts to the detriment of the Soviets.

This case, however, was rarely made, in part because the setting for the debate between the various Communists was on the Western side of the Yalta line, and involved far more than differences among Communists: NATO might be a casualty of the struggle, even if Soviet control over the international Communist movement also suffered.

But this was not the main reason for the lack of hardheaded analysis of the Eurocommunists. For the most part, American newspapers, magazines, television commentators, and academic experts were quite optimistic about Eurocommunism itself, as can be seen from some typical definitions taken from leading American publications of the period:[4] "a tendency in some Western Communist parties to stress independence from Moscow and opposition to coercion"; "a mixture of socialism and Western democracy"; "a version of Marxism which stresses transition to socialism by parliamentary means"; "a Communist rule free of Moscow's domination, as advocated by the parties of Italy, France, and Spain, and free of the Soviet features of violent accession to power and repression to retain power."

The most prestigious American foreign policy publication, *Foreign Affairs*, published several favorable articles on the phenomenon, yet there was not a single article critical of Eurocommunism until early 1978, when an article appeared by Jean-Francois Revel; then a year later there was an essay on terrorism by Alberto Ronchey, which included an assessment of the PCI's historic responsibility for Italian terrorism.

The main competitor, *Foreign Policy*, repeatedly gave space to authors urging that the United States encourage or at least tolerate the presence of Eurocommunist parties in European governments. *Foreign Policy* published nothing systematically critical of the Communists, and *Foreign Affairs* actually declined to print two articles that had been formally requested, both of which were written by anti-Communists (Annie Kriegel on the PCF, Renato Mieli on the PCI).

The high-water mark in American enthusiasm for Eurocommunism came in the summer of 1977 on the editorial page of the *New York Times*. On July 1, the *Times* noted that Santiago Carrillo had been excoriated in the Soviet press "because, even more than his Italian and French comrades . . . Mr. Carrillo holds Communism to be compatible with constitutional democracy. That means he believes there is a higher law than the will of any Communist party, even in a Communist country."

In the view of the *Times'* editorialists, the consequences for world communism were grave indeed: Eurocommunism was a threat to the results of sixty years of Leninist and Stalinist repression, expansion, and consolidation:

> It is the idea that threatens the Soviet regime. . . . The idea is an even greater threat to the Soviet-sponsored regimes of Poland, Hungary, Czechoslovakia, and East Germany, which have all faced similar demands from their peoples, including Communists. . . . Once it is acknowledged that Communists may be challenged and defeated at the polls by non-Communist or even rival Communist parties, and that citizens enjoy rights of speech and assembly beyond those granted them by a ruling Communist oligarchy, there would remain no ideological defense for the East European dictatorships and not much difference between Europe's Communist and Socialist parties.

The *Times* editorialists warned that the evolution of the Eurocommunists was incomplete, but did not doubt its authenticity. Indeed, the *Times* warned of two dangers that might emerge from American action in Europe: a direct challenge might drive them back to a harder line, while an American endorsement might incite the East European countries to rise up against their Soviet taskmasters. The implication was that the United States should do nothing, hoping that the evolution from communism to democracy could be achieved without destabilizing the Soviet empire.

The *Washington Post* accepted the Communists' claims to have taken a position equidistant between the two superpowers, and enjoyed the reactions of the Americans and the Russians:

> It's comic, isn't it? . . . The advance of these Communist parties distresses the Americans because they don't see enough evidence of real independence from the Soviets. It distresses the Soviets because they see too much evidence. When they point out that their free-thinking comrades of the West are straying from the one true path, they are repaid with nothing but cutting remarks about Stalinism.

The "Reformation" Theory

Part of the enthusiasm for Eurocommunism came from the conviction that it offered a Western communism with a human face, capable of Europeanizing communism and also of radicalizing, or even communizing, Western Europe. This is an old Western dream for those who have been earnestly searching for an alternative to capitalism and bolshevism. Eurocommunism titillated many intellectuals who wanted to see in it a mass movement that laid claim to the legacy of European Marxism. They hoped the Eurocommunists would avoid the horrors of the Soviet experience at the same time socialism was created in the West.

The conviction that Eurocommunism might actually represent a solution to the problems of both East and West was not limited to radical intellectuals; it briefly found space on the editorial page of the *New York Times*. At the beginning of July, it explained the Soviet fear of Marchais, Berlinguer, and Carrillo in these terms: "Better a capitalist or socialist adversary who possesses nothing more than NATO bombs than a comrade infected by this dread virus." For the *Times*, then, the NATO countries had only military weapons, while the Eurocommunists had the ideas. The true carriers of the message of democracy were then the Eurocommunists, and not the traditional enemies of communism in the West.

It followed from this that the traditional anti-Communists had no right to attack Eurocommunism, a theme that Tom Wicker developed when he took Secretary of State Henry Kissinger to task for opposing any further advance by the PCI in the upcoming Italian elections:

> What ideology . . . forces Mr. Kissinger to find any and all Communist participation in Western European governments "unacceptable"—even though an Italian government with Communist participation might well

bring that country more prosperity and stability? Is Italian stability good for Western security, or should we prefer continuing economic chaos and political paralysis under the discredited Christian Democrats?

Like the *Times* editorialists, Wicker could see no ideological reason for opposing Eurocommunism; if anything, the ideological arguments seemed to be on the side of the Communists. And since Eurocommunism was taken to be as threatening to the Kremlin as to Washington, it seemed to represent an original solution to the problems of both blocs.

Unhappily, few seemed to remember that Italy had already offered a concept of the "third way" between capitalism and bolshevism, earlier in this century: fascism. And in the late 1920s and early 1930s, many luminaries of the West European intelligentsia were convinced that Mussolini's Fascist revolution had provided a new model for the old continent. They were enthusiastic about the "corporate state," which seemed to avoid the excessive repression and centralized planning of the Soviet system, as well as the licentiousness, greed, and lack of discipline typical of capitalism. That the trains ran on time was taken as evidence of the charisma of the *Duce* and the new spirit of harmony produced by fascism. By the early thirties, Mussolini spoke of exporting the Fascist revolution to the rest of the continent, and even to the United States.[5]

This was "Eurofascism," which culminated in an abortive effort in the early 1930s to create a Fascist international. It was quite different from Nazism, for the Italian-sponsored theory of fascism was largely free of racist doctrine and of the explicitly militaristic and expansionist elements so vociferously advanced by Hitler. Eurofascism had quite broad appeal: it was hailed by Catholics who admired the Concordat and the lack of apparent church-state conflict; by conservatives who applauded the continuation of the monarchy and the traditionalist approach of the regime's chief legal experts; by radicals and even some anarcho-syndicalists who were attracted to the theory of corporatism and to the experiments in the trade union field. Finally, Mussolini received considerable support from avant-garde artists who were excited by the presence of some top futurists in the Fascist ranks.

Eurocommunism attracted a similarly variegated group of supporters. On the one hand, the resort to a Gramscian strategy meant that the most threatening elements of traditional Communist rhetoric were generally absent in Western Europe, and this helped make the Eurocommunists acceptable to the politically moderate middle classes. On the other hand, the repeated calls for a thorough transformation of society and the installation of "real socialism" retained the support of a convinced and militantly Stalinist base. One could therefore pick and choose among the various faces of Eurocommunism; for those who were unable to study the phenomenon at first hand, it was easy to be deceived (indeed, even some of the participants were fooled, at least for a while).

Taking some selected elements of the Eurocommunist rhetoric at first hand, and ignoring those themes that caused them difficulty, many Western academics, politicians, and journalists concluded that the Eurocommunists had decisively embraced Western democratic values, and that Eurocommunism might eventually reform both the Soviet Union and the United States. People holding this view of the world were of course not bothered by the obvious fact that the presence of Eurocommunists in European governments would greatly disturb the United States; this fact was held to be further demonstration of American wrongheadedness. As for the Soviet Union, it was held to be vulnerable to a sort of "reformation": the Eurocommunists were held to menace the Muscovite mother church with a mass schismatic movement. Victor Zorza, one of the most celebrated "Kremlinologists" of the seventies, expressed this theory in its clearest form in the *Washington Post* on June 29, 1977:

> Some European Communists suspect that important forces in the Kremlin might welcome the breakup of the Western Communist movement. Otherwise it might emerge as a cohesive force that could press Moscow to proceed with international political reforms more in keeping with the democratic traditions to which the European Communists lay claim.

Even *Time* magazine, the most careful American periodical on the subject, agreed that "Moscow's deepest concern is probably the possible reverberations that Eurocommunism, if allowed to develop unchecked, might have among the captive regimes of Eastern Europe." According to *Time*, a rampant Eurocommunism would threaten the Kremlin by undermining its ideological control over the satellites, and this in turn would destabilize the East-West balance of power. *Time* thus echoed the warning of the *New York Times* that American support of Eurocommunism might risk insurrection in Eastern Europe (a view reminiscent of the misnamed "Sonnenfeldt doctrine," according to which the United States should encourage the evolution of a more "organic relationship" between the U.S.S.R. and the satellites, in order to prevent dangerous destabilization).

Such warnings were irrelevant to the direction of American policy, for neither the Carter nor the Ford administration was likely to endorse Eurocommunism (although some of Carter's people toyed with a more "open" posture). They recognized that the Communist parties threatened NATO and the political coherence of the Atlantic Alliance, and were thus not inclined to give any positive signals to the Eurocommunists.

This concern for the Atlantic Alliance was not generally shared by the elite American press, nor, for that matter, by the leading European publications. C.L. Sulzberger of the *New York Times*, for example, was quite certain that the Italian Communists were committed to NATO, independent of Moscow, and thoroughly democratic:

> Personally, I have been impressed in long talks with Berlinguer and it seems to me he is being logical when he insists his party wishes at present to continue Italy's membership in NATO. . . .
>
> The reason is that Berlinguer not only believes in developing a different form of socialism—with democratic guarantees—in his country but also recognizes the very real possibility of a Soviet or pro-Soviet putsch in neighboring Yugoslavia some time after Tito's death.
>
> And Berlinguer . . . doesn't fancy the idea of a Soviet or Soviet-puppet neighbor for the independent Italy whose independent future he is now . . . helping to plan.

Sulzberger's colleague at the *Times*, Tom Wicker, went him one better by arguing that the elevation of the PCI to the Cabinet might be a good thing even if it entailed a breakdown in the American alliance system. "If new structures of Western security have to be built or old ones adapted because of European political developments," Wicker speculated, "that may be easier than trying to forestall those developments with American threats and CIA money." In any event, Wicker did not think the PCI was subservient to Soviet foreign policy or aligned with Soviet ideology. And that, in his words, "is one good reason for its increasing acceptability to Italian voters."

I have concentrated on the statements of American journalists, since they are so clear and concise, but similar views were held by the vast majority of American Italianists (particularly those at Harvard University, such as Peter Lange and Stanley Hoffmann, and those at MIT, such as Donald Blackmer and Sidney Tarrow).[6] Furthermore, many members of the PCI, the PCF, and the PCE genuinely believed that their parties were indeed on the verge of a decisive transformation; some of them were enthusiastic, while others opposed this shift, but the conviction was quite widespread. There was a fascinating sort of cross-fertilization of ideas at work in the seventies, as each hint of change from leading Eurocommunists was pounced upon by sympathetic Western observers as evidence that the decisive shift had already occurred, and this in turn intensified the debate within the Communist parties, and between them and the Kremlin. The phenomenon eventually became so complex that many of the participants themselves undoubtedly were confused; indeed, one of the finest (and by far the wittiest) books written about the subject was entitled *l'Italia spiegata al popolo*, "Italy explained to the people."[7]

The Americans

As has been seen, there was considerable sympathy for the Eurocommunists among American intellectuals, based upon their desire to see the success of a Western communism "with a human face." In addition, there was a certain reflexive opposition to the stern anti-Communist pronouncements of Secretary of State Kissinger—a continuation of the intellectuals' opposition to his policies in Vietnam, Chile, and Angola—and a carryover from the debates of a decade before over the Opening to the Left.

The opposition to Kissinger was not only the result of a broad-based criticism of his policies, but also the legacy of McCarthyism. Senator McCarthy's anticommunism not only wreaked direct and terrible havoc on the academic, intellectual, and policymaking communities, but it had the additional long-term effect of discrediting anticommunism for decades to come. In effect, McCarthy deprived anticommunism of intellectual legitimacy, and in cultured American circles in the sixties and seventies, the dominant world view is best described as anti-anticommunism. The liberals, who by the sixties had the greatest weight in the creation of the conventional wisdom for the major newspapers, movies, and radio and television networks, were not inclined to take a strong position against Eurocommunism, as this would have smacked of "reactionary" anticommunism.

These deep-rooted psychological and ideological reflexes help explain the remarkably uncritical treatment accorded Eurocommunism by the American intellectual establishment precisely at the time when investigative journalism and critical analysis of everything done by the American government were at an all-time high. There was virtually no critical investigation of the Eurocommunists. As the Watergate era and the aftermath of Vietnam slowly wound down, the dark warnings of Secretary Kissinger were widely discounted as an unfortunate residue of the Nixon era. Eurocommunism was thus never subjected to the kind of critical analysis reserved for the American president, secretary of state, and their associates.

Finally, there was the legacy of the debates over the Opening to the Left. Many remembered the heated fight over Pietro Nenni and the PSI, and tended to view the discussion of Eurocommunism in the same light. Some of the protagonists in the debate over the "Opening" were still in the bureaucracy in the mid- and late-seventies, and explicitly viewed Kissinger's opposition to Berlinguer, Carrillo, and Marchais as a replay of the stereotypical anticommunism that was aimed against Nenni fifteen years earlier. They argued that just as Nenni had converted to democracy, so could the Eurocommunists. This was the position of Arthur Schlesinger, Jr., who, while agreeing with Kissinger in 1977 that the West European Communists had not magically transmogrified into social democrats, nonetheless maintained that "the rise of Eurocommunism, with its declarations, sincere or fictitious, in favor of a pluralist political system, demonstrates the vitality of the democratic idea."[8] Schlesinger approvingly quoted Prime Minister Andreotti to the effect that the autonomy and independence of individual Communist parties would continue to grow in the West, so long as detente prevailed, and he fully embraced the notion that Eurocommunism threatened the Soviet Union at least as much as it menaced the West.

Similar views came from within the Ford administration itself, and would be picked up and amplified by others, following the inauguration of Jimmy Carter. The Bureau of Intelligence and Research in the Department of State, for example, had several analysts who felt that there were definite tendencies toward autonomy and democracy among the European Communists, and that these tendencies—like those of the Socialists earlier—could eventually produce full-fledged conversions. The CIA was not totally alien to this point of view, as is demonstrated by a secret research study in February 1976 dealing with "Emerging Eurocentrism in the European Left." This document stated that "Italian, French, and Spanish Communist assertions of independence from Moscow and the need for European ways to socialism are particularly troublesome for the Communist party of the Soviet Union and for Soviet state interests in keeping East Europeans in line."

On the question of NATO and the possibilities of East-West conflict, the CIA study was in substantial agreement with the "conventional wisdom" regarding the fundamentally pro-Western allegiances of the Communists, although the agency's analysts took the security problem more seriously than did most of the academics and journalists:

> (The PCI's) position in an Italian government would pose serious security problems for NATO, where the Italians have been members of the Nuclear Planning Group since its inception. Nevertheless, there seems little question that its response to a clearcut test such as a Soviet military invasion of Western Europe would be consistent with the probable reaction of other major European political groupings: a willingness to go along with NATO-ordered military counterattack.

The same tone was present in the responses to NSSM 242 in May 1976, when, just before the Italian elections, the various elements of the bureaucracy were invited to evaluate American policy in the light of a possible electoral triumph by the Italian Communists. The responses suggested that the United States should adopt a "wait and see" attitude if the Communists advanced, unless a government of the Left were formed, or Communists were installed in crucial ministries (like defense). In that unlikely case the Pentagon recommended the immediate withdrawal of nuclear weapons operated by a so-called double key system, and possible adoption of a mild quarantine of Italian officials from high-level NATO meetings, along the lines of the procedures adopted during the Portuguese crisis in the mid-seventies.

Oddly, most of the analyses were based on the conviction that the Italian political scene was relatively stable, and that it would be possible to form a new Center-Left government after the elections. The experts in State, Defense, the intelligence community, and the NSC were inclined to regard the responses to the NSSM as an abstract exercise, since there seemed to be no pending crisis, even if the worst (a PCI victory in the elections) actually occurred. Yet even so, it is surprising that prior to May there were no fully developed contingency plans for relocating the Sixth Fleet or providing for the replacement of the Italian bases if a government hostile to NATO came to power. Indeed, some classified studies in the same year urged consideration of *expanding* American bases in Italy, in the event of possible losses elsewhere (Turkey, for example, where the terrorist wave had reached pandemic proportions).

Although many of the government bureaucrats shared the same attitudes as the majority of the intellectual establishment, the responsibilities of the policy community were quite different (and the policy makers had to account to a secretary of state who held strong views). Accordingly, even those who were quite optimistic about the evolution of the Eurocommunists were reluctant to propose any American "opening" to the far Left. This latter posture remained confined to the pages of publications like the *Nation*, the *New York Times*, the *Washington Post, Foreign Affairs*, and *Foreign Policy*. For policy makers, there was simply insufficient hard information to warrant the conclusion that the entry of the Eurocommunists into their governments would be acceptable to the United States.

The Soviet Union and Eurocommunism

Any discussion of the Soviet Union must begin with the standard caveat: we know quite little about the U.S.S.R., above all about those things we most desperately need to know—how political decisions are made, the relative weight of various individuals inside the Kremlin, basic policy lines, and secret operations. In part this is due to a successful effort by the Soviets to keep such things secret; in part it is the result of our own failure to obtain such information. In the case of Italy, the latter probably accounts for the greatest part of our ignorance.

In the immediate postwar period, we had an enormous volume of information on Soviet activities in Italy, most of it coming from liaison with Italian intelligence services, with some of it the result of the compartmentalized operations run by Angleton and his protégés (notably Ray Rocca). As one might expect, the evaluation of the information obtained in that period varies widely from person to person. In general, those involved in the Angleton/Rocca projects felt that they had excellent information; those in the more traditional sort of liaison and the very limited number of independent operations in the late forties and early fifties, believed that they were being deluged with information of wildly variegated quality. Much of it was considered "smoke," claims of dubious accuracy designed to get the Americans excited and give greater support to Italy.

Since the bulk of the documentation from the late forties and fifties remains classified (and almost everything related to the Angleton operations is either still classified or missing from the files), and since the members of each group tend to remain loyal, one can only report the existence of the conflict without coming to a firm conclusion on the merits of the case. The debate is almost circular: Angleton's supporters claiming that they and only they had access to the *real* information, while their critics argue that if that was so, they still had nothing to show for it, so how good could the information have been?

The debate (which did not end even when the two most famous protagonists—Angleton and Colby—retired from public life) concerns the forties and fifties, for once the sixties began, the CIA's entire method of operation in Italy was changed. By that time, whatever remained of the Angleton network had been closed down, and the CIA's operations were centered in official structures, run through the embassy in Rome and the various consulates around the country. Under the direction of Tom Karamessines, for the first time since the war, the CIA in Italy (or at least that part of it that reported back to Washington through the normal channels) determined to collect its *own* information and even conduct some of its own operations, because the top officials of the agency had concluded that the quality of information obtained through normal liaison was so poor that some additional work needed to be done.

As for the earlier period, it is hard to assess the quality of the information gathered through the new methods. On the one hand, it is known that the CIA managed to recruit some members of the PCI, so that the American government no longer had to depend upon second-hand sources for information about the Italian Communists. On the other hand, some of the most active "players" in the Italian game in Washington—like Arthur Schlesinger—knew very little about the PCI, were not worried about the infiltration of Communists in the PSI and other parties, and did not care much about the clandestine PCI apparatus. Thus, even if the information from Italy had been spectacularly good (and it probably wasn't; it is almost impossible for a new program to generate outstanding results right away), it would have been difficult to change the minds of the policy advocates in Washington.

By the seventies, information about the internal operations of the PCI was quite sparse. There were only three full-time CIA men in the Rome station assigned to the PCI, and this was hardly sufficient to cover such a complex phenomenon in a time of rapid change. Above all, given the traditional lack of information from the Soviet bloc, the Americans were poorly placed to evaluate the relationship between the Kremlin and Berlinguer's party.

The situation was much the same in France and Spain, although there was a significant political difference between these countries and Italy. In Rome, the Communist bandwagon had advanced to the point where even intelligence officials were compelled to tailor their reporting to the possibility that Communist leaders might soon be "consumers" of the "intelligence product." In other words, an intelligence professional who came down hard on the PCI might find himself in deep political trouble in relatively short order; the tendency throughout the seventies was to tread lightly (hence information damaging to the Communists was hard to come by, both for the American government and for American journalists). In Paris and Madrid, on the other hand, there was little likelihood that the Communists would in the short term achieve such power, and hence many governmental officials subjected the Communists to intense surveillance. The political differences can be easily seen by the sorts of books and articles that appeared in the mid-seventies. In Italy, most books on communism were sympathetic to the PCI; in France and Spain, a series of shocking revelations about the Communists came out, one after another.[9] These ranged from confessions of Spanish Communists about the role of Santiago Carrillo during the civil war to investigative works in France about the secret finances of the PCF and the role of the Soviet bank in Paris.

It was easier to evaluate the state of relations between the French and Spanish Communists, on the one side, and the Kremlin on the other, than it was to evaluate the PCI-Kremlin relationship. But this fundamental question remained fuzzy throughout the seventies and into the eighties. The Spanish press announced that some 200 cadres from the Spanish *comissiones obreras* had been sent to East Germany for training in the autumn of 1978,[10] thus suggesting that the feud between the PCE and the Kremlin might have been somewhat less intense than advertised, but there were many, both within and outside the Spanish Communist party, who believed that the chasm between Carrillo and Moscow could no longer be bridged. In other words, even in the cases when relatively more was known, the question of Soviet control over the Eurocommunists remained unanswered. It was clear that it was more difficult for Brezhnev to give orders to Berlinguer than it had been for Stalin to command Togliatti, but what were the limits on Berlinguer's actions? And what were the methods that Brezhnev used to underline his points? Clearly, money played a major role, but were the Western parties not drawing on growing independent sources of income? And to what extent could the Kremlin turn the financial spigot on and off? Finally, there was the question of command, control, and communication. In the forties and fifties, the Soviets installed command structures within the European parties, wherein Communists loyal to the Kremlin guaranteed the obedience of the local party members. Were there still such groups? If not, were individuals within the Eurocommunist parties assigned the tasks previously performed by the likes of Anna Pauker in the PCF? The Americans could not answer these questions with any confidence. The analysis of Eurocommunism was therefore primarily a political one.

It might still have been possible to obtain more illuminating information about the European Communists if the local intelligence services had been more aggressive, or if the CIA had been capable of mounting a major effort to gather more intelligence. But by the most reliable accounts, neither was possible. First of all, many of the European agencies were plagued by problems: the Germans found again that they had been infiltrated by Soviet agents at a high level; the Italians were in the midst of a long period of self-inflicted wounds and self-destruction (actively encouraged by the PCI) that eventually rendered them almost impotent by the time of the Moro disaster in 1978; the French, under Alexandre de Marenches, alternated between brilliant operations and ham-handed embarrassments; and the British, who generally had the most reliable European intelligence service, were fairly effective but lacked the manpower to take up the slack.

Most important of all, the crisis of the CIA—and particularly the spectacular leaks of classified information to the press—inevitably reduced the quantity of information at the disposal of the American government. Sources were reluctant to take risks on behalf of a government that was palpably unable to keep secrets. The same held true for foreign intelligence services; they began to withhold some sensitive information from the Americans, fearing it might become public.

The basic assessment of Eurocommunism was therefore based on less than satisfactory intelligence, but even so the view of American policy experts during the Nixon and Ford administrations was quite different from that presented by so many in the media, the bureaucracy, and academia. Kissinger and his closest associates did not accept the notion that the Eurocommunists would be tolerable members of NATO governments. Unlike the critics of anticommunism, those at the highest level of the American government (including most of the Carter people as well) refused to take Communist rhetoric at face value, and looked at four fundamental ingredients of Eurocommunism that were clearly hostile to American interests:

First, the internal organization of the parties, known as "democratic centralism." To be sure, none compared with those of Eastern Europe, China, Southeast Asia, and Cuba in rigidity and ruthlessness, but there were few signs of any genuine democratic evolution. And, as has been seen, when a handful of PCI leaders tried to challenge the Leninist organization of the party in the winter of 1976, they were quickly headed off, and no basic changes were made.

Second, while Berlinguer, Marchais, and Carrillo used a Western vocabulary, their words didn't have the same meanings that they did for democratic politicians. The definition of "pluralism" offered by the PCI was a typical example:

> Pluralism can not be reduced to an abstract democratic game as an end in itself. It is entirely legitimate for a party which is the bearer of new social and ideal values to pursue the route toward hegemony based on consensus and which aims, not at a recurring alternation of progressive and conservative governments, but toward the historic goal of the transformation of society.[11]

Third, the Eurocommunist parties remained closely attached to the purse strings of the Kremlin, both through direct subsidies and a variety of import-export and consulting operations with the Soviet bloc and Soviet allies in the Third World.

Finally, there were no major deviations from what Berlinguer described to the London *Times* as the "peace policies of the Soviet Union." This was of course the point that most concerned the Americans, because it meant that Communists, even Eurocommunists, wanted to shift the foreign policies of their countries in a direction hostile to American interests.[12]

All of this did not mean that the Eurocommunists were viewed as puppets of the Kremlin, as hopelessly and forever totalitarian, or unalterably opposed to American interests. There were certainly French, Italian, and Spanish Communists who were anti-Soviet, and many others who wished to be truly independent of the Kremlin and even free of the Leninist totalitarianism that governed the internal affairs of their party. But it was one thing to accept the good intentions of some individual Communists; it was quite another matter to believe that the parties themselves had crossed the line from East to West, and could be reliable partners in a Western alliance against the Soviet empire. In the event, the American policy makers were right, and the intellectuals wrong, for in the one significant test—the open conflict between Santiago Carrillo and Soviet spokesmen in 1976-77—the three leading Communist parties of Western Europe failed to demonstrate either their independence from the Kremlin or any internal coherence among themselves.

The Reformation Betrayed: Carrillo vs. the Kremlin

The litmus test for the Eurocommunists took place in June 1976, and was followed by three other important events: the "Eurocommunist summit" in Madrid the following March, a meeting between Berlinguer and Marchais in late April, and the visit of a three-man PCI delegation to Moscow in July. During this period, only Carrillo undertook a systematic criticism of the U.S.S.R., and Carrillo alone was censured by the Kremlin.[13]

If there was a moment at which one could have reasonably spoken of Eurocommunism, that came at the Berlin Congress of all (East and West) European Communist parties in June 1976. At that time the Soviet Union grudgingly announced its acceptance of the principle that all Communist parties should be free to pursue their own national strategies toward socialism. Yet oddly enough, Carrillo himself called Eurocommunism "an unfortunate idea, which doesn't exist," and his West European comrades were not supportive of Carrillo's call for strongly independent national strategies (Flora Lewis of the *New York Times* noted that the Spanish leader "went well beyond what the Italians and . . . French have been saying").

Carrillo's statements in Berlin—later reinforced in his book *Eurocommunism and the State*[14]—challenged both the Soviets and the other Eurocommunists. The Soviets were disturbed by Carrillo's claim that Moscow could no longer function as the Vatican of the international Communist church, and by his call for each party to develop its own doctrine in keeping with its national traditions. The French and Italian Communists were alarmed as well, for the Spaniard threatened to back them into a corner where they might be forced to choose, immediately, between continued harmony with the Kremlin and the assertion of Western values that would strain relations with the mother church. Carrillo, perhaps inadvertently, called the bluff of the French and Italians, for if they were truly independent of the Kremlin, did they not have to perform a self-analysis similar to what Khrushchev had done in the Soviet Union? None of the three parties (including the PCE, for that matter) was willing to undertake such a profound self-reappraisal. Indeed, to this day, not one of the three has ever published Khrushchev's "secret speech" about the horrors of Stalin's regime. As Enzo Bettiza has written:

> Carrillo took the step that neither Berlinguer nor Marchais wanted to take. He said, in clear terms, that which they don't want to say: true socialism must now be created in the West in opposition to, and not by imitation of that false socialism that has endured for more than half a century in Russia.[15]

To what extent was Carrillo really determined to break with the Kremlin? Unfortunately, we still do not know very much about the secret relations between the PCE and Moscow during the long period of Franco's dictatorship, when the Spanish Communist party was a totally clandestine organization. Only some bits and pieces of Carrillo's activities are known, and some of this information was provided by Ion Mihai Pacepa, the former deputy director of the Rumanian Intelligence Service, when he defected to the United States in 1978. Pacepa knew Carrillo well, because Carrillo kept a considerable quantity of the PCE's funds in Rumanian banks (the rest was largely in French accounts in Paris), and he spent long periods of time in Rumania, where his favorite doctor lived. Many Spaniards were trained in Rumania as well, and this suggests that Carrillo's independence of the Kremlin was of the same sort as Ceausescu's: that is to say, motivated more by personal ambition than by any fundamental ideological divergence. While Ceausescu has certainly made life difficult for the Soviets in his country, his basic loyalties to communism and to Soviet foreign policy objectives are not in doubt; the same may be true of Carrillo.

In any event, Carrillo was the best-placed of the three Latin Communist leaders to launch a campaign for autonomy, for his was the smallest party, and the most tightly disciplined as a result of the decades of clandestinity. He had none of the problems of the mass party that Marchais and Berlinguer had to deal with, and, as the *Economist* noted, Carrillo's Leninist control of the PCE made it possible for him to quickly alter the party line and have the change unanimously approved.[16]

Marchais and Berlinguer could not reject Carrillo, for his critique of Soviet socialism was a commonplace in Western Europe. To brand him a heretic would have meant identifying themselves with Soviet ideology, yet to embrace him would have risked excommunication. The French and Italians would have undoubtedly preferred a middle course, but this was doomed by the events of 1976-77.

Shortly after the Berlin Congress, the Soviet Union began to apply pressure throughout the Communist world. First of all, the Soviet press stressed that nothing fundamental had been given away by the Kremlin at Berlin. Ideological fundamentalists like Suslov and Ponomarev wrote that the Soviet Union remained the pole star for the European Communist parties, and that proletarian internationalism—the code phrase for Soviet domination—remained operational. Hardly a mention was made of the two concessions granted by Brezhnev: autonomous paths toward socialism, and toleration of some criticism of the Soviet model. Within the bloc, Soviet strategy was to claim that nothing had happened. Indeed, Brezhnev claimed a success in holding the congress at all.

Outside the Iron Curtain countries, the Russians encouraged a return to the old line. Throughout the fall and winter, various hard-liners were dispatched on speaking tours to Rome and Paris, where they announced that Eurocommunism did not exist, that the old rules still applied, and that any criticism of the U.S.S.R. was anti-Sovietism. These visits clearly embarrassed the Latin leaders, but there was no formal rebuttal. And in February, Berlinguer told a national television audience in Italy that there would be no ideological break between his party and the Kremlin.

All of this was a continuation of previous patterns of behavior. Beginning in the summer of 1975, the Russians had both tolerated the carefully phrased claims of relative independence from the French and Italians and issued stern warnings against these tendencies. The Soviet ideologist Konstantin Zarodov had criticized the tactic of alliances with the bourgeoisie (a criticism directed against both Marchais and Berlinguer), recalling Lenin's pamphlet *The Two Tactics* of seventy years before. But there was little in the way of an open break, and for good reason: the PCI's strategy had brought about the greatest success story in the history of West European communism, and the PCF's design to reenter the French government after nearly thirty years in opposition held considerable promise. Unless there were a pressing reason to do so, the U.S.S.R. was probably willing to wait and see.

The pressing reasons arrived in the second half of 1976 and the first months of 1977. In the first place, the tone of the Eurocommunist rhetoric changed with the publication of Carrillo's book (early 1977). Even in the best circumstances, the Kremlin would have had to respond forcefully to this challenge, and there were now other reasons for a strong reaction. Brezhnev's policies were in trouble on several fronts: his efforts to convince Tito to modify his opposition to the Soviet Union and reenter the international Communist fold had failed; the months following the East Berlin Congress had not seen a warming of relations with the West European Communists; and finally, Jimmy Carter had announced his human rights campaign. This last produced a remarkable internal reaction: the Soviets were convinced that Carter was determined to bring about an uprising against their rule, and the KGB was ordered to carry out an intensive investigation of the Soviet empire to find out which groups had been organized by the White House. From Moscow's vantage point, the human rights campaign meant that the new administration was changing the rules of detente and returning to a more aggressive posture. This impression was heightened in March, when Secretary of State Vance took new SALT proposals—calling for massive arms reductions—to Moscow. The Soviets therefore girded for a possible return to a Cold War atmosphere.

Thus, the international situation did not permit the Kremlin to coolly wait to see if the electoral gains of the Eurocommunists would match the costs to the Soviets in control and prestige. In addition, there was a small but nevertheless real possibility that some of the Eurocommunists might openly support some of the leading Soviet dissidents, and thus precipitate an internal crisis within the bloc.

An electoral breakthrough by one of the Latin Communist parties would seriously compromise detente, for it would challenge the political coherence of NATO, alarm the West, and in all likelihood provoke an anti-Communist backlash from America to the German Federal Republic. Whatever the prudence of the American administration, the political consequences of an historic compromise in Italy or a government headed by the Union of the Left in France would be quite serious. While the Soviet Union might conceivably be inclined to take such a risk in the case of Italy—where entry of the PCI into ministries in Rome might prove irreversible—it was more risky in France, where the PCF was the junior partner in the Union of the Left, and would remain a distinctly junior partner in a government of the Left, as indeed proved to be the case in the eighties when Mitterrand was elected president of the French Republic. So the victory of the *Union de la Gauche* was probably not worth the risk of an end to detente.

Of course, we do not know the Kremlin's analysis, as we do not understand the degree of control the Kremlin held over the Eurocommunists. In all probability, the major considerations were international: a desire to maintain detente while Soviet power grew steadily, and the determination to put the Communist house in order in the face of what was taken to be a serious ideological challenge from Washington.

The Soviets accordingly mobilized the Communist parties of the bloc, in order to show that nothing had changed in the international Communist movement and to limit the margins of maneuver for the Eurocommunists. But any hope for moderate damage control was dashed by the publication of *Eurocommunism and the State*. Even if Carrillo's opus was a hoax, designed purely to legitimize the PCE in post-Franco Spain, the Soviets had to react. For once, they did so with a certain cunning, waiting until after the 1977 elections before issuing a direct response, in the meanwhile directing their attention to the French and Italians.

Brezhnev had long maintained the distinction between the so-called mature parties—those in a tight Soviet orbit—and the "immature" ones that had to be slowly reintegrated around the Soviet pole. This phraseology was used to indicate Soviet acceptance of the demands for autonomy by some foreign Communist parties, and it permitted Brezhnev to soothe some of the more doctrinaire comrades by increasing control over the bloc.

By early 1977, stronger measures were required for the "immature" Eurocommunists, and Brezhnev first moved to have the "Eurocommunist summit," originally scheduled for February, delayed for a month. In the interim, representatives of the PCF and PCI were summoned to Moscow for consultations. So that when the Eurocommunist delegates arrived for their summit at the Hotel Melia in Madrid in March, they discovered that an "antisummit" had been organized in Sofia, where representatives of the bloc parties were gathered. The effect was immediate: after hasty consultation with PCI "foreign minister" Sergio Segre, Carrillo announced that the Eurocommunists had no intention of creating conflict with "any of our fraternal countries." And the Madrid summit was an anticlimax thereafter. Above all, the document that issued from the Melia begged the central question: the Soviet model of society. Although there was considerable rhetoric about the values of democracy, there was not the slightest indication that this concept was in conflict with the goals for the world Communist movement headed by the Kremlin. The omission was all the more notable because it was known that Carrillo had prepared an explicit reference to the failure of the Soviet Union to achieve full democracy. As Frane Barbieri wrote in *il Giornale* after the summit:

> If the missing part was not written it means that there does not exist a model of that which should be global application of Eurocommunism. If the missing paragraph was cancelled, the fact can only be attributed to a concession to Soviet pressure. The three leaders deny it; however, it is nonetheless true that the most critical and aggressive formulations prepared by Carrillo, dealing precisely with dissent and the regime existing in the East, were suppressed following the French and Italian contacts with Moscow.[17]

The toughest paragraph in the final declaration was a call for the integral application of all elements of the Helsinki Final Acts by all governments. The spokesmen for the Eurocommunists let it be understood that this was actually a criticism of the Soviet bloc for its maltreatment of dissidents. But such obscure references to Soviet repression hardly added credibility to the claims of the Eurocommunists to have achieved independence from the Soviet Union, or to have fully embraced democratic values.

There were even some tense moments between the Eurocommunist leaders themselves, as when Marchais remarked that Spain was still far from democracy, a line that prompted Carrillo to rally to the defense of Spanish President Adolfo Suarez. And Berlinguer took pains to observe that there had been no major step forward toward the creation of increased coordination and cooperation between the three parties. In short, the summit fell far short of expectations, and was a tribute to Soviet pressure.

This was only the beginning of the Soviet offensive. Immediately following the Sofia conference, Konstantin Katuschev, CPSU secretary in charge of relations with ruling foreign Communist parties, was removed from his post and assigned to deal with relations with the Comecon countries. His job was assigned to Boris Ponomarev, one of the most rigid and aggressive of the old Stalinists. And Ponomarev immediately convened a meeting of the secretaries of seventy-eight Communist parties in Prague at the end of April, at which time he reminded his comrades that proletarian internationalism was the basic criterion for the legitimacy of Communists throughout the world. "The testing ground of each of the elements of the Communist movement," he said in Prague, "is its relationship with the Russian Communist party."

At the same time, Marchais and Berlinguer were meeting in Rome, and before their session Ponomarev's right-hand man, Vladimir Zamyatin, stopped off in Rome for a conversation with Berlinguer. The results, once again, were satisfactory to the Kremlin: nothing but vague homilies came from the Berlinguer-Marchais dialogue. This established a pattern for the year. Whenever pressed on the basic question of whether "true socialism" existed in the Soviet Union, Marchais and Berlinguer always answered in the affirmative. Berlinguer went on national television more than once to assure the Italians that there would be no break with the Kremlin, and in the early spring the Italians were forced to swallow a heavy-handed interference in Italian internal affairs by the Soviet Union.

Every two years the Venice *Biennale* is devoted to a specific theme; in 1975 it was focused on "fascist Chile," and received considerable favorable attention from the PCI and from Soviet "cultural commentators." In 1977, the Socialist leaders scheduled a *Biennale* devoted to "cultural dissidents in Eastern Europe." The Soviets were irritated at this, and had quietly lobbied against the *Biennale* for over a year. The PCI had also criticized the choice of theme, and since there were Communists on the board of the *Biennale*, they were able to slow down the initiative. The result was that the Communists were able to attack the *Biennale* on the grounds of poor preparation.[18]

The Soviets, however, were not content with this rear-guard action, and preferred a direct assault. In early March, the Soviet ambassador to Italy formally asked the Italian government to have the program cancelled. The Foreign Ministry passed the request to the *Biennale*'s president, the Socialist Carlo Ripa de Meana, who promptly resigned in protest. In the debate that followed, not a single Communist leader criticized the Soviets for this interference in Italian affairs. The celebrated "liberal" Communist mayor of Rome, the art historian Carlo Giulio Argan, asked whether it was necessary to stage a "Solzhenitsyn parade" in Venice, while others simply condemned the initiative on grounds of anti-Sovietism.

By July, it was clear that the PCI would neither support Carrillo in his now open fight with the Kremlin, nor voice moral encouragement for the East European dissidents. In an interview with *Der Spiegel* on July 11, Gian Carlo Pajetta was asked whether the Eurocommunists encouraged dissent in the bloc, and he replied with characteristic bluntness: "First of all, these movements in the East bloc are not really relevant political forces. They are symptoms of uneasiness. We very much hope the governments in the East will implement what they are promising."[19]

Paradoxically, the most pro-Soviet and Leninist of the three Eurocommunist parties, the PCF, was the most supportive of the bloc dissidents. Marchais, who clearly had no intention of either introducing greater democracy into the party or challenging Soviet "socialism," actively supported individual dissidents (such as Leonid Plyutsch) to reach the West. Thus, Paris retained its historic reputation as a sanctuary for political exiles.

The Soviet Offensive

With the French and Italians in line, and the Spanish elections over, the Kremlin could now move directly against Carrillo. Marchais having announced that there was no Eurocommunist "movement," and Berlinguer having refused to endorse Carrillo's claim that genuine democratic socialism could only come from the West, the Spanish leader was exposed to the direct Soviet ideological offensive. His position was further weakened by a surprisingly poor showing of the PCE in the Spanish general elections in June. After preelectoral polls predicting as much as 25 percent of the popular vote for the Spanish Communists, the party got a meager 9 percent. Carrillo could thus be denounced both as an ingrate and a failure.

In a series of articles in the Soviet publication *New Times*, Carrillo was excoriated as anti-Soviet, a divisive element in the Communist world and an asset to bourgeois forces. The Soviets took pains to stress that this attack was not directed against "other fraternal parties," and the Soviet publication complained about attempts in the Western press to portray the conflict as one between the Kremlin and all the Eurocommunists. Carrillo was further condemned as a man who had not given a single speech in which he had not attacked the U.S.S.R., the CPSU, "the Soviet Communists and the Soviet people in general."[20]

But while the Kremlin was careful to exclude Marchais and Berlinguer from its assault, it was clear to everyone that the Soviet Union was laying down the law to all of the Eurocommunists. In the past, the Soviets had permitted the French and Italians to carve out a certain autonomy for themselves without challenge, but in the face of the rejection by Tito, the failure of the soft line in Africa, and the menacing words from Washington, the PCI and PCF were forced to choose between the apostasy of Carrillo and the rigorous Moscow line.

The situation was particularly painful for the PCI, which was entitled to believe that it could shortly achieve a share of national political power if only it were left undisturbed. But Berlinguer could only succeed in the context of detente between the superpowers, for any direct challenge to his party from Moscow or Washington threatened his delicate tightrope act. In early July, the PCI sent a small delegation to Moscow to discuss the situation with the Soviet trinity of Suslov, Zagladin, and Ponomarev. Once again, all parties repeated the ritual statement that the Soviet attack was directed solely against Carrillo (or, in some variations, against Carrillo's *book*), and that there were no fundamental conflicts between the U.S.S.R. and the two other Latin parties. The Italians subsequently added a few private complaints about the tone of the Soviet criticisms of Carrillo, and authorized the publication of the Italian edition of *Eurocommunism and the State* by the official party publishing house. But on the important question, Carrillo was left to hang. There was no word of support for the theses of the Spaniard, and no protest against the content of the Soviet criticism.

Carrillo fully appreciated what had happened; as he told a friend in Madrid, "Berlinguer ha fallado" (Berlinguer failed to act).[21] Until that moment, Carrillo seems to have believed that the Italians would eventually give him at least some support. He had told friends in Madrid that the PCI and PCF had been unable to defend him earlier because the Soviets were so concerned about Carter's human rights campaign. But by summer, he thought, the situation was calmer and he expected Berlinguer to express his true feelings.

It is not known what Berlinguer's true feelings were, but his eloquent silence was undoubtedly the politically wise statement for the Italian leader. He could not survive the kind of criticism that the Kremlin had directed against Carrillo; that would have produced an internal crisis that would threaten any further political gains by the PCI. So there would be no break with the Kremlin, no West European alternative to Soviet Communism. The only meaningful link between the French, Spanish, and Italian Communists remained—communism.

The End of the Myth

Over the eight-ten years since the vogue of Eurocommunism, events have effectively demolished the high expectations that so many people held. It is important to recognize that some of the most fervent believers in the new gospel of Eurocommunism were themselves members of the Latin Communist parties, men like Sergio Segre of the PCI (excluded from the official slate for the Chamber of Deputies in the 1979 elections) and Jean Ellenstein in France (isolated by Marchais after his criticisms of the PCF line after the defeat of the Union of the Left in 1978). One of the most eloquent of these men is Carlo Galluzzi of the PCI, who was in charge of the foreign relations of the party for eight years, from 1962 to 1969. Galluzzi's criticism of the Soviet Union, as early as 1968, was every bit as pointed as Carrillo's, and his memoirs show the frustration of a man who tried without success to move his party firmly into the Western world. Reflecting on the repression of *Solidarnosc* in Poland in December 1981, Galluzzi wrote:

> Above and beyond the errors of the ruling group ... there were however more profound causes, tied to the structure of the regime itself, and to the model of society that it was attempting to install. That model, and the ideas that underlay it, were mechanically imported from the Soviet Union of the Stalinist period at the end of the Second World War. That created a contradiction between the structures of the regime and the reality of the country, opening an abyss between the political society and civil society, between institutions and the popular masses.
>
> But they not only imported a model that was extraneous to the true reality of the country ... they imported an obsolete model that already showed signs of a disastrous involution.[22]

Galluzzi believed that the PCI finally embraced its European vocation with its condemnation of the Polish repression, but subsequent events have not demonstrated this. Indeed, in the winter of 1985-86, the Italian Communist most closely linked to moderate social policies and to the West European trade union movement, Luciano Lama, was soundly defeated in a debate over economic policy. So violent were the condemnations of Lama by other party leaders that even some sympathetic observers wrote of the Stalinist methods of the PCI:

It may be that some day there will be a genuine change in the soul of the PCI or some other European Communist party, but if and when that happens it will not be necessary to put the subject under a microscope to discover it; the change will be so clear that it will be impossible to misunderstand the phenomenon. Until then, professions of new faith must be treated with extreme scepticism, as a mixture of self-deception, political convenience, and outright manipulation.

Perhaps the silliest of the myths about Eurocommunism was the "Reformation Theory." According to this view, the U.S.S.R. feared Eurocommunism because of the appeal it offered to the Communists in Eastern Europe. Thus, Carrillo, Berlinguer, and Marchais might inspire the bloc countries to demand greater independence from Moscow. The theory was patronizing to the East Europeans, who hardly needed the Eurocommunists to tell them that life would be better without Soviet tanks in their cities and without Soviet censors blocking the pursuit of truth. Furthermore, as events demonstrated, the Eurocommunists had no stomach for a challenge to the Soviet system, even without the Red Army in their streets. As Enzo Bettiza has wisely observed, "If this Eurocommunism, that seems inhibited by a castration complex with regard to its father, does not manage to support even the 'legitimate dissent' of a Carrillo, what kind of support will it ever be able to give to the 'illegitimate dissent' of a Sakharov?"[23]

We may never know the full story of the real relations between the Eurocommunists and the Soviet Union, but if we could gain access to the archives of the Kremlin we might well discover that the mid-seventies resembled the immediate postwar period more than we suspect. When Togliatti and Thorez returned from exile at the end of the Second World War, they understood what Stalin expected of them: no insurrection, a policy of tranquilizing the Americans, cooperation with all "democratic" elements in their countries, steady infiltration of the national institutions and of the rival parties of the Left. Communist access to power was to be gradual, in keeping with the needs of Soviet foreign policy and domestic requirements in Italy and France. But this strategy was suddenly and violently transformed at the Polish meeting where the Cominform was created.

The drastic shift in line took place against the background of several changes in the national and international arenas. The Communists had been removed from the governments of France and Italy, and the United States had adopted a policy of aggressively challenging Soviet expansion. And while the French and Italian Communists believed that their exclusion from government was only temporary (a belief that may well have been encouraged by the Kremlin for a short time), the Soviets were more realistic. They knew that a return of the Communists to government in Western Europe would not take place for a long time.

A similar situation may have existed in the mid-seventies, as the Soviets tried to evaluate the new Carter administration. At first, prior to the inauguration, there was a phase of optimism, when it appeared Carter would be far "softer" than Ford or Nixon. Then came the alarm that followed the double-barreled initiatives on human rights and SALT. Finally, they discovered that Carter had no intention of seriously challenging the continued expansion of Soviet power.

The Eurocommunists may have been trapped in the switches, the victims of a misunderstanding on the part of the Soviets and a confused policy from Washington. To anticipate the argument of the final chapter, most West Europeans were convinced that Carter would be far more open-minded to phenomena such as Eurocommunism than his predecessors had been, and thus, that there was a far greater margin for political experimentation in Europe than there had been in the recent past. The Communists were encouraged to believe that a continuation of the "soft" Togliattian strategy would produce favorable results in the fairly short term.

But this evaluation ran headlong into the Soviet panic in early 1977, and at the very moment that the Eurocommunists were convincing themselves that the American veto was falling, the Soviets were preparing for a new Cold War with Jimmy Carter. The prime victim of this conflict in analysis was Santiago Carrillo, who probably wrote *Eurocommunism and the State* under the illusion that Eurocommunism would be acceptable to Washington if only the Communists put sufficient distance between themselves and the Kremlin. But such a tactic could only work in the context of detente (or, to put it differently, if the Soviets could sit long enough to let the tactic bear fruit). Once the atmosphere changed, Carrillo could no longer sustain his position either with the Soviets or with the Americans.

His last chance came in the autumn of 1977, when Carrillo visited both capitals. True to his basic conviction that he could obtain some legitimacy from the United States, he played his final cards. During the celebrations of the Bolshevik Revolution, he deliberately arrived too late for his prepared remarks to be delivered as scheduled. When the Soviets refused to change the schedule for the following day, Carrillo complained about censorship and left the Soviet Union in righteous indignation. The following month he travelled to the United States, where he fully expected something to happen that would indicate at least some sort of American acceptance of Eurocommunism. He was not entirely clear in his own mind about the form this American gesture might take, but he was quite certain it would occur. When his visit passed without any such act, it was finally clear that American policy had not changed. Henceforth there was nothing to do but mend his fences with Moscow (insofar as this was possible), and revert to a long-term strategy.

There is no way to be certain of this analysis, but it has the merit of calling attention to one of the central ingredients of the "Communist question" in Western Europe: it must always be analyzed in the context of both Soviet and American foreign policies. And just as Stalin's tactics in the forties were based on repeated misunderstandings of American intentions, so those of Brezhnev, Berlinguer, Marchais, and Carrillo thirty years later were undoubtedly the fruit of misconceptions about Carter's world view.

Notes

1. Speech by Henry Kissinger, *cit.*
2. Cf. also Pelisik's comments on the tenth anniversary of the Soviet invasion of Czechoslovakia in *il Giornale nuovo*, 3 August 1978.
3. Frane Barbieri, interviewed by Manfred Steinkuhler in *Deutschland Archiv* (Cologne, April 1977).
4. The quotations are from the *New York Times*, the *Washington Post*, and the *Christian Science Monitor*. For a lengthier discussion, see Michael Ledeen, "The 'News' about Eurocommunism," in *Commentary*, October 1977. This article contains the quotations below from the *New York Times*, the *Washington Post*, Tom Wicker, Victor Zorza, and C.L. Sulzberger.
5. Cf. Michael A. Ledeen, *Fascismo Universale; the theory and practice of the Fascist International* (New York, 1978). The Italian edition was done by Laterza & Figli (Bari and Rome): *L'internazionale Fascista*.
6. Cf. Donald L.M. Blackmer and Sidney Tarrow, eds., *Communism in Italy and France* (Princeton, 1975); Peter M. Lange, "What is to be done—about Italian Communism," in *Foreign Policy* (Vol. 21, #2, 1975); Stanley Hoffman, *Primacy or World Order* (New York, 1978).
7. Gianfranco Piazzesi, *L'Italia Spiegata al Popolo* (Milan, 1977). This wonderful book is one of the few analyses of a deadly serious subject written with a splendid sense of humor.
8. The quotation is from an article in the *Wall Street Journal*. For a longer discussion, see Arthur M. Schlesinger, Jr., "Eurocommunism and Detente," in *Current* (October 1977).
9. In France, for example, there was Jean-Francois Revel's *La Tentation Totalitaire*, Jean Montaldo's *Les Finances du PCF* and his *Les Secrets de la Banque Sovietique en France*, and the exposes of the PCF by Daix, Robrieux, and others. Interestingly, when Italian Communists wanted to write critically of the PCI, they often did it in France, as in the case of Maria A. Macciocchi (*Apres Marx Avril*, whose introduction contains a devastating attack on the PCI's efforts to spike the Italian edition). This general rule of going outside Italy to state ideas unpopular among PCI leaders was also followed by Macciocchi's husband, Alberto Jacoviello, who wrote an article sympathetic to Mao in *Le Monde*. He was harshly criticized by the party in Italy.
10. And *Cambio 16* ran an exhaustive series on the KGB's financial activities in Spain in virtually every issue of the magazine in October, November, and December, 1978.

11. Cited in Bettiza, *op. cit.*, 104-105.
12. Cf. Michael Ledeen, "Italian Communism: the Soviet Connection," *cit.*
13. The best treatment of Carrillo's dispute with the Kremlin is in Frane Barbieri's articles in *il Giornale nuovo* and in Bettiza, *op. cit.*, 166 ff.
14. *Eurocomunismo y Estado* (Barcelona, 1977).
15. Bettiza, *op. cit.*, 119.
16. This very important point—that Communist parties are able to shift their positions with a speed and unanimity unthinkable in democratic parties, precisely because of the undemocratic nature of the Communist organizations—was often overlooked in the general confusion of the mid-seventies.
17. Frane Barbieri in *il Giornale nuovo*, 5 March 1977.
18. Cf. Michael Ledeen, "Eurocommunists Exposed," in *The New Republic*, 26 March 1977, and Marcello Staglieno in *il Giornale nuovo*, 6 March 1977.
19. Things reached such a level of passion that the president of the Biennale, the Socialist Carlo Ripa de Meana, said "after the menacing Soviet protest, carrying out the Venice Biennale this year as it was planned, that is, dedicated to dissent in the East, is a question of national sovereignty. It is a matter of establishing who's in charge here. . . ."
20. Carrillo responded, "what a shame they didn't attack me before the elections; I'd have gotten more votes." Cf. the articles by Frane Barbieri in *il Giornale nuovo*, 25 and 28 June, 4 and 7 July.
21. Barbieri in *il Giornale nuovo*, 7 July.
22. Carlo Galluzzi, *La Svolta* (Milan, 1983), 256.
23. Bettiza, *op. cit., 126.*

7

The Question of American Policy

> *Although at the present time Eurocommunism is meeting with resistance chiefly on the part of the Right, I believe it can only really be overcome from the Left. A new ideology that succeeded in striking a balance between freedom and security and made its basis the inviolability of human rights would mean the end of the ideology of communism.*
> —Andrei Amalrik, 1977

The Carter administration that took office in late January 1977 was determined to revise the bases of American foreign policy. The president's top advisers—above all, Secretary of State Cyrus Vance and National Security Advisor Zbigniew Brzezinski—believed that Henry Kissinger's approach to international affairs was morally bankrupt and a practical failure. Regarding "Eurocommunism," the objections to Kissinger's approach were basically three:

First, the blanket veto on the entry of Communist parties into West European governments was considered unduly conservative, based on a desire to maintain the status quo at all costs. The Carter people thought of themselves as more "progressive" than the Kissinger group, and openly preferred parties further to the Left. Thus, Carter and his top advisers considered the European status quo a failure; their basic sympathies lay with the opposition parties in many countries. They had little sympathy with the views of leaders like Giulio Andreotti in Italy or Adolfo Suarez in Spain. They preferred politically more progressive figures like François Mitterrand in France and Felipe Gonzales in Spain. In Italy, their preferences tended toward the Socialist party, but they recognized that the PSI was a feeble reed (nonetheless, it was hoped that a more liberal ambassador might help the Italian situation).

Second, the policy of exclusion of all Communists was viewed as both counterproductive and immoral. As candidate Carter put it in his notorious *Playboy* interview: "For (Communist) leaders in countries like Italy,

France, and Portugal, I do not want to close the door of communications, consultations, and friendship. This would mean pushing them almost automatically into the Soviet sphere of influence."[1]

Not only did the veto policy drive the Eurocommunists into the arms of the Soviets, it also—at least in the eyes of the new administration—produced an anti-American backlash, and in some cases actually favored the Communists' advance. It was believed that excessive American fulminations led some Europeans to vote Communist out of spite.

Finally, Kissinger's warnings were considered an unacceptable American interference in the internal affairs of European countries. After years of revelations about presumed CIA illegal activities, the Carter administration was anxious to reassure the public that nothing of the sort would occur under the new president. Henceforth the American government would avoid all such "meddling."

There were actually some—most notably Secretary of State Vance—who believed that the participation of the Eurocommunists in their governments might actually turn out to be a net gain for the United States. Vance told Arnaud de Borchgrave in a *Newsweek* interview two months before the inauguration that the entry of the Eurocommunists might make relations between the U.S.S.R. and Eastern European countries very difficult, while he was not convinced that this event would destabilize the Atlantic Alliance.[2] And candidate Jimmy Carter had told an Italian television interviewer the previous July that if the PCI entered the Italian government, "It would not be a catastrophe. It would not be my choice, but it would not constitute a threat to world peace."[3]

By the time the new president took office, then, he and his leading advisers were on the record with statements that gave the West European Communists every reason to hope that henceforth they would not encounter strong American opposition. And While Carter, Vance, Brzezinski, and the others strove to give the new foreign policy a new image, they evidently failed to consider the effect that the new rhetoric would have. Had they recognized the expectations they raised, they undoubtedly would have taken far greater care with the first official pronouncement on Eurocommunism—on April 6—timed to coincide with the swearing-in of Professor Richard N. Gardner as ambassador to Italy. The State Department stressed that the Communist question had to be decided by the people of the country itself, and not by foreign powers. Hence, "we do not propose to involve ourselves in the process by which they reach their decision." This was the principle of "noninterference," so dear to those who felt Kissinger was improperly active in the past.

However, this did not signify that the United States was neutral on the participation of such parties in the governments of Western Europe. Indeed, the April 6 statement went on to express some doubt that the United States would be able to work in close harmony with other Western governments "if these governments came to be dominated by political parties whose particular traditions, values, and practices are foreign to the fundamental democratic principles and the common interests upon which our relations with Western Europe rest." This was the principle of "nonindifference."

The dual policy of noninterference and nonindifference survived until January of the following year, at which time a more traditional policy was resurrected. And the eventual about-face on Eurocommunism stemmed directly from some of the effects of the original rhetoric. So certain were the Europeans that Carter was basically open-minded about West European communism, that the phrase "governments . . . dominated by political parties" was taken to mean that the new administration was willing to accept Communist *participation*. For several weeks following the statement, the Italian, French, and (to a lesser extent) Spanish press gravely observed that the State Department had spoken only of domination, not of participation. Hence the policy appeared to have shifted dramatically.

The persons who drafted the April 6 statement had of course not intended to make any such subtle distinction; they believed that American opposition to the presence of Communist parties in West European governments was crystal clear. But the confusion was such that the president was forced to spell it out again repeatedly in the next two months, when he constantly took pains to point out that "we prefer that (allied) governments continue to be democratic governments, and that the totalitarian elements do not acquire an influential or dominant role."

It might have been hoped that this formulation would be the last word on the subject, but it was not. Indeed on May 3, just before his departure for the London summit, Carter gave an amazing answer to a European newsman's question:

> Q: What's going to be your attitude if there are someday Communist leaders participating in governments as cabinet members? . . . And how do you see the impact of this question?
>
> Carter: That's a question that is hard for me to answer, and I have got a lot to learn from other leaders of the nations with whom I'll be meeting in London. President Giscard can help me a lot to understand that question. So can Mr. Andreotti. We have taken the basic position that it's not up to us to tell other people how to vote or how to choose their leaders or who those leaders should be.
>
> Secondly, we strongly favor the election of leaders who are committed to freedom and democracy and who are free from Communist philosophy, which quite often has been dominated from the Soviet Union or other nations.[4]

In other words, after more than three months in office, the president had not gotten a handle on the Eurocommunist question. This admission was the result of back-channel communications from both the French and Italian governments, protesting against the confusion from Washington and the apparent readiness of the Carter administration to accept Communist ministers in those two countries. As a result, the National Security Council rejected a "feeler" from French Socialist leader François Mitterrand in May for a trip to Washington, telling his representative (the PSI foreign policy expert, Robert Pontillon) that Mitterrand could not expect to meet with the president or with Vice President Mondale. And in response to Italian complaints that American rhetoric—along with a new policy in issuing visas to foreign Communists—seemed to favor the *compromesso storico* in his country, Premier Giulio Andreotti was invited to Washington for a July meeting.

The West European leaders (particularly West German Chancellor Helmut Schmidt) stressed the importance of this theme at the London summit in May, and Carter returned to Washington with a new sense of resolve. He told a delegation of top congressional leaders that he was seriously worried about the prospect of Eurocommunist participation in allied governments, was determined to prevent this if he could, and was planning to go to France in the autumn to show his support for French President Giscard d'Estaing.

A slow shift in the thinking of the Americans had begun, for the president was prepared to take these steps even though his basic sympathies were with the Socialists. The shift was occurring primarily because of the lessons learned from the likes of Schmidt, Andreotti, and Giscard, and also because it was simply impossible for the American government to support a French Socialist party that had an electoral alliance with the Communists. Nonetheless, the shift was only beginning in May, and there was still a firm commitment to distinguish Carter"s views from those of his predecessors. In particular, the secretary of state and the domestic political advisers felt it was important to give the public the impression that the administration was not going to get involved in worldwide activities to counter Communist thrusts, whether political or paramilitary.

The president accordingly reversed himself again on May 22 in a major foreign policy address at Notre Dame University, where he announced that the United States had lost its "inordinate fear of communism."[5] This seemed to confirm the fears of the Europeans that the president, at a minimum, was far more open to the possibilities of Communist gains than his predecessors had been. And this impression was reinforced by several actions by the new government. First was the support given to the change in visa policy embodied in the McGovern Amendment, reversing the traditional practice on issuing waivers to foreign Communists. Previously such waivers required a specific decision bolstered by supporting evidence, but it was henceforth assumed that the State Department would issue the waiver unless there were an overriding motive to reject the request. This was not a particularly dramatic move, and in practice very few requests had been denied over the years; but the previous policy had made it easier for the government to block potentially embarrassing visits (as in 1976, when PCI foreign policy spokesman Sergio Segre had been invited to speak to the Council on Foreign Relations. He was informed that no visa would be issued and he decided not to apply for one). The change, however, was viewed as a positive gesture toward foreign Communists.

Ironically, there had long been a consensus that the visa policy needed to be changed. Kissinger and Sonnenfeldt both recognized that the real issue was not whether but when to change the regulations, and for the last several years of their tenure this was simply impossible. For the year or two prior to 1975, it was unthinkable, given the events in Portugal. And the great leap forward by the PCI occurred in 1975, thus precluding any American gesture that might look like a policy change vis-à-vis communism.

When McGovern's proposal came early in 1977, it was welcomed by the Carter administration, but they soon discovered that the new visa requirements were a mixed blessing. First of all, the change seemed to confirm a larger pattern of acceptance of European communism, and exposed the administration to attacks from the Right. Secondly, there was considerable opposition from the leaders of the AFL-CIO, who were concerned that visas not be issued to Communists from Eastern Europe posing as "trade unionists." The most intense opposition to the new policy thus came from a sector of the Democratic party that unhesitatingly and enthusiastically supported the president's human rights policy. The Carter team—along with the State Department advocates of a more liberal line—were learning that liberal anticommunism still counted in American political life.

The second shift in emphasis regarded official contacts with Communist parties. Unlike every other Western country, the United States had for many years avoided any contact between American officials and Communist leaders. The practice dated to the Cold War, and was called into question with the increasing liberalization of American political culture in the sixties and seventies. The problem was less ideological than political: having established the "cold shoulder" policy for such a long time, any change would inevitably be viewed as a political gesture in favor of the Communists. For example, had the American government issued a visa to Sergio Segre in the spring of 1976, this would have been widely interpreted as a sign of greater American acceptance of the PCI.

Nonetheless, the Americans were not prepared to cut themselves off from *all* contacts with the European Communists, and starting under Nixon, contacts had gradually been established in Paris, Rome, and Madrid. Working through intermediaries (in one case, an American journalist, in another, an American scholar, in the third, a member of the foreign ministry of the country in question), a single member of the political section of the American embassy was authorized to begin formal and regular conversations with a member of the local Communist party. Begun in the late sixties in France, in 1973 in Italy, and in 1977 in Spain, this was the only known official contact throughout the Kissinger years and the first year of Jimmy Carter, and it did not yield great benefits to either side. In fact, at the very time that Kissinger was being criticized for his unyielding opposition to communism, and the American government was urged to widen contacts, the actual officials involved in the discussions were profoundly disappointed by the attitude of the Communists themselves. The Eurocommunists showed no great enthusiasm for the discussions, rebuffed American suggestions that they might be expanded, and displayed very little interest in enhancing their understanding of America or American policy. The Communists looked at the contacts instrumentally: they wanted an American gesture, not serious discussion.

The hue and cry surrounding the suggestion that the American government should expand its contacts with the Communists finally encouraged the PCI to try something on its own. Supported by then-Prime Minister Francesco Cossiga, the PCI sent a two-man delegation to Washington in the autumn of 1978 to meet with the "secret government" of the United States: a handful of key senators and former top (Republican) administration officials including former CIA officers Ray Cline and William Colby. The two Communists, Napoleone Collajani and Romano Ledda, were preceded by a wave of rumors, all suggesting that the PCI was ready to announce a clean break with the Soviet Union, and to embrace democratic principles.

The trip was a fiasco, first of all because it showed that the PCI had not understood the nature of the American government (there was no deal to be made with the people they saw; although Cline and Colby, along with men like Senator Domenici and former National Security Adviser Brent Scowcroft, were certainly distinguished and influential, they were in no position to make a commitment for the Carter administration).[6] But it succeeded only in embarrassing the two Communists and their supporters, for Ledda and Colajanni simply mouthed variations of the "third force" doctrines of the 1950s. There was no expression of willingness on the part of the PCI representatives to fundamentally alter the party's foreign policy line, no indication of condemnation of Soviet expansionism, and no indication of any basic change in the nature of the party itself.

Nonetheless, throughout the Carter period the American advocates of a more "progressive" stance urged greatly expanded contacts, even if this risked having American behavior exploited by the Communists. In 1976, when Segre was denied a visa, the members of the Council on Foreign Relations, along with Kissinger's former colleagues at Harvard University, roundly denounced the action, even though (or, in some cases, probably *because*) they knew that a Segre trip during the election period would have been construed in Italy as a change in policy, and an American "kiss"—or at least a wink.

If issuing a visa to a foreign Communist leader represented an unacceptable risk of misinterpretation and Communist propaganda exploitation, expanded contacts in Rome, Paris, and Madrid were even more dangerous. Nonetheless, it became an ingredient on the agenda of the new administration. The expectation of those pushing for the change was that the "point man" in this operation would be the new ambassador to Italy, Professor Richard N. Gardner. A distinguished expert in international law, with a long and close association with Italy (his wife came from one of the most famous Italian Jewish families, the Luzzattos), well versed in the language and on close terms with many leading intellectuals and politicians, Gardner seemed perfectly suited to this role. In the months prior to his departure for Rome, there were widespread expectations that Gardner would be far more open than his predecessor (John Volpe). Indeed, so general was this impression that when Gardner made an obligatory protocol call on the Communist President of the Chamber of Deputies, Pietro Ingrao, columnists Evans and Novak in Washington interpreted the event as an "opening to the Communists."[7] Gardner did expand secret contacts with Communists, doing some of it himself, but so long as the contacts remained discreet (and, above all, so long as there was no Communist interest in real dialogue), there was no impact on policy. Indeed, as even the Carter people discovered that no change in the PCI was imminent, enthusiasm for the Eurocommunists dropped markedly. In any event, in addition to the additional contacts, embassy restrictions were eased (American officials did not have to consult all guest lists in advance to make sure no Communists would be present, since it was judged that no disaster would occur if an American met an Italian Communist at a dinner party). On the other hand, the embassy carefully checked a guest list for a luncheon offered by Premier Andreotti in honor of visiting Secretary of HEW Joseph Califano in Rome during Gardner's first year, and cancelled the date when it was discovered that a top Communist had also been invited.

Similar easing of restrictions was implemented by Ambassador Arthur Hartman in Paris, and by Ambassador Wells Stabler in Madrid. In each case the official liaison with the Communist party was a political officer, and no other systematic encounters were established. But casual meetings and chance conversations were permitted.

These changes, in and of themselves, would have been of little moment. Dozens of Communists visited the United States in the first year of the new visa policy, with little impact on America. To be sure, the Communists, particularly in Italy, attempted to use the visits to convince the electorate that American opposition to communism had ended; but the visa policy probably had greater impact on the Christian Democratic leadership (playing the game of appearing to be "soft" on the PCI while encouraging the Americans to be tough) than on the general public. Similarly, the slightly expanded contacts between Communists and the embassies did not permit the Communists to ballyhoo the change. But neither did it produce any benefits for American policy, aside from easing the social requirements for embassy officials.

However, against the background of the various statements by American officials, the new policies added some emphasis to a perceived shift in direction. The leaders of France and Italy thought they saw a new pattern of American behavior, pointing toward greater openness toward Eurocommunism. These European concerns were heightened by the Notre Dame address, especially since it came so soon after a London summit at which Carter had seemingly understood their anxieties and had promised to take appropriate action.

It was for this reason that Kissinger broke his period of self-imposed silence in early June 1977, with a major speech on Eurocommunism, in which he both spelled out his objections to the European Communists and warned of the consequences of continued American incoherence:

> We must avoid giving the impression that we consider Communist success a foregone conclusion by ostentatious association or consultation with Communist leaders or by ambiguous declarations. Communist success is not a foregone conclusion. United States hesitation or ambiguity can, however, contribute to it.[8]

Kissinger saw that American incoherence encouraged the Communists in France, Spain, and Italy, and was attempting to prompt the Carter administration to restate its position in terms everyone would understand. He had discussed his speech with the State Department before delivery, and had avoided any explicit criticism of the new administration. It was therefore possible for State to maintain that there were in fact no substantive differences between the old and new secretaries of state.

This happy superficial unanimity was short-lived. Within a week Secretary of State Vance had told the Washington correspondent of *Il Tempo*,

Marino de Medici, that the entry into government of a Eurocommunist party might be more destabilizing for the Soviet bloc than for NATO. This was dynamite, and *Il Tempo* deleted the passage when they printed the interview,[9] but the State Department later related the full text, thereby giving the Italian Left a glorious opportunity to underline the significance of Vance's peculiar position. For if the Carter administration believed that the progress of Eurocommunism represented a net gain for the West, then there would be little reason for the Americans to fight the Communists.

Ambiguity came from the White House as well. In an October interview with Jonathan Power, printed in the *Washington Post*, [10] Brzezinski said that the very existence of the Eurocommunist parties encouraged "a change in the nature of Communism." Under the circumstances it would be unwise for the United States to interfere in the process, since the Eurocommunists might in time become "symbols of national independence." Brzezinski went on to stress that the United States didn't want these parties to rise to power in Western Europe, but his earlier words reinforced the belief that the Carter administration saw positive elements in Eurocommunism. In the same month Brzezinski told a closed meeting of the Trilateral Commission that the Carter government would be inclined to treat governments with Eurocommunist ministers "without prejudice."[11]

On the other hand, in the October issue of *Reader's Digest* the president himself said that he was deeply concerned about Eurocommunism, and that the entry of such parties into European governments would raise grave concerns about the viability of NATO. To be sure, he added, this did not necessarily mean that the country or countries in question would have to leave NATO, but there would certainly be serious questions about the basic loyalties of at least some of the Communist ministers. This in turn might place at risk some advanced military systems and future military plans.[12]

While Carter and his advisers were pondering the meaning of Eurocommunism, the parties themselves were making steady progress. Carrillo's prestige in Spain was enhanced by the Soviet attack in *New Times* (even though it came too late to help him in the elections). Prior to the sudden and unanticipated crisis within the Union of the Left in France in September, all the polls were predicting a victory in the spring 1978 elections. In Italy, the PCI was moving relentlessly forward, signing a "programmatic accord" with the DC in July. And the Andreotti visit, designed to reassure the Italians about America's unchanged attitude toward communism, instead became an occasion for Andreotti to reassure the Americans that the PCI would not be given ministries without a clear electoral approval from the Italian people.

Andreotti arrived in Washington with a carefully calibrated presentation: after describing the parliamentary balance in Rome, he explained that he was compelled to obtain some support from the PCI in order to govern at all. He did not reiterate what had already been made clear to the American government earlier—that Washington's ambiguities about Eurocommunism were making it more difficult for the Christian Democrats to resist Communist pressure for further concessions. And neither Carter nor his advisers felt it necessary to make any further statements, even though they had recently further clouded the atmosphere with their various remarks.

While it is not known precisely what Andreotti reported to his government and party colleagues in Rome after the trip, it may be presumed that he was convinced that the Americans were willing to tolerate the consequences of their ambiguous position. He had every reason to draw this conclusion: after he had protested the ambiguities, Kissinger had picked up the same theme, and yet the administration had persisted on its course. Was this not a deliberate choice? Was it not possible that the Americans wished to use the Eurocommunists as potential allies in the human rights campaign against the Soviet Union? This would give some sense to Brzezinski's remarks to *Business Week* in early September, when he said that the problem facing the Carter administration was not that of greater or lesser sympathy for communism in Western Europe, but rather the selection of the most effective tactic "both in terms of the internal political framework of the various European countries, and in terms of the impact of Eurocommunism on Eastern Europe and the Soviet Union."[13]

Interestingly, this interpretation probably corresponded to the Soviets', who could not permit the possibility that the Eurocommunists might be enlisted by the West in the campaign on behalf of the dissidents. As has been demonstrated, the Soviet leaders acted to block this possibility throughout the spring of 1977, and moved against Carrillo as soon as it was profitable. But the Italian Christian Democrats might be forgiven for believing that the Americans were pursuing a coherent vision. It was difficult for them to appreciate the real situation: the ambiguity and incoherence of the Americans' statements reflected a genuine political incoherence in Washington.

The Italian Crisis

Unlike France, where American opinions are considered interesting but hardly decisive in shaping political decisions, Italian politics have long been closely tied to American attitudes. True, American influence has long been overrated, even in periods when considerable quantities of sound dollars were poured into the coffers of the non-Communist parties, but it was highly unlikely that non-Communist forces in Italy would reach a major decision that ran clearly counter to the interests and desires of the United States. Italy was not about to risk ostracism by the United States—and by extension, NATO as well—by effecting the *compromesso storico* over American objections. As a matter of fact, American opposition to Communism became an essential theme in the DC's reluctance to negotiate power-sharing arrangements with the PCI.

The Christian Democrats were themselves sharply divided over the most advantageous course of action; many believed the historic compromise was inevitable and merely discussed various tactics to minimize the cost. Others were violently opposed, and felt it should be contested to the very last. But most of the Christian Democrats were convinced that the eventual operation would not depend upon Italian circumstances, but rather on the international situation. According to the most thoughtful Christian Democrats, the American positions were decisive, both directly (U.S. attitudes toward the PCI) and indirectly (the state of American-Soviet relations). The PCI agreed: Berlinguer realized that his party could not survive direct attack from either the United States or the Soviet Union. The historic compromise therefore required an international atmosphere in which the experiment could be carried out without seeming to upset the balance of power. In short, detente was an absolute requirement, along with some sort of additional American toleration of the Italian adventure.

Prior to the advent of the Carter administration, one of the central requirements for the historic compromise was lacking: American acceptance. While Kissinger's detente policy unintentionallly favored the Eurocommunist advance by minimizing the perception of East-West conflict (and permitting Communist legitimization by analogy: if Nixon could do business with Brezhnev, why could Moro not deal with Berlinguer, or Giscard with Marchais?), he was explicitly opposed to the *compromesso*. But the situation changed with Carter.

The notion that the American veto on Communist participation in the government had ended was sounded most clearly and persistently by the left-wing press, reaching its zenith in the pro-Communist Roman daily *Paese Sera* on December 23 when it announced that "America will not come to the aid of those who wish to impede the entry of the Communists into the Italian government." The story was of course self-serving, but it reflected accurately the state of opinion among well-informed people in Rome.

As often happens in such cases, once the Italians had convinced themselves that a basic change had occurred, the symptoms quickly multiplied as a bandwagon effect took over. Key figures in the DC told American officials that they could no longer promise—as Andreotti had in Washington the previous July—that the political agreements would not change before new elections. In conversations throughout the fall, American diplomats discovered that the Christian Democrats were preparing to make major concessions to the PCI without obtaining electoral support for such moves.

The architect of this operation was Aldo Moro. A profoundly complex and subtle man—to the point where references to his sphinxlike intellect had become commonplace in Italy—Moro was convinced that great cunning was necessary to resolve the Italian crisis. Like so many of his generation, Moro had held several different political positions in the course of his distinguished parliamentary and governmental career, from outspoken anticommunism to one of the most vigorous advocates of the Opening to the Left, and his Catholic pessimism was reflected in this belief that most social problems were beyond human solution. He accordingly concentrated his considerable energies on political maneuver.

Moro had become convinced that Communist entry into the government was inevitable, and that American resistance had disappeared. Unlike Andreotti, who was a keen student of international affairs, and who enjoyed discussing foreign policy, Moro demonstrated an almost total lack of interest in the subject (despite a stint as foreign minister). His analyses of problems were deeply rooted in his profound understanding of Italian politics and on a superficial reading of the American position.

Moro's role was crucial, for as president of the Christian Democratic party and the most prestigious figure in its ranks, he alone could hold the party together during the pressure-packed process that would accompany the entry of the PCI into the Council of Ministers. He was supported by most of the major figures in the DC: Fanfani, Piccoli, Galloni, Zaccagnini, and Forlani. All of these, when asked if the DC maintained its pledge that there would be no major change without new elections, replied that they could no longer guarantee it. While they all told top embassy officials that they doubted it would be possible to bring Communists into the government without new elections, they also said that it was conceivable that the PCI might enter the parliamentary majority as a result of a governmental crisis. In some cases, the Americans were told in some detail how this particular slice of salami would be cut. Fanfani asked Gardner point blank "how far the DC could go" without provoking American opposition, and he was told that Italy had reached a sorry state indeed if the only thing preventing the entry of the PCI into the Italian government was the attitude—real or imagined—of the president of the United States.

To be sure, there were some American efforts to convince the DC that the operation would carry a significant cost. One of DC Secretary Zaccagnini's top assistants (Pisanu) had gone to Washington in December to sound out American opinion, and had been told by NSC Special Assistant for Western Europe Robert Hunter and by the Italian desk officer that the American government viewed the possibility of Communist participation in the Italian government with considerable alarm. And Ambassador Gardner, who had no interest in seeing Italy "go Communist" during his tenure, had made his concerns known to leading Christian Democrats.

These warnings were not accepted as authoritative by the key figures in the DC. And they may have judged the situation correctly, at least in the short run. On at least two occasions, the group concerned with Italian problems in the State Department had sent memoranda for the president via the secretary, urging that serious preparations be made in the event of a new Italian governmental crisis. They warned that the situation was accelerating, that Moro and others were prepared to make dangerous concessions to the Communists, and that it was desirable for the secretary to consider taking steps to prevent this from coming about. Vance was not convinced, and he returned the memos with the written comment that he "did not want the president to worry about Italy." It was not explained whether this was because he thought there was nothing the president could do (and thus shouldn't worry unnecessarily), or because Vance did not think that a new advance by the PCI was something that should disturb the president.

The Italian experts at State were not alone in their concerns: Gardner wanted the president to make a clear public statement about American wishes and concerns. Finally, the same tone was to be found in the communications from the CIA station chief in Rome at the time. But there was still no reaction. In fact when an American response finally emerged in January 1978, it was of a most bizarre sort, consisting of a speech that was misinterpreted, a widely ballyhooed conversation that in fact never took place, and a crucially timed article in the *New York Times* that appeared by accident at the crucial moment, having been delayed for several days by editors who did not understand its significance.

The American Response

The misinterpreted speech was given by Carter in Paris on January 3, when he said that when democracies face difficult challenges, their leaders must firmly "resist the temptation of finding solutions among nondemocratic forces." There had been dozens of statements of this sort in the past, generally referring to the president's conviction that the United States should ally itself with "progressive" forces and not support the likes of the Greek colonels, Franco, or Pinochet. However, the Paris speech was taken to refer to the Italian situation and to the PCI (indeed, the precise wording was subsequently transferred to the State Department declaration on Eurocommunism of January 12, thus reinforcing the claim), and some persons attributed the phrase to Gardner. In all probability, there was no such intention on the part of the president, whose own frame of mind was pinpointed on the last day of his French visit, January 6. The day began with a meeting with Socialist leader Mitterrand, and Carter praised him for the useful role he had played in France. This was a typical example of the president's preference for "progressive" political leaders.

That the president was insensitive to the delicacies of French politics was confirmed by the briefing on the meeting with Mitterrand given to the press on the presidential airplane en route from Paris to Brussels. The pool representative (as luck would have it, former presidential press secretary Pierre Salinger) was told that Carter had expressed to Mitterrand "in general terms his concern about the possible alliance with the Communists." Salinger was told that this concern was placed in "a general European context." However, it is clear from Salinger's exceptionally well-drafted pool report (and confirmed by administration spokesmen) that Carter in fact said nothing of the sort to Mitterrand. The statement to Salinger was concocted after the event, when it was realized that Carter had praised Mitterrand without saying anything at all about the Socialists' alliance with the PCF. The French Socialist leader must have wondered what Machiavellian strategy the president was pursuing; he could not have been expected to believe that Carter had simply failed to understand the central issue in French politics, or had forgotten to allude to it.

Regardless of the actual facts, however, it was the pool statement that became history; the world believed that Jimmy Carter had sternly warned François Mitterrand about communism. Thus, two elements of the new policy were in place: the Paris speech, and the warning to the Socialists. The third piece came from developments in Rome, New York, and Washington.

As has been seen, the tempo of PCI advance toward the Cabinet accelerated in the fall, culminating with a joint foreign policy statement issued by the PCI and the DC members of the Foreign Policy Commission of the Chamber of Deputies in November. This broke a long-standing guarantee by the Christian Democrats that there would be no collaboration on foreign policy with the Communists, and the significance of the event was properly emphasized in the Communist press. The Americans were profoundly disturbed, and the ambassador made his discontent amply clear to the Italian government, only to find an even more disturbing response: "How can we say 'no' to a Communist endorsement of our policy?" This of course begged the question of the political significance of a *joint* statement, something quite different from a Communist endorsement.

Still, there was little to be done so long as Secretary Vance maintained his attitude of lofty sanguinity. Even when the Andreotti government was placed in jeopardy by a crisis in December, there was no sign of an American initiative. The opportunity finally arrived in January, with Carter, Vance, and Brzezinski all on their European swing. At this point, the State Department professionals, with full consultation with their colleagues in Rome, decided it might be wise to recall the ambassador to Washington for consultations. This would at least show the Italians that the United States was alert to what was going on.

The invitation to Gardner was prepared at the end of the first full week in January, when Carter was meeting with Mitterrand. The fact of the invitation was leaked to *New York Times* correspondent Richard Burt in Washington on the sixth, and published on the morning of the seventh. The story had all the signs of a calculated policy leak, for it announced that Gardner was being recalled for consultations on the Italian crisis, that State Department officials were very concerned about the possibility that Communist pressure might lead to a new agreement with the DC within a month, and that such a development might represent a dramatic challenge to the "low profile" policy of the administration. This, Burt wrote, "would be an ironic development in light of previous indications according to which President Carter and his principal collaborators appeared less concerned than the Ford administration about the Communist advance in Europe." Burt went on to describe the recent Italian developments, and reported that some American officials were openly calling for a return to the Kissinger policy of publicly condemning the growing Communist role in Italy.

Just as in the cases of the Carter speech and the warning to Mitterrand, the timing of the Burt article seemed more carefully planned than it was. For Burt had filed a story about State concerns about Italy nearly a week before, and it had been held up because the *Times*' foreign desk did not feel that a story about State Department officials concerned about Italy warranted publication. It was only printed—on a Saturday at that—when the "hook" of Gardner's recall became known.

In any event, the Carter administration now had a Eurocommunism policy, the logical consequence of the three "events" of early January. Three days later, the American correspondent of the *Corriere della Sera*, Ugo Stille, was able to write that the administration had decided it was necessary to send a clear signal to Italy, and the only real debate was over the nature of the signal:

> Some maintain that the recall of Ambassador Gardner for consultations, along with the "officials' comments" that preceded it, constitute an adequate "signal."

> Others sustain the necessity of underlining the "preoccupation" of the United States . . . with some additional moves. . . . This decision will depend to a large degree on the analysis that Gardner will present to Carter.[14]

The advocates of the second line prevailed, and on January 12 the State Department issued a statement dealing with the Communist parties of Western Europe. After an initial pretense that "our position is unchanged," spokesman Hodding Carter announced a new departure: "We are not in favor of such participation (of Eurocommunists in their governments) and would like to see Communist influence in the countries of Western Europe reduced." Moreover, Carter said, the American government did not believe that the Communists shared the "profound values and democratic interests" that the United States and Italy shared.

The declaration had an enormous effect in Italy. The suddenness of the change in attitude, the appearance of a carefully planned campaign, ranging from Paris to Rome and Washington, made a great impression. Some considered it a gross interference in Italian affairs, somewhat embarrassing to the leading Christian Democrats (especially those who by now were involved in compromising embraces with the Communists), and infuriating to the PCI. Giancarlo Pajetta actually claimed that the Communists had greater popular support in Italy than Carter had in the United States:

> (The hope of seeing Communist influence diminish) is a bit grotesque, since the threats and interferences of the past have perhaps helped us win the confidence of more than 34 percent of the Italian electorate. This is a higher percentage than that of barely over 25 percent of the American citizens that constitute the electors of Jimmy Carter.[15]

The rage of the Left was not simply a political response to an American initiative; virtually the entire left-wing media had enthusiastically propagated the thesis that Carter would do nothing to prevent the Communist advance. Events thus demonstrated that they had not understood the American political reality.

The most violent attacks came from the Soviets, always eager to make their enemies pay the maximum political price for any success. For the next several weeks the Soviet press devoted thousands of column inches to the alleged American "interference" and called upon all Italian political forces to reject the initiative. This was too much even for the *Corriere della Sera*, whose excellent Moscow correspondent Piero Ostellino noted acidly that when the Soviets called for the entry of the PCI into the government (as it had done regularly for three decades), this was deemed to be a legitimate expression of national concern. But if the Americans announced that they preferred a different outcome, that was "interference."[16]

In any event, the true measure of any policy is not its popularity but its effect, and the declaration undoubtedly slowed the engine of the *compromesso storico*. Indeed, its most vociferous American critics condemned it precisely for that reason. Arguing that the policy of excluding the PCI from the government was doomed from the outset because of the powerful position the Communists held, a group of academic experts in Cambridge, Massachusetts contended that "the Italian economic and social crisis and the increasing cooperation between the forces of the Center and the Communists have rendered the ideology of unconditional anticommunism irrelevant to the contemporary situation in Italy."[17]

These words were published nearly a year after the January 12 declaration, and flew in the teeth of the events in Italy itself. In retrospect, one can see that the PCI began its descent shortly after its great electoral triumph in June 1976. The PCI lost virtually every electoral test from that day onward (save for a national explosion of sympathy after the death of Enrico Berlinguer), and its continuing forward advance was only made possible by the connivance of elite groups in and out of Parliament, not by popular consensus. The Americans were thus fully democratic when they insisted that Moro and Andreotti kept their promise that a step of such magnitude as the elevation of the PCI to the role of a "party of government" not be undertaken without the explicit approval of the electorate. The January statement prevented the elites of the PC and PCI from achieving the *compromesso storico* (or a major step in that direction) over the heads (or behind the backs) of the Italian people.

The importance of the American declaration lay in its braking effect on the Italian political world, thus permitting the elites of the two major parties to digest the change that had already taken place in the country. The Communists and Christian Democrats were largely unaware that a process of rejection of the PCI had begun, and in certain areas (the South, and the cities recently placed under Communist mayors, like Rome, Naples, and Turin) had gone quite far. Basing their strategies on the results of the June 1976 elections, the leaders of the two parties were determined to accelerate a process that was viewed wth growing antipathy by a majority of Italians.

The elites were prevented from carving a full slice of political salami and had to settle for half: instead of moving into the parliamentary majority (which was probably Moro's plan), the PCI had to content itself with participating in something called a "programmatic majority." This Moro invention, which permitted the PCI to join a vote in the chamber for the program of the new government (but not the government itself), was approved on the last day of Moro's life as a free man. On the morning of the vote, he was kidnapped by the Red Brigades and was never seen alive again.

The PCI's little step forward thus turned out to be a pyrrhic victory, for it placed them in an impossible position: henceforth coresponsible for the government's performance, the Communists had to answer to the restive base of the party for their open collaboration with the hated Christian Democrats. At the same time, the Moro kidnapping and his subsequent assassination by terrorists calling themselves "Red" and historically linked to Prague, produced an anti-Communist backlash. The party's efforts to put space between itself and the Red Brigades did not work. While Berlinguer's firm refusal to negotiate with the Red Brigades for the release of Moro impressed the public, it was clear to everyone that the language of the terrorists was the same the PCI had been using for thirty years, prompting Rossanna Rossanda's famous statement that the documents of the Red Brigades read like "an old family album." Coming from the leader of the "manifesto" group that had broken away from the PCI in the late sixties, everyone knew what she was talking about.

Thus, while few people believed that the PCI leaders had any operational responsibility for the Moro affair, many held that the Red Brigades were an historical legacy of Italian communism. This cost them dearly in the local elections of May 1978.

The entire affair was not without irony; prior to the Moro tragedy, the activities of the Red Brigades had strengthened the Communists' position, for they were able to claim that law and order could not be established without active Communist participation in the goverment. This argument was fairly convincing at the time (especially as the Andreotti government showed little ability or determination to move against the terrorists), but the execution of Moro altered the picture, for it focussed attention on the *political* goals of the Red Brigades. Henceforth the issue was no longer "law and order," it was the survival of the Italian state. And while the Italian people learned that terrorism could not destroy Italy, they were equally convinced that the terrorist fire could not be put out by well-known arsonists.

The effects of the Moro affair were not limited to Italy; in all probability it influenced some of the voters in the French general elections of the same period. Moro's body was found in Rome just before the crucial second round of voting in France, and probably contributed to Giscard's margin of victory over the *Union de la Gauche*. The Red Brigades may well be said to have contributed to the defeats of the two leading Communist parties in Western Europe; no mean achievement for such a small organization.

Of course, both the French and Italian Communist parties, along with the Soviet disinformation apparat, attempted to suggest that the United States was secretly behind Italian terrorism, and that the Red Brigades were manipulated by the CIA. But it was inconceivable that the Carter administration—and the CIA under the hapless Stansfield Turner—were capable of such a diabolical scheme. The indecisiveness of the Americans, and the grave weakening of the CIA were by now evident to all concerned, and the insinuations were hardly taken seriously. Indeed, far more credibiliy was given to a rumor that Berlinguer had asked the Soviets to unleash the KGB on the Red Brigades (as has been seen, he certainly asked the Rumanians for help).

The Moro affair and its aftermath accelerated the rate of decline of the PCI, even though the basic causes for the decline were quite different. Aided by the clear American position, anti-Communist elements within the Christian Democratic, Socialist, and other lay parties were encouraged to become more aggressive. The emergence of Bettino Craxi at the head of the Socialist party was an event of major import, for it meant that the PCI could no longer count on manipulating the Socialists to its own ends. Indeed, Craxi was probably the single Italian political leader most hated by the Communists, for he was the incarnation of the sort of progressive anticommunism that they most feared.

The electoral results in Italy and France had a great psychological effect, for the myth of the inevitability of Communist victory was definitively shattered. No longer could the Eurocommunists claim that they were marching in step with the engine of history. No longer did the political opportunists automatically align themselves with the Communists. No longer did the progressive media automatically tailor their articles in order to avoid offending Communist leaders. In a word, the Gramscian strategy of communizing the political culture in order to achieve a smooth conquest of political power came unstuck. Communist cultural hegemony was revealed to be far weaker than believed. Indeed, by 1979 the vogue in French intellectual circles was no longer the "pidgin Marxism" so well described by Jean-Francois Revel,[18] but a more realistic and tough-minded anticommunism with such heroes as Vladimir Bukovsky, Leonid Plyutsch, and Alexander Solzhenitsyn. And when the decline of the PCI, already evident in the school elections of December 1976, was confirmed by the parliamentary elections of June 1979 in Italy, the historic compromise was relegated to the dustbin of history, at least for the moment.

Lessons and Prescriptions

With the return of the French and Italian Communist parties to positions of opposition in 1978-79, and the confirmation that the PCE in Spain would remain at a mere 10 percent of the electorate, the great vogue of Eurocommunism came to an end. The vogue having passed, the question of American policy toward the Communists became far less pressing. Yet the question in all likelihood will require attention in the future. This is particularly true in the Italian case, where the PCI remains one of the two most powerful political parties regardless of the failure of the strategy of the *compromesso storico*.

The great hue and cry over Eurocommunism shows how easy it is to be misled, for not only did the great majority of American academic specialists, foreign correspondents, and editorial writers embrace the mistaken notion that the Communist parties of France, Spain, and Italy had converted to Western and democratic ideas and broken with the Kremlin, but they were also inclined to believe that there was considerable harmony between the three. These opinions were shared, albeit to a far lesser degree, by many of the policy makers in Washington, and the consensus thus arrived at in turn produced the pressure for a more open American approach to the Eurocommunist question (hardly anyone would propose American open-mindedness toward Stalinist parties coming to power in NATO countries). Thus, the policy recommendations were based in the first instance upon bad analysis.

The distorted analysis was in part due to developments within the American government. The progressive enfeeblement of American information-gathering organizations made it virtually impossible to gain a full understanding of the internal dynamics of the Communists and their relationships with the Soviet Union. The analysis of Eurocommunism became primarily political, and the Americans had to evaluate the *intentions* of the Communists; a virtually hopeless task. To say this is not necessarily to criticize those who were forced to deal with the problem in the 1970s; it is only to suggest that they paid a high price for errors in judgment and some devastating personnel changes that began years earlier. Given the paucity of reliable information, Washington could hardly arrive at convincing analyses in the seventies.

However, this was not the only source of confusion, and many of the errors were the result of ideological bias. For many opinion makers and professional policy makers had been captured by the fashionable myths of the post-Vietnam period: that America was powerless to achieve fundamental change in most of the world; that many of the unpleasant things that had happened in the past were the result of misguided or sinister American activity, and hence American actions should be limited wherever possible; and that under no circumstances should the United States meddle in the internal affairs of other countries (unless they are, or were, friendly dictatorships, of the Pinochet, Marcos, or Duvalier variety, or hateful but allied systems like apartheid). All of these self-fulfilling prophecies combined to condition a series of reflexes at the highest levels of the American government that led to either inertia or self-defeating policies. As Daniel

Patrick Moynihan put it, the American political elite emerged from the Vietnam and Watergate period so confused and so guilt-ridden that it ended by accepting our enemies' view of the world.[19]

In the mid-seventies, the strongest corrective influence on this highly confused and masochistic elite came from our allies. In the case of Eurocommunism, the leaders of the NATO countries repeatedly implored Jimmy Carter to stop giving the impression that the United States was benevolently disposed toward Marchais, Berlinguer, and Carrillo. But the Carter administration was too clearly oriented in the opposite direction, and a basic identification with those West European forces deemed to be "progressive," along with a desire to differentiate its own policies from those of Nixon and Kissinger, made it impossible for the administration to take a clear position. True, Carter was temporarily swayed by Andreotti, Giscard, and Schmidt, but the effect was brief. The policy of resolute non-interference, combined with generic indications of a preference for non-Communist governments, remained the official line.

This policy was misguided on several levels. First, the pious claim to noninterference simply disregarded the realities of the American relationship with Western Europe. Every American action and expression of intent constitutes an interference in European politics. But the effect is strongest when there is a break with traditional policies. In the case of Eurocommunism, the constant promise that America would not interfere, along with the refrain that all decisions affecting the old continent would be left to the Europeans, was more of an interference than Kissinger's warnings that there would be serious consequences for the Alliance if Communists entered allied governments. In short, the so-called policy of noninterference was actually the reverse of that. Carter's policy encouraged the Eurocommunist advance, and he should have known that would happen. That the consequences of their policies were not foreseen is best explained by the ideological blinders worn by most top policy makers in the first year of the Carter presidency.

To be sure, expressions of American preference, and even a violent ideological campaign initiated from Washington, vary in their effect from country to country. Just as the Communist parties of France, Spain, and Italy are quite different from each other, so American policy toward each country must be differentiated. But to advance the notion that the United States is impotent, and that any effort to effect positive change in keeping with American interests is doomed in advance, is to encourage unfavorable results and undermine American leverage.

Second, the Carter team evidently believed that a policy of noninterference would restore luster to the American image in Europe. The president and the secretary of state probably expected that their line would quickly convince Europeans that the United States was acting more democratically, permitting the old continent to pursue its own destiny. Instead, the Carter line pleased only the radical-chic intelligentsia, and the opponents of American interest. For the Europeans did not want the United States to withdraw from the old continent's battles; what they wanted, above all, was clarity. As one experienced European diplomat put it, "We can live with a dovish America, or with a hawkish America. We can not survive an America that does not know which it is." In other words, the Europeans wanted—and want—the United States to play its leadership role with vigor and clarity.

This role had to vary from country to country. In Italy, men like Andreotti wanted the United States to hold firm to its anti-Communist line so that he could pursue tactical objectives under the American umbrella. In France, there was no need for dramatic American action, for Giscard (and Chirac, of course) were quite capable of waging an effective anti-Communist campaign by themselves. Moreover, unlike Italy, where foreign attention and action is expected and discounted in advance, French politics are considered untouchable, and there is considerable negative reaction to any outside attempt to influence electoral results. This applies to American endorsements and to Soviet pronunciamenti. Thus, there was no need for the Americans to participate directly in the campaign prior to the historic elections of 1978, and good reasons to maintain a fairly low profile. But when Carter and his advisers began to suggest that a basic change had occurred in American attitudes toward Eurocommunism, Giscard properly protested, for this favored his opponents. Like Andreotti in Italy, Giscard wanted his people to have the impression that American attitudes toward communism were constant, and that any basic change in the French political firmament would risk alienating the Americans. The threat from Washington was that this basic touchstone of the Atlantic Alliance would be taken away.

In Spain, the matter was rather more complex, because of the historic ties between Washington and the Franco regime, and also because a considerable part of the political debate in Spain was over the cultural affiliations of the Spanish people. Yet for Don Adolfo Suarez, it was important to be able to show his countrymen that there were important advantages to having close ties with the United States. And he was deeply frustrated by the apparent lack of recognition he received from the Carter administration. Suarez, along with King Juan Carlos, performed a major political miracle in guiding their country from dictatorship to democracy without grave internal conflict. Suarez's discontent with the Americans deepened with Carter's opening to Eurocommunism, and then when his major opponent, the socialist Felipe Gonzales, was invited to Washington and greeted by leading figures in the American government.

The third basic shortcoming of the Carter line was its failure to comprehend the way in which Europeans view the United States. The American government is invariably singled out for particularly harsh treatment regardless of its policies. When Washington acts aggressively to lead the Alliance, it is criticized for arrogance and lack of consultation; when instead Washington awaits European decisions before proceeding, it is criticized for cutting Europe adrift. But in all circumstances, the United States' role is overstated, and American motives often wildly misinterpreted. Even our closest and oldest allies have a difficult time understanding the American political process, and they can rarely if ever bring themselves to believe that American foreign policy is as often the result of confusion as of ratiocination. This has been seen in the case of the Carter approach to Eurocommunism: each and every actor in the farce insisted on discovering the "hidden logic" behind the apparently contradictory pattern of American behavior. They could not accept what was under their noses.

American behavior will always be subjected to this kind of interpretation, and we must take this into account in designing our policies. Insofar as it is possible, we must also try to educate other branches of the government to understand the implications of *their* actions. When Senator Frank Church's Subcommittee on Multinational Corporations flooded Western Europe with leaks about American bribery in 1975, Europeans were certain that his actions were part of a broader foreign policy initiative. And when Americans from the private sector travel in Europe and speak to the press, their words are often taken to be those of the government. (The opposite misunderstanding occurs in America, where it is rarely appreciated that representatives of European businesses, universities, and political parties often speak for their governments.)

The lesson is that policy makers have an extremely broad canvas on which to paint; the range of initiatives available to the government at any moment is vast indeed. Signals can be sent through myriad channels; it is not always necessary for the president or the secretary of state to pronounce on all subjects. Indeed, one of the most serious developments in recent years has been the compulsion of the president himself, along with a handful of experts, to take complete charge of the conduct of foreign affairs. This unduly limits the parameters of American diplomatic activity.

It must also be appreciated that silence is also a form of activity; while most recent architects of American foreign policy have had a passion for exposition, clarification, and dialogue, there is much to be said for studied silence, vague hints, and misdirection. This is particularly useful nowadays, when the United States has deprived itself of many of the traditional instruments of action. Lacking them, it is far better to permit others to believe that something has replaced them rather than insist that things have fundamentally changed (our denials may be treated as disinformation, after all).

The Outlines of Good Policy

An effective American policy rests upon the recognition that the United States must contest any Communist party in Western Europe. Better to challenge such parties while they are in opposition than to have to conduct a more difficult struggle once they have entered government.

The challenge is above all political and ideological, and we have every reason to believe that we will win it. The values of the United States are those of most West Europeans. Communism has produced tyrannies and disastrous economic and social policies wherever it has triumphed, and we should attack it relentlessly. In doing so, there is no need to sink to the level of visceral anticommunism; we need not exaggerate the horrors of communism, nor attempt to portray it as a vast monolithic conspiracy. The reality is sufficiently dreadful without overstating the case. Ideological war, then, provides the United States with a legitimate and highly effective card to play. Indeed, even the Carter human rights campaign, for all its inconsistencies and brief life span, was highly effective in exposing the Soviet Union and the Eurocommunists to punishing criticism.

The ideological challenge to communism also permits the United States to carry out a political litmus test on the evolution of European Communists. It may well be that someday one or another of the European parties—or, more likely, some European Communists—will choose to break with their traditions and abandon communism. For all that this is not likely, it is nonetheless in our interests to keep the option open, for we prefer that our allies have stable internal debates rather than intense internal conflict.

Parties do change, and although there is not a single example of this sort of transformation *en bloc* (there are thousands of individual ex-Communists, of course), the past is not always a reliable guide to the future. But it is folly to believe that such a difficult transformation will take place without considerable external pressure from the United States. Without it, the Communists will be tempted to try to fool us (and perhaps themselves as well) as they have in the past. The Italian Communists, often cited as the most likely candidates for this transformation, would prefer that we accept them as they are, without making the hard choices that divide their ranks and split them off from Moscow. Premature acceptance of the PCI would guarantee that these choices will not be faced. A sustained challenge might conceivably encourage the transformation.

A final note on the matter of a democratic "conversion" on the part of Eurocommunists: if this ever happens, one will not have to put the party under a microscope to find the evidence. For the event will be luminously clear to all observers, and the behavior of the Soviet Union will undoubtedly provide us with a good deal of the evidence. At a minimum, we will have to see a decisive change in the internal structures of the party, and significant shifts in its foreign policies.

Second, the United States should demonstrate that it is willing to help its friends, and fight alongside them. This means not only verbal, but also material support when required. When democratic parties in Western Europe are challenged by Communist parties that receive considerable covert support from the Soviet bloc, the United States should be willing to help, especially in critical electoral campaigns and in crucial political and cultural arenas. This recommendation flies in the face of much current "wisdom," for it has become fashionable to criticize payments to American allies abroad. Financial assistance, especially when it is secret, to pro-American political parties, trade unions, and cultural organizations, is widely considered immoral. Yet is it reasonable that democratic parties are required to conform to American standards of political morality, while antidemocratic parties are permitted to function in accordance with different standards? Should the United States run the risk of seeing its enemies strengthened merely because they are wealthier and more corrupt than American friends? And, to take a concrete example, was it not proper for the democratic Socialists of Western Europe (along with the United States) to send covert support to the Portuguese Socialist party in the mid-seventies when Mario Soares and his comrades fought the Communists of Alvaro Cunhal for the future of Portugal?

It is common practice in all democratic countries to give financial assistance to cultural organiations that might not otherwise survive. Why should the United States be required to withold aid to similar organizations abroad? In a country like Italy, where Communists and their friends spend millions of dollars to coopt the levers of cultural power, American assistance to democratic individuals and organizations (from scholars and journalists to newspapers, and radio and television stations) may be required to support a genuinely free flow of ideas. If it be feared that such aid is inevitably corrupting, this should be balanced against the fear of a more likely development: that potential democrats might make their peace with the totalitarians because of the lack of a viable alternative. I have seen the plight of young university students in Europe, privately opposed to the dominant culture, forced to conform to the official line because the alternative was unemployment. In such circumstances, it is better to take foreign money than to surrender to certain manipulation by the local totalitarians. And although the context of these observations is the "Communist problem," the same applies to tyrannies of the Right. Just as the American trade union movement spent money well in the forties and fifties to keep free trade unions afloat in the face of repression from both political extremes, so the American government should not hesitate to support democratic forces where this appears necessary.

This principle is accepted throughout the Western world, most recently in the United States, where the National Endowment for Democracy was created precisely for this purpose. In the past, the debate in America was characterized by a pious hypocrisy, as in the case of the Church Committee hearings. At one point, Church was told by a top Lockheed official that there were numerous instances in which the Soviets had engaged in precisely the same sort of activity for which that corporation was being attacked in the Senate. Yet Senator Church and his associates were not sufficiently interested to ask for details. This double standard is not only hypocritical; it is damaging to our interests and demoralizing to our friends. In the best of worlds, we would prefer not to do such things. But in this world, it is reasonable enough to help our friends.

To be sure, the enterprise is not without risk. Many of our friends would like assistance, but they cannot acknowledge it. This means that secrecy is sometimes required, and if it cannot be maintained, it is better not to do it at all. This points to two conclusions: assistance should be open whenever possible; and if the money can be raised and administered by private sources, all the better. In Europe, where political parties have substantial resources and are willing to spend their money on international activities, the coins do not have the same odor as those that come from governments. The United States has created the National Endowment for Democracy in an attempt to acquire this sort of capability, but there are often alternatives to government channels, and these should be exploited.

Furthermore, if the aid is important and secrecy is required, then the United States government must have channels that guarantee secrecy will be maintained. And the secrecy must be of an enduring sort; it will not do to support a democratic party for some years only to have it sabotaged by untimely revelations at a later date. In all likelihood, some change in the current approach to the Freedom of Information Act will be required to make this stick.

Finally, we tend to forget that financial assistance to friends abroad runs the risk of creating organizations that are excessively dependent upon American support. Oddly enough, *we* then tend to become hostage to the organizations we help. This is clearly the case with the Italian Christian

Democratic party, which although a long-time recipient of American aid, became almost totally unmanageable. The employer of the piper does not by any means always call the tune; often he is sent a bill for a concert he detests. Our interest is in the establishment of independent and democratic parties. Thus, our support should tend to be limited in time, if this is feasible.

The Strategic Dimension

The problem of communism in Western Europe, as elsewhere in the world, is linked to the role of the Soviet Union in international affairs. The overall balance of power is therefore central to the analysis of American policy. For if there is a decisive strategic shift in favor of our enemies, the most brilliant diplomacy will not save us. By the same token, no degree of military power can substitute—on our side of the Yalta line, at least—for ineptitude in the management of foreign policy. But the crucial element is the balance of power. If the Soviet Union is widely perceived to be decisively stronger than the United States, the intermediary powers will be forced to make their peace with the inevitable victors.

There is a bandwagon effect in world affairs, and the peoples of the world are often swayed by shifts in the global balance. When, as in the mid- and late seventies, the Soviet Union successfully extended its power through direct and indirect intervention from Central America to the Horn of Africa, without once encountering an effective American response; when Soviet strategic power is permitted to grow relentlessly for years without response in kind from the West; when the leaders of the United States exert their influence to topple mildly unsavory allies while accommodating the preferences of the Kremlin in one theater after another, the rest of the world concludes that the tide is running in favor of the East. In the long run, these trends do more to favor the advance of Communist parties than the most brilliant Gramscian strategy.

In the postwar period the desires of the United States were decisive in most of Western Europe because there was sufficient military and economic power to guarantee that America would prevail in any showdown that involved our vital interests. While there was confusion in the early postwar period (with the usual great rush to demobilize, bring the troops home, and get back to "normalcy"), by the time of the turning point in 1947-48 the disparity between the two camps was undeniable: the Soviet Union was ruined by the war, while the United States was intact in all its vital functions. In the last analysis, American will was supreme because American military and economic power were supreme.

This situation no longer exists, and today's overriding problem is to prevent an inversion of the relationship between the superpowers, with all the attendant geopolitical consequences. Some Europeans have already been "Finlandized," and if the negative strategic trends of the past continue, these symptoms would multiply.

One should beware, however, of overstating the connection between the gradual development of Soviet might and the success of communism in Western Europe. While one is tempted to say that the great leap forward for the Eurocommunists came at precisely the moment of vital American collapse following the defeat in Vietnam and the trauma of Watergate, it would then be difficult to account for the collapse of Eurocommunism half a decade later when the Soviet Union was sending its Cuban centurions around the world, and the United States was threatened as never before by hostile regimes in its own hemisphere and by distant suppliers of raw materials who controlled the lifeline of the Western economy. In other words, there is no immediate causal relationship (although there would be if there were a decisive shift in the balance of power). But the progressive weakening of the United States certainly had an effect on parties like the Italian Christian Democratic party, which had based a good deal of its anticommunism on American strength. And the weaker the United States, the less resolve such parties are likely to evince.

It should be added, however, that several very encouraging events took place during those dark years, above all the abandonment of many of the myths of the Left in Western Europe. Democratic socialism seems to have lost much of its historic inferiority complex in all three of the countries where Eurocommunism was knocking at the government's door, and Eurosocialism is today far more significant than Eurocommunism. The growth of Soviet military power has produced signs of resistance alongside evidence of Finlandization, perhaps because the sight of the gallows marvelously concentrates the mind. But whatever the explanation, it is inevitable that Europe will fall under Soviet influence unless it is evident that the United States will be willing and able to defend its allies against Soviet might.

Thus, after thirty years, the strategies of the superpowers are curiously inverted. At the end of the war, it was the Soviet Union that pursued an ideological campaign in Western Europe, since it was unable to challenge the United States on any other grounds. In the 1980s, we find ourselves fighting with similar weapons, because the strategic superiority of the forties is gone. If the strategic balance remains satisfactory, then we shall find politics, ideology, and diplomacy effective weapons indeed. If the balance shifts badly against us, our diplomacy will become a study in aesthetics. Only those powerful enough to do so are permitted the luxury of designing diplomacy to achieve national desires.

Notes

1. The Carter interview was in *Playboy* (November 1976).
2. In *Newsweek* (13 December 1976).
3. Carter interview with RAI-TV (TG2), 14 July 1976.
4. The interview was published by *La Stampa, Le Monde,* The *Times* (London), and *Die Welt.*
5. This speech profoundly disturbed many West European leaders, who while they publicly hailed Carter's words, privately felt it important that the United States continue to have a healthy fear of communism.
6. The selection of interlocutors by the PCI shows how poorly the Communists understood the United States. Instead of going to the government actually in power, they spoke with what they evidently believed was the "real government"—the "secret government." They spoke with many people from the world of the secret services, who had very little to do with real political power in Washington, whatever their considerable intellectual merits.
   This crazy approach to the United States led the Communists to talk to people who, with rare exceptions, couldn't have helped much even if they had wished to—and the presentations of Ledda and Colajanni guaranteed that none of the Americans was convinced in any case.
7. The *Washington Post* (31 March 1977).
8. Kissinger's speech on Italy and Eurocommunism, *cit.*
9. *Il Tempo* (18 June 1977).
10. 9 October 1977.
11. The discussions of the Trilateral Commission are generally not made public. This information has been confirmed by more than five persons present at the session.
12. *Reader's Digest* (October 1977).
13. Brzezinski said substantially the same to Italian TV (14 November 1977).
14. Stille did not know that Ambassador Gardner, who had been skiing when the crisis hit, had been very reluctant to interrupt his vacation for a trip to Washington. Yet again, the only thing that mattered was the *Italian* perception; and that was embodied in Stille's remarks.
15. Pajetta in Paese Sera (13 January 1978).
16. Ostellino in *il Corriere della Sera* (14 January 1978).
17. The group included Lange, Vannicelli, Blackmer, and Tarrow, and, if memory serves me correctly, Stanley Hoffman.
18. Revel, *La Tentation Totalitaire, cit.*
19. Senator Daniel P. Moynihan, interviewed by Michael A. Ledeen in *The Washington Review of Strategic & International Studies* (I, 1, 1978).

Index

SUBJECTS

Abortive insurrection, 41-44, 45-46
Action Pact, 16, 17, 71-72, 80, 81-82, 89
AFL (American Federation of Labor), 51, 83-87; —CIO, 85-86, 165; support in Europe, 84
Allies: advance in WW II, 3, 15; counterintelligence, of 12-13; failure in Italy, 9; and Italian Resistance, 2, 27n.51, 65; in Italy, 4, 8, 13
American Federation of Labor. *See* AFL
Anti-Fascist: campaign, 13; credentials, 9; forces, 3, 4, 5, 8, 10, 21; rhetoric, 14
Apertura a Sinistra, 87-92, 97; and the Kennedy administration, 92-95. *See also* Opening to the Left
Ardeatine Caves massacre (1943), 15
Armed party. *See Partito Armato*
Atlantic Alliance, 72, 73, 82, 96; and Eurocommunism, 139-40

Badoglio government, 4
Balance of power, 114-15
Bari resolution for the abdication of the king, 8
British Special Operation Executive (SOE), 3, 23n.9
Bulgaria's training operation, 126

Capitalism, 20, 127, 137; anti-, 86, 138
Carabinieri, 33, 36
Carter administration policy on Eurocommunism, 161-62, 164-65, 167, 169, 175, 182; ambiguity in, 168-69, 170, 179, 181-82; changes in, 167-68; shortcomings of, 179-84
CGIL (Italian trade union movement), 18, 43, 73, 77, 83-84, 86-87, 97, 106
Chinese communism, 135
Christian Democratic party (DC, Italy), 16, 51, 54, 66, 71-73, 78, 83, 86-87, 91, 92, 96-97, 103-4, 107-8, 121, 174, 177; blamed as "fascist," 128-29; and U.S. policy, 168, 170-73, 174
CISL. *See* Italian Catholic unions
Cold War: in Italy, 29-46; Soviet initiative for a new, 158; and U.S. policy, 57
Cominform Conference, 59-61, 64, 157
Comintern, 5, 13, 20, 61, 117, 118
Comitati di redazione (worker's groups), 105-6
Communists. *See* name of individual parties
Compromesso storico (historic compromise), 105-7, 108-9, 116, 120, 125-26, 171, 177, 179; failure of, 121-22, 179-80
Confederazione Generale Italiana del Lavoro. *See* CGIL
Continental military conspiracy, 36
CPSU (Soviet Communist party), 66; Twentieth Party Congress of the, 68, 76, 79, 80, 81
Cultural hegemony. *See* Gramscian strategy of cultural hegemony
Czech: connection with Red Brigades, 123; intelligence, 119
Czechoslovakia, 57, 58, 61;

DC. *See* Christian Democratic party
Democracy, 10, 58, 77, 116, 127; and communism, 46; European, 29; threat to, 30, 51
Democratic centralism, 110, 127
Detente, 62, 108, 114, 115, 122, 151, 171
Doupov training center, 123, 125

East European: countries, 59, 60, 117; delegates in Cominform, 60; gains by Stalin, 61; Socialists, 117
L'envoi, 21-22

l'Espresso magazine, 105
Eurocommunism, 7, 25n.26, 56, 59, 80, 116, 125, 126; anticapitalism, 138; anti-Soviets, 138; concept of, 134; development of, 11, 136; and fascism, 138; and Gramscian strategy, 138; independence from Soviet Union, 135-36, 148-52; leaders: Carrillo, Marchais, and Berlinguer, 134-35, 137, 141, 147, 149-50, 153, 155, 157; as a mass movement, 137; myth of, 133-59; and the "reformation" theory, 137-41, 148-54, 157; the Soviet Union and, 143-48, 149-56; Soviet offensive against, 154-56; as a threat to NATO and the Atlantic Alliance, 139; as a threat to the U.S. and U.S.S.R., 138; and the U.S., 141-43, 147; U.S. policy toward, 161-88; as pro-West, 134; West European intelligence and, 138
Eurocommunism and the State (Carrillo), 151, 155, 158
Eurofascism, 138
European Communists, 79, 118
European Center-Left, 56
European Left, 56, 72, 157; anti-Communist parties of, 89
European Right, 60
European social democrats, 56

Fascism, 1, 2, 9, 74, 138
Fascist seizure of power in Italy, 9
Finland, 57
Foreign Affairs, 136
Foreign Policy, 136
France: aid to Italy, 51; expelling Communists from government, 52; intellectuals in, 179; Italian Communists in, 38-39; Labor agitation in, 30; and the Moro affair, 178; and NSC, 56; threat to democracy, 30; Union of the Left in, 151, 169, 178
French Communist party (PCF), 30, 57, 59, 60, 61, 99n.32, 118; and the myth of Eurocommunism, 133-59 passim; and Spanish Communists, 145; pro-Soviet and Leninist, 154, 174
French Socialists, 72, 164, 174
Fried group, the, 91, 99n.32, 118

Genoa group (Ciruzzi's), 124

Germany, 14, 15
Gramscian strategy of cultural hegemony, 73-77, 81, 105, 128, 138
Great Britain; and NSC, 56; policy on postwar Italy, 1-4, 13; and the United States, 1-3, 13
Greece, 57, 60

Helsinki Final Acts, 152
Historic compromise. *See Compromesso storico*
Hungary, the Soviets in, 81-82

Intellectuals: American, 134, 141; and Eurocommunism, 137, 141; French, 179; intimidation of, 130n.4; and the PCI, 73, 74, 81; and the PSI, 76; Soviet, 80
Israeli intelligence, 79
Italian Action party, 8, 16
Italian Catholic unions (CISL), 85, 86
Italian Communist party. *See* PCI
Italian peninsula, 1, 9, 12
Italian Resistance, 1-22, 32
Italian Social-Democratic party. *See* PSDI
Italian Socialist party. *See* PSI
Italian trade union movement. *See* CGIL
Italy: abortive insurrection in, 42-44; Allied-occupied, 8, 13; Center-Left of, 94, 96, 101n.443; Center-Left coalition, 71, 96; coaltion of DC and PSI in, 71-98; Cold War in, 29-46; Communist cultural hegemony in, 105-7; 1948 anti-Communist vote in, 104; crisis in, 51, 170-73; "economic miracle" in, 92; 1948 elections in, 29, 58, 59, 66, 72, 104, 121; 1976 elections in, 121; government of, 46, 126; fascism in, 75, 138; free trade unions in, 84; importance for Allies, 19, 20; intelligence services of, 6, 123; intelligentsia of, 81; Labor agitation in, 30, 42-43; the Left in, 31, 73, 77, 78, 96, 103, 122, 126, 169, 176; media of, 105-6, 128-29; monarchy in, 8-9, 16; Nazi-occupied, 15; the North of, 2, 3, 9, 34, 36; politics in, 50-51, 73, 91, 129; postwar, 2, 25n.25, 59, 74, 84, 86, 91, 103-4, 112; POW of, 12; purges in, 5-6; the Right in, 73, 122; Right-Center coaltion in, 73; the South of, 9, 13; and the *svolta*, 7; surrender of, 4; threat to democracy in, 30, 51; and the

Index 193

United States, 49-68, 129, 170-71, 173-79; pro-Western sentiments in, 129. *See also Compromesso storico Partito Armato; Partito Nuovo*

Kennedy initiatives in Italy, 92-96

Latin Communists. *See* West European Communist parties
Leninist: roots of PCI, 122, 126-30; strategy, 44; theory, 11; uprising, 12
Lincoln Brigade, 3
Lubiana, Yugoslavia, 36

McGovern Amendment, 164-65
Marshall Plan, 21, 29, 30, 52, 56, 57, 59, 60, 84, 86
Mass party, 15, 38, 86, 89, 105, 149; and its enemies, 109-117
Masses, the, 74
il Messagero moves to the Left, 105
Middle classes, 121, 138; lower, 73
Milan *il Corriere della sera*, 105-6, 112, 113, 128, 176
Milan *il Giornale nuovo*, 105, 128-29, 130n.2, 134, 152
Moro affair, 126, 178, 179
Myth. *See* Eurocommunism/myth of

National Security Council. *See* NSC
NATO (North Atlantic Treaty Organization), 78, 82; and Eurocommunism, 135, 137, 139-40; modernization of nuclear forces, 114-15
Nazi-Maoist group, 119
Nazism/Nazis, 1, 12
New party. *See Partito Nuovo*
New Republic, 106
New York Times, 79, 91, 136, 137, 139, 173
NKVD (Soviet intelligence), 7, 35
NSC (National Security Council, U.S.), 55-56, 58, 164
Nuovi-argomenti, 80

Opening. *See* Opening to the Left
Opening to the Left, 56, 71-98. *See also Apertura a Sinistra*
Organization. *See* PCI/ clandestine apparatus

OSS (Office of Strategic Services), 12, 14, 22, 22n.2
OSS Research and Analysis branch (R&A), 1-3, 13, 15, 25n.46

Panorama magazine, 105
Paris Commune, the, 133
Partisans. *See* Italian Resistance
Partito Armato (Armed party), 20, 31, 32-33, 34, 35-36, 38, 41, 42, 44-45, 66, 68; and the Red Brigades, 123
Partito Nuovo (New party), 11, 31, 38, 41, 66, 109
PCE. *See* Spanish Communist party
PCI (Italian Communist party), 18, 20, 22, 30, 35, 51, 60, 81-83, 89-90, 93, 98n.3, 103-130; ambivalence of, 125-26; anti-American, 41, 57, 61, 113-15, 126; as antidemocratic, 127-28; and the attack on Togliatti, 42-44; Central Cadre Office of the, 35; Central Committee, 6, 38, 40, 127; and the CIA, 144-45; clandestine apparatus, 5, 25n.25, 36, 44, 45, 53, 58, 68, 122; clandestine vs. "legal," 36-37, 45, 72, 118; and CPSU, 66; and the DC, 171; decline of, 121-22, 177, 179; and detente, 108; and Eurocommunism, 133-59 passim; failure of, 104; and fascism, 7, 39; Fifteenth Congress of, 110; foreign policy, 111, 113, 114-16; and Gramscian strategy, 74-76; hegemony, 77, 83; historic compromise of, 105-7, 108-9, 116, 120, 121-22; independence from Kremlin, 36, 1200; infiltrating the administration, 53; and Italian Resistance, 1-22 passim; leaders, 6, 36-37, 82, 116, 119, 120, 127, 129, 131n.13; Leninist roots of, 122, 126-30; and Marshall Plan, 57; as mass organization, 15, 119; members in New York, 13; and the monarchy, 8-9; and NATO, 111-15, 116; new face of, 107-9; participation in government, 173-74; and pluralism, 128, 129, 147; and postwar Italy, 76, 157; and Prague, 122; and PSI, 77-81; purges in, 5-6; rank-and-file vs. leaders, 116; and Red Brigades, 122-26, 178; pro-Soviet, 41, 57, 111, 113-15, 116-20, 126-27; and the Soviet Union, 18,, 20, 25n.25, 34-35, 42, 54, 59-64, 65-68, 87, 111, 113-14, 119-20,

157; "Sovietization" campaign of, 129; split of leadership, 120; Stalinist methods of, 156-57; underground armed force, 31-41, 44, 58; and the United States, 13-17, 166, 169, 173-79. *See also Partito Armato; Partito Nuovo*; Secchia; *Svolta*; P. Togliatti
Poland, 81-82
Postwar period, 10, 29-31, 117, 118, 157
Prague, Czechoslovakia, 31, 122. *See also* Radio Prague
PSDI (Italian Social-Democratic party), 46, 51, 79, 81, 84, 85, 86-87
PSI (Italian Socialist party), 16, 18, 22, 56, 71-73, 81-83, 84, 85, 86, 88-90, 92, 94, 96; failure, 104; leaders of, 17, 76; opposition to NATO, 78; an the PCI, 44, 72, 76, 77-81; and the Soviet block, 71-72; and the Soviet Union, 72, 77, 79; split of, 46, 51, 84, 96-97; and Stalinism, 76, 77; and the United States, 77, 78, 100n.42; pro-Western foreign policy, 96
Purges: of the Paris group, 6; in the PCI, 5-6, 39; in Russia, 35, 37

Radio Prague, 33, 122
Realpolitik, 135
Red Brigades, 76, 121, 122-26, 178; Catholic tradition of, 125
Rome Communist Federation, 46
Rumanian secret service, 126, 149
Ruptures of 1956, 81-83

Six Party Congress (1948), 32-33
Socialist block, 117
SOE, 14
Soviet: block and PSI, 71, 79; GRU (military intelligence), 118, 123; intellectuals, 80-81; KGB, 80, 90-91, 118; liberalization, 81; "Trust," 48n.18
Soviet Communist party. *See* CPSU
Soviet intelligence. *See* NKVD
Soviet Union: aggressive action in Europe, 30; and detente, 108, 114; hegemony on European Communists, 59, 77, 108, 118, 150; influence in postwar Italy, 4, 5, 8, 35; initiatives in Europe, 29, 118; invasion of Afghanistan, 114; in 1943-45 Italy, 17-21; offensive against Eurocommunism, 154-56; an the *Partito Armato*,

35-36; and the PCI, 6-7, 34-35, 59-68, 80, 117-20; and Santiago Carrillo, 148-54, 170; secret intelligence services, 6, 25n.25, 26, 35; strategy in Italy, 3-4, 5, 9-10, 35, 153-54; and the United States, 16, 52, 59, 63, 170, 176; and Western Europe, 20, 57, 63, 72, 119. *See also* Two stage theory
Spanish Communist party (PCE): and Eurocommunism, 138-56 passim; and the French Communists, 145; and the Soviet Union, 146
Sphere of influence theory, 23-24n.4, 57
Spring of 1944, 5, 7-13
Stalinism, 80, 81, 138
Svolta di Salerno, 5, 7, 14, 17, 31, 39, 63
Time magazine, 139

Truman administration, 49
Truman Doctrine, 52
Turin *La Stampa*, 106
Two stage theory, 10-11
Telemontecarlo, 128-29
Terrorism/Terrorists, 122-26, 127, 136, 178

UIL (lay union), 85, 86
Unions. *See* name of individual unions
l'Unità (PCI's official paper), 42, 43, 112, 113, 127
Unity of Action Pact. *See* Action Pact
United States: anticommunism, 3, 56, 86, 88, 95, 137, 141, 157; CIA, 26n.46, 30, 31, 47n.3, 79, 84-85, 88-91, 92-93, 119, 142, 146; and the Cold War, 58; anti-Communist activities in Italy, 46; and the Communists, 13-17, 30; economic support in Italy, 49-50, 54, 84, 93, 96; and Eurocommunism, 134, 134-37, 140, 141-43, 146-47; and European nuclear forces, 114-15; and European democrats, 56; FBI, 23n.9; information gathering, 33-34, 36, 44, 45, 143-45; intellectuals, 134, 141; intervention in Europe, 29, 52, 58; and Italian abortive insurrection, 44-46; and Italian DC, 87, 96-97, 171-73; and Italian Resistance, 1-3, 13-17, 39; and Italian socialism, 83-87; failure in Italy, 96-98; policy in postwar Italy, 5, 13, 16, 20-22, 29, 31, 49-64, 66, 87-92; 92, 93-96; missile modernization, 114-15;

and Nenni, 141-42; and the Opening of the Left, 87-92, 141; outline of good policy for the, 184-87; policy change, 52-53, 54-59; policy on Eurocommunism, 161-79; policy in Western Europe, 61-62, 63; propaganda campaign of, 55; Republican party, 92; response to communist threat in Italy, 49-68; response to Italian crisis, 173-79; and the Soviet Union, 8-9, 13, 16, 52, 59, 79, 157-58; and P. Togliatti, 9, 37, 54; State Department, 56, 58, 78, 92, 94, 95, 162-63, 165, 168-69, 173, 176; threat to security of, 127; union movement in, 83. *See also* AFL; Labor party, NSC

United States Labor party, 56

Vatican, the, 58, 66
Venice *Biennale*, 153-54, 160n.19
Volante Rossa (1945-49), 32-33, 44, 47n.7

Washington Post, 137, 139, 169
West European Communist parties, 60, 62-64, 72, 80, 103, 133-59 passim; Soviet offensive against, 154-56, 157. *See also* Eurocommunism; name of individual parties
West European Socialist parties, 103, 153
West European leaders, 164
Workers, 42, 105-6
Working classes, 19, 73, 74, 83, 121

Yugoslav Communists, 59, 60, 135

NAMES

Alberganti, Giuseppe, 33
Alexander (General), 14
Amendola, Giorgio, 7, 45, 76, 110, 120
Andreotti, Giulio, 164, 169-70, 182
Angleton, James J., 34, 79, 90, 91, 144
Are, Giuseppe, 109-110, 113, 132n.27

Badoglio, Pietro, 1-3, 5, 8, 9
Barbieri, Frane, 134-35, 152
Barzini, Luigi, 105
Beltramini, Alessandro, 124
Berlinguer, Enrico, 44, 82, 104, 107-8, 110-13, 116, 119, 121, 122, 124-25, 126, 127, 131nn.11,12, 155, 171, 178; And Carrillo and Marchais, 133-59 passsim; and NATO, 110-13
Berti, Giuseppe, 6, 38-41; purged by Togliatti, 39
Bettiza, Enzo, 75, 157
Bocca, Giorgio, 32
Brezhnev, Leonid I., 150, 152
Brown, Irving, 83-85, 89
Brzezinski, Zbigniew, 161, 169, 170
Burt, Richard, 175

Calimodio, Marisa, 124
Carrillo, Santiago, 136, 158; and Berlinguer and Marchais, 133-59 passim; vs. the Kremlin, 148-54; Leninist control of PCE by, 149; Soviet offensive against, 154-55
Carter, Jimmy, 150-51, 158, 161-64, 167-71, 173-75, 181, 189n.5
Ceausescu, Nicolae, 126, 149
Cervetti, Gianni, 127
Churchill, Winston S., 1-2, 4, 13
Ciruzzi, Aristo, 124
Claudin, Fernando, 10, 60, 61
Colby, William, 88-91
Cossuta, Armando, 127
Craxi, Bettino, 96, 98n.3, 103, 121, 125, 179
Croce, Benedetto, 3
Curcio, Renato, 122, 124-25

Dozza, Giuseppe, 6
Dubinsky, David, 83-84
Duclos, Jacques, 59
Dunn, James, 33, 40, 45-46, 49-51,54, 58

Ehrenburg, Ilya, 80
Ercoli. *See* Togliatti, Palmiro
d'Estaing, Giscard, 182

Fanfani, Amintore, 83, 87, 93, 94, 96, 172
Felix (pseud.), 90
Feltrinelli, Giangiacomo, 122-23

Franceschini, Alberto, 122

Galluzzi, Carlo, 156
Gardner, Richard N., 167, 172-73, 175
De Gasperi, 16, 42, 46, 49-52, 53, 71, 73, 76; government, 43, 50, 52; and the United States, 51-52
Giolitti, Antonio, 82
Golitzyn, Anatoli, 90-91
Gramsci, Antonio, 7, 73-75; and fascism, 74; vision of totalitarianism of, 74-75. *See also* Gramscian strategy of cultural hegemony
Grieco, Ruggiero, 6

Harriman, Averell, 93-95
Hart, Liddell B.H., 15
Heacock, Roger, 45
Horsey, Outerbridge, 95, 97
Hughes, H. Stuart, 57-58

Kennan, George F., 56-57, 61-63
Khrushchev, Nikita, 68, 76, 79-80
Kissinger, Henry, 126-27, 131n.7, 133, 137, 141, 147, 161-62, 168, 170, 171
Komer, Robert, 94-95

Laqueur, Walter, 15
Lama, Luciano, 156
Lazagna, Giovanni Battista, 124
Lichtheim, George, 74
Lizzadri, Oreste, 84
Longo, Luigi ("Gallo"), 15, 31, 35, 37, 42-43, 46, 47n.3, 59-60, 66, 119, 132
Lovestone, Jay, 83-84, 89
Luce, Claire Booth, 91

McCarthy, Joseph R., 88, 141
MacFarlane, Noel, 4, 5, 7-9
Marchais, 154; and Carrillo and Berlinguer, 133-59 passim. *See also* Eurocommunism
Mieli, Renato, 40, 118, 129
Mitterrand, François, 164, 174
Montanelli, Indro, 125
Moro, Aldo, 76, 83, 96, 121, 126, 172, 177-78. *See also* Moro affair
Moscatelli, 35
Moynihan, Daniel Patrick, 180-81

Mussolini, Benito, 74, 138; fascist revolution of, 138

Nenni, Pietro, 16-17, 22, 56, 71-73, 76, 78, 79-80, 81-83, 84, 86, 89-90, 93-94, 97-98, 98n.3
Nixon, Richard, 166
Novella, Agostino, 44

Onofri, Fabrizio, 81

Pacepa, Ion Mihai, 149
Paggio, Giulio, 33
Pavone (General), 3
Pirani, Mario, 124
Ponomarev, Boris, 153, 155

Reagan, Ronald, 122
Reale, Eugenio, 8, 59-60, 63, 82
Reinhardt, Frederick, 94-95, 97
Reuther, Victor, 93, 95
Reuther, Walter, 85, 95
Roasio, Antonio, 35, 43
Rocca, Ray, 90, 91, 144
Rodano, Frando, 64
Ronchey, Alberto, 122-23, 136
Roosevelt, Franklin D., 1

Salinger, Pierre, 174
Saragat, Giuseppe, 51, 72, 81-82, 84, 86, 89, 93, 97
Schlesinger, Arthur M., Jr., 82, 92-93, 94-95, 97, 142
Scicluna, 18-19
Secchia, Pietro, 31-32, 33, 35, 37, 38, 40-44, 45-46, 47n.3, 64, 79, 122; vs. Togliatti, 64-68
Sengia, Giulio, 67-68
Sejna, Jan, 123, 132n.28
Sereni, Emilio, 6
Serge, Sergio, 165, 167
Sforza, Carlo, 4-5, 8-9, 13
Spadolini, Giovanni, 121
Stalin, Joseph, 3, 5, 7, 10, 11, 20, 23-24n.14, 26n.35, 27n.65, 30, 38, 39, 42, 45, 46n.2, 57, 60, 61, 63-67, 77, 124, 157; anti-, 80-81; Khrushchev's denunciation of, 79, 81; myth of, 72, 80
Stevenson, Adlai, 13
Stone, Ellery, 21

Sqarez, Don Adolfo, 153, 1182
Sulzberger, C.L., 140

Tarchiani, 49-50, 51-52
Tasca, Henry J., 52-54
Terracini, Umberto, 7, 36, 39-41, 74; rebellion against the *svolta*, 39; against the United States and Soviet Union, 39
Thorez, Maurice, 60, 157
Tito, 60, 67, 119, 150
Togliatti, Palmiro (pseud. Ercoli), 3, 5-9, 11, 14, 17, 20, 24n.19, 25n.34, 27nn.65,66, 31-32, 33, 35, 59, 60, 63-64, 71-72, 74, 76, 78, 79-81, 82, 86, 109, 118-19, 157; the attack on, 42-46; and the Communists, 7-13; as leader of PCI, 36-41, 45; and the purges, 37, 39; vs. Secchia, 64-68; as a Stalinist, 38, 39; two-faced, 41
Togliatti, Vittorio, 124
Trilisser, M.A. (pseud. Moskvin), 6
Truman, Harry S., 29, 51-52, 57. *See also* Truman administration; Truman Doctrine

Vance, Cyrus, 161, 162, 168, 173, 174
Vishnisky, Andrei, 4
Vittorio, Giuseppe di, 43, 83

Welles, Sumner, 54
Wicker, Tom, 137-38, 139

Zhdanov, Andrei A., 61, 63
Zorza, Victor, 139